# The War of Civilisations

# has begun

75 Essays on the West's War against Islam

Aabed Moustapha

مكتبة اسلامية   MaktabaIslamia

## MaktabaIslamia Publications

www.maktabaislamia.com
info@maktabaislamia.com
www.facebook.com/everythingislamic
www.twitter.com/maktabaislamia


2016 CE – 1437 H

Translation of the Qur'ān


It should be perfectly clear that the Qur'ān is only authentic in its original language, Arabic. Since perfect translation of the Qur'ān is impossible, we have used the translation of the meaning of the Qur'ān throughout the book, as the result is only a crude meaning of the Arabic text.

Qur'ānic verses appear in speech marks proceeded by a reference to the Sura and verse number. Sayings (*Hadith*) of Prophet Muhammad ﷺ appear in speech marks with their relevant references.

# CONTENTS

# Introduction

All praise belongs to Allah (swt) the Lord of all Mankind, and may the blessings and peace of Allah (swt) be upon His Messenger Muhammed (SAW). The last and final messenger sent to mankind.

Since September 11 2001, the West has intensified its confrontation with Islam. This struggle is not a clash of civilisations as misunderstood by some; rather it is a war of civilisations and the Muslim world is the foremost of battlegrounds. Western powers are waging this brutal war with all of their might and wealth to ensure the survival of their political, economic, cultural and military domination of the Muslim world.

The growing Islamic revival we witness today constantly shakes the thrones of the agent rulers and threatens West's hegemony over the Muslim *Ummah*. What the West fears most is the re-emergence of the Caliphate which will radically alter the international situation and displace America, as the world's sole super power.

Against this backdrop, I have authored a plethora of articles about several subjects that readers will find intriguing and intellectually stimulating. The articles challenge the very nature of the conventional views held by the West and their surrogates in the Muslim world.

The articles have been grouped together into six sections. Where appropriate, I have modified some of the articles to ensure consistency and readability.

Part 1 is a rebuttal of some of the common accusations levied by western writers against Islam. Part 2 exposes the collaboration between the West and the Muslim agent rulers regarding the colonisation of the Muslim lands. Part 3 sheds light on the inability of Western Capitalism to solve its problems at home. Part 4 expounds on the failure of the West to prevent Muslims from yearning to live under the Caliphate. Part 5 explores the various facets of the Arab uprising and the subsequent political changes in

Arab world. Special attention has been paid to include articles on Egypt and Syria, as both countries historically have played a major role in shaping the political future of the Arab world. Part 6, looks at the events in the broader Muslim world, especially Afghanistan and Pakistan. This section also details aspects of West's continued war against Islam and also touches on the hot contemporary subject of the decline of America and Western civilisation.

This book will appeal to those who are interested in pursuing and understanding the events in the Muslim world. Care has been taken to stimulate political thinking about such events, and the book relies heavily on political texts to explain the motives of major powers and their agents, as well as exposing their plans.

It is my hope that despite the brevity of the topics, readers will be sufficiently encouraged to explore many of the ideas and views presented in the book.

Aabed Moustapha
January 31, 2015
11 *Rabi' Atthani* 1436

# Part 1
# War of Ideas: Western Capitalism versus Islam

# 1

## Using the Sword to Spread Western Values

*"History makes it clear however, that the legend of fanatical Muslims sweeping through the world and forcing Islam at the point of the sword upon conquered races is one of the most fantastically absurd myths that historians have ever repeated."*

*--De Lacy O'Leary*

Whenever Western governments mention weapons of mass destruction (WMD) and Muslims in the same breath, the Western media immediately breaks into a wild frenzy warning its people that a catastrophic event of epic proportions is about to unfold.

Old European fables of Muslims spreading Islam by the sword are reinvented to convey the impression that Muslims are extremely dangerous, highly irresponsible and pay scant regard to human life. Hence the mantra of disarming Muslim countries of WMD has become the rallying cry of the West directed against the Muslim world.

In some cases the arguments are extended to justify the West's ongoing policy of regime change in Syria, Iran and perhaps Pakistan. However, a close study of Islamic rule in the past contradicts the popular western myth that Muslims are bloodthirsty people anxious to wipe out the rest of mankind in the name of Islam.

The same however, cannot be said about the West. The West armed with its secular doctrine and materialistic world-view proceeded to exploit, plunder and colonise vast populations in order to control resources and maximise wealth.

In pursuit of these newfound riches the West succeeded in destroying numerous civilisations such as the Incas, American Indians, Aztecs, and Aborigines. Those who survived colonisation were forcibly converted to Christianity, stripped of their heritage and sold into bondage to Western companies. For the indigenous people of Africa, India, Asia, Middle East and others, the promises of freedom quickly evaporated and were replaced by colonial rule. Rather than show remorse towards such atrocities the West could only gloat at its achievements.

Technologies such as cannons, pistols, steam engines, machine guns, aeroplanes, mustard gas etc only hastened the acquisition of colonies and the exploitation of its people. Resistance offered by the natives towards their colonial masters was met by brute force—often resulting in the destruction of entire communities. When the West was not destroying the natives they were too busy annihilating each other in a desperate bid to cling on to their precious colonies. World Wars I and II are prime examples of the destructive nature of Western values.

This is a description of the Old World where countries like England, France, and Germany built empires and accumulated immense wealth on the death and destruction of millions of innocent people. Is the New World (America leading the West) any different today?

Take the example of the New World and its relationship with Afghanistan and Iraq. Liberation has become occupation; democracy has given way to colonial rule, devastation is termed as precision bombing and the slaughter of innocent Muslims is described as collateral damage. Meanwhile, American and British oil companies are queuing up to exploit the oil wells of Iraq and transport the energy reserves of the Caspian Sea to Europe via Afghanistan.

The Islamic Caliphate in the past never treated mankind in such a barbaric fashion. Neither did the Caliphate spread Islam by force nor destroy civilizations. When Islam spread to Egypt, many Coptic Christians did not embrace Islam and today they still number approximately 7 million. Likewise, when India was opened up to Islam the inhabitants were not coerced into accepting Islam. India today has a population of more than 750 million Hindus.

Compare this to extermination of Muslim and Jews in the courts of the Spanish Inquisitors during the much-coveted European renaissance. Those Jews that survived this Spanish holocaust were warmly welcomed by the Ottoman Caliphate. In Islamic Spain they flourished and became important members of the Islamic society.

Today the world has more to fear from the destructive nature of Western values than WMD. In the past these values were enforced upon nations either through direct colonial rule or through tyrannical regimes loyal to the West. Presently, the greatest danger facing mankind is the constant threat of the West imposing its values on the rest of the world through WMD.

February 17, 2008

# 2

## Unveiling Secularism

*"I believe that pluralistic secularism, in the long run, is a more deadly poison than straightforward persecution."*

*--Francis Schaeffer*

Former British Foreign Secretary Jack Straw again courted controversy by suggesting that Muslim women should remove the veil. Previously, Straw caused immense outcry amongst Muslims and non-Muslims alike, when he authorised the war against Iraq, and denied any link between Britain's foreign policy and home grown terror. But Straw is not the only minister who is denigrating the Islamic character of the Muslim community in Britain. Ruth Kelly, the Communities Secretary, called for a "new and honest debate" [1]on the merits of multiculturalism. Home Secretary John Reid said that Muslims parents should spy on their children. It is obvious that the British government has embarked on a crusade to trounce its cherished principles of pluralism, and freedom of religion in a last ditch attempt to preserve secular Britain.

Since September 11, under the pretext of the war on terror, the West has undertaken a host of measures specifically aimed at Muslims living in the West. These measures include arbitrary arrests, physical torture, imprisonment without trial, surveillance of mosques, muzzling of Imams, and deaths in police custody. Some have even been forced to become spies. Muslims have also witnessed the endless vilification of Islam by the Western media.

---

[1] Kelly, Ruth. "Kelly urges 'honest debate' on multi-culturalism", The Independent, (August 24, 2006).

All this has left an indelible impression on Muslim minds that secular democracies in the West are incapable of guaranteeing Muslims the peace and security to practice their religion.

The plight of Muslims living under secular dictatorships supported by the West is much worse. In countries like Uzbekistan, Muslim males are routinely arrested for having a beard or visiting the Mosques too often. In Turkey, Muslim women who opt for university education are forced to abandon their hijab.

But the fiercest punishment is reserved for those who seek to criticize these tyrannical regimes; imprisonment, torture and extra-judicial killings can routinely be found in such countries. So we also find Muslims living in the Muslim world convinced that secularism is flawed and unfit to govern them.

Even non-Muslims living under secularism feel that their religion is vulnerable. Many Christians in the West view gay bishops, women priests, illegitimate children, and the commercialization of Christmas as malicious attempts by secular fundamentalist to subvert Christian values, replacing them with secular ones.

Likewise, secularism has failed to protect the Christian sects in Northern Ireland and safeguard the lives of Jewish, Christian and Muslim people living in Palestine. India, the largest secular state in the world, is prone to religious violence where Hindus, Christians, Muslims and Sikhs are all victims of secularism. So, just like Muslims, non-Muslims are also looking for an alternative system that can provide them with an opportunity to practice their religion in peace.

Islam is the sole ideology in the world where people of different faiths can worship and perform their religious duties without experiencing reprisals or insecurity. In practice, this is secured by the Caliphate state. In the past the Caliph safeguarded the rights of non-Muslims and Muslims alike, without discriminating between them. Take the case of Palestine: under the rule of the Caliphate, Muslims, Jews and Christians lived in harmony, a feat unrivalled in the history of mankind.

By pressing ahead with the forced secularization of Muslims, Christian and Jews, Western governments run the risk of alienating them. Instead, the West should re-evaluate its policy of coercive assimilation and critically address the broader question of our time, as to whether secularism can really guarantee the rights of people belonging to different faiths.

October 7, 2006

# 3

## West's Bigotry towards Islam Knows No Bounds

*"The Islamic teachings have left great traditions for equitable and gentle dealings and behaviour, and inspire people with nobility and tolerance. These are human teachings of the highest order and at the same time practicable. These teachings brought into existence a society in which hard-heartedness and collective oppression and injustice were the least as compared with all other societies preceding it....Islam is replete with gentleness, courtesy, and fraternity."*

*--H.G. Wells*

In the latest bout of West's defamation of Islam, an obscure writer Sherry Jones succeeded in the publication of her book Jewel of Medina, despite vehement protests from Muslim groups around the world. Once again Muslims are expected to subscribe to West's notion of freedom of expression and respect Sherry's offensive portrayal of the Messenger Mohammed (SAW) with his youngest wife Aisha (RA)[2]. Earlier in this year, at least seventeen Danish newspapers vowed to defend freedom of expression and reprinted a degrading caricature of Prophet Mohammed (SAW). The conservative broadsheet Berlingske Tidende wrote in an editorial: "Freedom of expression gives you the right to think, to speak and to draw what you like... no matter how many terrorist plots there are..." It is evident that both Europe and America did not learn anything from the outcry of Muslims that accompanied the newspaper Jyllands-Posten decision to publish the original cartoons in 2005.

In Europe Islam bashing is an epidemic that infected the whole continent. The Dutch government refused to take action against Dutch

---

[2] S. Jones, "The Jewel of Medina", LA Times, (October 6, 2008).

Member of Parliament Geert Wilders who made a derogatory video about the Qur'ān. The government defended Wilders's actions by citing freedom of expression. France and Germany have imposed a ban on the wearing of hijabs. European security forces routinely harass, arrest and torture Muslims for simply being Muslims. Writers and journalists are free to insult Islam and their right to do so is passionately defended by politicians. Take Oriana Fallaci, the Italian war correspondent wrote a book entitled 'Anger and Pride' in which she described Muslims as 'vile creatures who urinate in baptisteries' and 'multiply like rats'. To the horror of Muslims, Italy's Defence Minister, Antonio Martino, praised Fallaci for having the courage to write the book. In Britain under the guise of freedom and tolerance, government ministers routinely denigrate Islam and set new benchmarks for British Muslims to pledge their loyalty to the state.

In Muslims eyes, America the leading state of the West is notorious for the humiliation and torture of Muslims in Abu Ghraib and Guantanamo, responsible for the destruction and defilement of Iraq's mosques, the debaser of Muslim women and the slayer of tens of thousands of innocent Muslims. Testimonies from human rights organizations, journalists, lawyers, US officials, former prisoners and rape victims all tell the true horror of America's war on Islam. In this war, Western ideals of 'religious freedom' and 'freedom of expression' have given way to religious intolerance and anti-Muslim demagoguery.

Away from Washington, the US media, esteemed think tanks and leaders of the religious right who are counted among President Bush's closest allies exploited free speech to vilify Islam. Rev. Franklin Graham, described Islam as a "very evil and wicked religion". Evangelist Pat Robertson, called Prophet Muhammad "an absolute wild-eyed fanatic . . . a robber and brigand . . . a killer". Jerry Falwell called the Prophet of Islam a terrorist.

On the international scene the West was quick to sacrifice freedom of religion in preference for forging alliances with despotic regimes across the

Muslim world. The regimes of King Abdullah, Musharraf and Karimov that habitually torture, imprison and kill Muslims for expressing their Islamic beliefs became the vanguard for the West's crusade against Islam.

The West claims that individuals are free to worship whatever deity they choose. But in practice this leads to perpetual conflicts amongst people, as religious beliefs and practices professed by some can be interpreted as offensive and insulting to others. Hence, Western governments are constantly intervening in the disputes and resort to legislation to protect the religious rights of some people by depriving others. Often, the real benefactors of freedom of religion are those individuals or groups whose beliefs coincide with the interests of the government or those who possess the ability to exert influence over the government. That is why the religious right in America is allowed to attack Islam because their fiery rhetoric is in full harmony with President Bush's war on Islam. However, if the same conservative Christians were to insult Jews or the Zionist state of Israel the US government would adopt stern measures to curb their insults. The ostracizing of Jimmy Cater by the main stream media is a noteworthy example.

Western governments use religious freedom or freedom of expression to pry open societies closed to Western values or totally ignore freedom when it does not concur with their interests. In the case of Karimov's massacre of Muslims in Andijon[3], the West has chosen to dilute its response, as the protesters were avid practitioners of Islam and not democracy. Such hypocrisy only serves to underscore the perception amongst Muslims that America and Europe are solely interested in the utter destruction of Islamic values and practices.

Islam does not believe in the fanciful idea of freedom of religion or freedom of expression, where a handful of men decide which beliefs and thoughts are legally beyond reproach, and which beliefs and thoughts are

---

[3] "Slaughter 'signals end of Karimov regime", The Guardian, (May 18, 2005).

subject to unfettered criticism and legislation. Islam stipulates that life, honour, blood, property, belief, race and the mind are to be protected by the Islamic State. All the citizens of the Caliphate are guaranteed these rights, irrespective of whether they are Muslim or non-Muslims. Islam also protects the rights of non-Muslims to worship without any fear of retribution or vilification of their beliefs. The Messenger of Allah (SAW) said: *"One who hurts a dhimmi (non-Muslim citizen of the Caliphate), he hurts me and the one who hurts me, hurts Allah (swt)."*

Therefore, it is prohibited for a Muslim to insult the beliefs of a non-Muslim or to harm their places of worship. Islamic history is unrivalled in its capacity to guarantee the religious rights of non-Muslims under the shade of the Caliphate. Muslims living under the tyrannical rule of regimes supported by the West need to realize that holding demonstration or boycotting Western goods will not prevent the West from undertaking further acts of aggression against them. The only way to prevent the West and her surrogates from attacking Islam and humiliating Muslims is to re-establish the Caliphate. The rights of the Muslims were protected, until the very last days of the Caliphate. During the rule of Sultan Abdul Hamid II, Britain decided to stage a play, which depicted the life of the Messenger of Allah (SAW) in a derogatory manner. Hearing this, Sultan Abdul Hamid complained to the British government to stop the play. The British government defended its decision to hold the play citing free speech. But when Sultan Abdul Hamid threatened Britain with military action Britain immediately relented.

October 7, 2008

4

# Secularism Not Islam is the Real Enemy of the Vatican

*"During the period of the Caliphs the learned men of the Christians and the Jews were not only held in great esteem but were appointed to posts of great responsibility, and were promoted to the high ranking job in the government....He (Caliph Haroon Rasheed) never considered to which country a learned person belonged nor his faith and belief, but only his excellence in the field of learning."*

*--Dr. William Draper*

The inauguration of Cardinal Ratzinger as Pope Benedict XVI has brought to the fore a host of issues, which threaten to undermine his papacy. Chief among them is the challenge from Islam and the secularization of Christians in Europe.

The Vatican is somewhat divided on how to tackle Islam. Some cardinals are in the favour of reaching out to moderate Muslims and tapering the Vatican's attitudes towards Islam. "The next pope will need to be someone capable of dialoguing with the different religions of the world, and particularly Islam... Islam is on the rise, and Christianity, at least in the developed world, is in decline", said the Rev. Keith F. Pecklers, a Jesuit professor of theology at the Pontifical Gregorian University. This approach is reminiscent of the one articulated by Pope John Paul II who in 1986 became the first pope to visit a Muslim country. During the visit to Morocco he said, "We believe in the same God, the one and the only God, who created the world and brought its creatures to perfection." Hence the doctrine of inter-faith dialogue with Islam was born. For the next twenty years this doctrine defined the relations between the Vatican and the Islamic world.

Other cardinals prefer a much tougher stance towards Islam. John Allen, the Vatican correspondent of the National Catholic Reporter, is sceptical that there is such a thing as moderate Islam. "They [cardinals] think what is needed is tough love. The nightmare scenario is that one day we'll wake up and the Holy Land will be empty of Christians", Allen said. The views expressed by this group appear to be in unison with Pope Benedict XVI, who not so long ago scoffed at the idea of Turkey joining Christian Europe. Last August, Ratzinger said, "In the course of history, Turkey has always represented a different continent, in permanent contrast to Europe. Making the two continents identical would be a mistake." Back in November 2004, Ratzinger criticized Muslims for politicizing Islam and stressed that Muslims had a great deal to learn from Christianity. Ratzinger said, "Muslims should learn from the Christian culture the importance of religious freedom, and the separation between church and state."

In the real world, the challenges posed by Islam are not only overstated by the Vatican, but are miniscule in comparison to the influence of secularism on the world's billion or so Catholics. A far greater threat is the secularization of Catholics in Europe, which is significantly higher than any other continent. Only 21 percent of Europeans say that religion is "very important" to them, according to the European Values Study, conducted in 1999 and 2000 and published two years ago. A similar survey in the United States by the Pew Forum on Religion and Public Life put the number at nearly 60 percent. Beyond that, Mass attendance has significantly declined throughout Europe.

Among Catholics, only 10 percent in the Netherlands, 12 percent in France, 15 percent in Germany and Austria, 18 percent in Spain and 25 percent in Italy attend weekly Mass. Therefore it is not surprising to find some Catholics voicing extreme concerns for the future of Christianity in a secular Europe. "Some people look at Europe and see it spiritually tired, if not dead," said the Rev. John Wauck, who teaches at the Pontifical University of the Holy Cross in Rome.

Apart from the dwindling Christian population in Europe, the principal threat to the Vatican comes from the direction of secular fundamentalists who are adamant in recasting catholic truths as falsehoods. Catholic teachings regarding the inauguration of women priests, birth control, abortion, gay marriages, adoption by same-sex couples, euthanasia and the commercialization of Christmas bear the brunt of this onslaught. Commenting on this trend, Wauck said that the union (European Union) seems to be "infected" with a "radically secular culture". Ratzinger delivered similar assessment hours before the conclave got underway to elect the new pope. He said, "We are moving toward a dictatorship of relativism . . . that recognizes nothing definite and leaves only one's own ego and one's own desires as the final measure."

Now that Ratzinger has been officially installed as the new Pope he must decide on how best to protect Catholicism and its values. His immediate concern and those of the cardinals who elected him is to win over those who have shunned Catholicism in preference for an agnostic life-style. To accomplish this feat, Pope Benedict XVI cannot ally himself with the secular powers of the world or rely on any of the world's secular institutions to defend the Christian faith.

Secularism and its practitioners despite being a by-product of Judaeo-Christian history are not interested in defending Christianity or for that matter any faith. For instance, in May 2002 President Bush did nothing to prevent Israel from shelling the Church of Nativity, despite strong appeals from Pope John Paul II and leaders of other Christian sects. Similarly, before the American invasion of Iraq in 2003, President Bush refused to meet evangelical Christians who were opposed to the war, but continued to entertain lobbyist from oil companies.

Religion and people who profess religious beliefs is an anathema to secularist fundamentalists and are barely tolerated. The people of faith who wish to retain their religious identity become the object of abuse within secular societies. Secular authorities utilize instruments such as the media and the political medium to constantly hound those that resist secular values. This continues until they capitulate or change their beliefs to conform to the materialistic worldview of the secularists.

Catholicism as well as other Christian faiths has suffered immensely under the patronage of secular Western states, particularly European states. Retreating behind the veil of 'freedom of speech', and 'freedom of religion', secularists have relentlessly abused Catholicism and forced the Roman Church to adapt its views and practices. Today, Catholic teachings and truths are scarcely recognizable and face imminent extinction, unless the Vatican takes a firm stand against the secular powers.

Forming an alliance with other world faiths such as Judaism, Hinduism, Sikhism and other Christian denominations will not alter the fate of the Roman Church. These religions are unable to stand up to the menacing ideology of secularism and they too have fallen prey to the secular powers. This is because of two reasons. First, they are all founded on an emotional creed that does not possess the intellectual dynamism to challenge the ideology of secularism. Second, they are based on creeds that only offer a spiritual perspective on human existence and are unable to present a social-political system of life that is a real alternative to secularism.

Islam is the sole ideology in the world that is able to counter secularism and offer genuine protection to people belonging to different faiths. Islam is able to achieve this, because at its heart is a spiritual and political creed that provides spiritual nourishment to its adherents and offers a comprehensive social-political system, where Muslims and non-Muslims are treated equally before the law.

In the past, when Islam was implemented practically, as in Islamic Spain, Jews, Christians and Muslims living in the Spanish cities of Toledo, Cordoba and Granada, enjoyed unrivalled tolerance and prosperity. Martin

Hume wrote in his book Spanish People[4]: "Side by side with the new rulers lived the Christians and Jews in peace. The latter rich with commerce and industry were content to let the memory of their oppression by the priest-ridden Goths sleep".

However, when the Catholic monarchs Isabella and Ferdinand took charge of Spain in 1492, they did not reciprocate tolerance but proceeded to expunge Spain of its Jewish and Muslim populace. Similar acts of cruelty with the blessing of the Pope were carried out in other lands controlled by Muslims such as the island of Sicily and Jerusalem.

Today the Islamic world is experiencing a radical transformation from secularism to Islam. Muslims across the Islamic world are rebelling against the secular order that has been forcibly imposed upon them by Western powers and their surrogates. Muslims are working day and night to over throw these secular autocracies and to re-establish the Caliphate on their ruins. With the establishment of the Caliphate, millions of Christians who were previously denied their rights under the secular regimes will have their rights restated in full. History bears witness that unlike the Roman Empire and the secular order of today, Christian doctrines and teachings were not changed under the Caliphate to agree with Islamic values.

Against this background it would be wise for Pope Benedict XVI to reconsider his position towards Islam and the Muslim world. Instead of opting for a harsh stance against Islam and Muslims, the new pope should support the right of Muslims across the Islamic world to overthrow their secular regimes and re-establish the Caliphate. In this way, the pope will be saving Catholicism, protecting the rights of his flock in the Muslim world and sending a good omen for future relations with the Caliphate.

May 07, 2005

---

4 "The Spanish People: Their Origin, Growth, and Influence", (1901).

**5**

## Tsunami: Why the West has No Compassion and Respect for Human Life

*"We must be aware of the superiority of our civilisation, a system that has guaranteed well-being, respect for human rights and - in contrast with Islamic countries - respect for religious and political rights, a system that has as its value understanding of diversity and tolerance..."*

*--Silvio Berlusconi*

The belated response from Western governments in pledging aid to the victims of the tsunami disaster was frowned upon by Westerners and victims alike. America's initial pledge of $35 million was described by a US senator as equivalent to what the American military consumed in Iraq before breakfast. Eventually, the aid was increased to $350 million, but did little to stem the growing tide of criticism directed at the Bush administration. In Britain too, the government was censured for pledging a meagre amount to the relief fund. Sensing humiliation the government hastened to match the British public's donation of £90 million.

These are the very same governments that never tire of preaching equality, human rights to the rest of the world, and setting up human rights commissions, but when given the opportunity to foster these ideals in some of the poorest countries of the world they are suddenly overcome with amnesia.

The failure of Western governments to respond adequately to the catastrophe in Asia is not an act of God, but is the result of the capitalist ideology that makes materialism as opposed to humanitarianism the discerning factor in the disbursement of aid. Take the US for example:

approximately 0.1 percent of US gross national product annually goes towards foreign aid. The amount of aid offered by other Western countries is slightly better, but still way below what is needed to return the disaster stricken areas back to some degree of normality.

In marked contrast, the West spends vast amounts on exploiting the world's precious resources, creating new markets for their companies and tying developing countries to Western financial institutions. In June 2004, America's cost of waging war in Iraq and Afghanistan reached $151 Billion and is expected to surpass $200 billion mark in 2005. The inequality in spending between aid and war is due to the capitalist ideology that drives Western governments to prioritise materialism above anything else.

In their view, the sanctity of human life and respect for fellow human beings comes a poor second to the pursuit of profit. For instance, since the beginning of the war in Iraq, an estimated 100,000 Iraqi civilians have been killed according to the Lancet medical journal. This means that the US government is paying the Pentagon on average $ 1.5 million per Iraqi civilian killed in order to secure the oil fields of Iraq. On the other hand, the US government eager to avoid the label 'stingy' has pledged $ 35 per person in humanitarian assistance to the million or so displaced victims.

Still there are some, who boast about the size of the West's generosity in comparison to other countries. As evidence they cite the huge contribution made to the tsunami relief fund by Western governments and their willingness to impose a moratorium on debt relief.

However, West's kindness has a notorious history of rebounding and leaving a bitter taste amongst the receipts of aid. Victims of the Bam earthquake in Iran are still living in abject poverty because only $ 17 million of the much-publicised $ 1 billion aid was delivered. Afghans, ravaged by coalition bombs are yet to receive 40% of the $ 5.4 billion in aid promised to them. Back in 2002, Bush declared that African countries would receive up to $5 billion a year in development assistance[5]. Two years on, and not a single dollar has been dispersed. There is also overwhelming evidence that aid given to Maldives was attached with the condition that democratisation process should continue.

Similarly, freezing debt repayments only to be resumed at a later date will do little to alleviate the economic plight of the countries in the region. These countries are saddled with mountains of debt and are forced to endure tough IMF measures which in most cases reverse the economic recovery. For instance, Indonesia's overall external debt is about $ 150 billion; suspending the payment of $ 3.1bn in principal and $ 1.3bn billion in interest payments as suggested by some European countries will not lift Indonesia out of poverty or help the tsunami victims.

If the West is serious about assisting Indonesia and other countries, then it should retire the debt altogether and cancel the IMF conditions imposed on its economy. This will enable Indonesia to become economically self-sufficient and less reliant on external aid. This strategy will not only help the Indonesia people stand on their feet, but also help them prepare effectively for future tsunamis. But Western governments will never tolerate economic parity between themselves and the developing world, as it hurts cooperate profits and loosens their grip on valuable resources.

Materialism and the constant quest for resources have allowed Western governments to squander another opportunity to win the hearts and minds of the Muslim people reeling from America's war on terrorism.

But if the West's adherence to capitalism has made it devoid of compassion and insolent of human life then the same can be said for the rulers of the Muslim world. Instead of taking advantage of the catastrophe in Asia to help their fellow Muslims and win the hearts and minds of the

---

[5] "Bush and Foreign Aid", Foreign Affairs, (September/October 2003).

non-Muslim victims, their first priority is to protect the economic interests of Western powers followed by their own thrones. Take Saudi-Arabia. After the events of September 11, it launched a multi-million dollar media campaign in the US to improve the public image of the royal family. In comparison, its response to tsunami crisis remains low-key and underscores how enamoured they have become with capitalism.

What the world needs today is an ideology and a state that is not forever preoccupied with securing resources and protecting its markets when faced with people deeply distressed by natural disasters. But is able to face up to victims of such catastrophes with compassion and respect for human life.

Only the Caliphate can win the hearts and minds of both Muslims and non-Muslims who have been afflicted with calamity. When the sworn enemies of Islam, the Quraiysh were stricken with famine, it was not the Romans or the Persians that rushed to their rescue, but the infant Islamic state in Madina under the leadership of the Messenger of Allah (SAW) that provided relief and won their hearts. In 650, during the reign of the Caliphate of Umar (RA), Madina was devastated by famine and it was the Muslims of Egypt that sent forth aid the likes of which was not seen before. In addition to sending aid over land, a sixty-nine mile canal was dug to connect the River Nile to the Red Sea, so that ships laden with vast quantities of food could reach Jeddah the port for Madina. The whole project was completed in six months and Medina's food shortages were permanently solved.

Jan 15, 2005

# 6

# European Union Fearful of Islam Downgrades Turkey's Entry Talks

*"If any religion had the chance of ruling over England, nay Europe within the next hundred years, it could be Islam"*

*--George Bernard Shaw*

European politicians have started to raise doubts in public about Turkey's entry with the EU. Austrian Finance Minister Karl-Heinz Grasser said that Turkish membership "would make excessive demands of Europe." Spanish Foreign Minister Miguel Angel Moratinos acknowledged two weeks ago, after the French and Dutch referendums, that "without a doubt" the two rejections were "going to affect" further expansion plans. Polls in France and the Netherlands showed that opposition to Turkey's membership was one of the key reasons voters gave for opposing the EU constitution.

The latest developments pour cold water on Abdullah Gul's claim last December that the European Union's decision to extend membership talks with Turkey contributes to the Muslim country's stability and gives it a new position in Europe and the Islamic world. Thus European Union's relationship with Turkey no longer rests on Turkey undergoing extensive political and economic reforms. Rather future relations between the two will be decided by two major factors.

The first is the 'clash of civilisations' and is pretty obvious to politicians as well as the peoples of both Europe and Turkey that this clash is inevitable and ongoing. Valery Giscard d'Estaing, the former French president once said that the entry of Turkey, as an Islamic and mostly Asian power, would spell "the end of Europe". Today Giscard's remarks are not only echoed by fellow European politicians, but are widely shared amongst the populations of Britain, France, Germany and several other countries. There is a deep sense of Islamophobia, which has swept the region and rekindled past memories of the Ottoman Caliphate dominating the affairs of Europe. Equally, the Muslims of Turkey are opposed to joining the EU. They fear that they will be stripped of their Islamic identity and forced to adopt Western values. For example EU's chastisement over Turkey's plan to outlaw adultery was quickly reversed by Ankara. This angered many Turks and only heightened their anxiety that Europe was intentionally targeting Islamic values.

This in part is born out of the climate of fear produced by America's war on Islam and in part is due to the centuries old conflict between Christendom and Islam. This polarization in attitudes is impossible to overcome, unless the ideological differences between the two cultures are debated and settled. To proceed in the absence of such a dialogue will result in failure, no matter what progress is made towards achieving the political and economic goals set out by the EU.

The second is that Europe has failed to accommodate its own Muslim populations, so what are the odds that it can successfully manage the inclusion of 70 million Turks. Take the example of Britain. Muslims are the most socially deprived ethnic group. In October 2004 the Guardian newspaper reported: 'Muslims had the highest rate of unemployment, the poorest health, the most disability and fewest educational qualifications. In most respects Muslim women fared worse than Muslim men did.' [6]

Muslims in France and Germany fair much worse. The banning of the hijab, the random interrogation of young Muslims and the withholding of citizenship are at the forefront of discriminatory acts carried out against Muslims. Add to this, the reluctance of the European powers to intervene

---

[6] "Census shows Muslims' plight", The Guardian, (October 12, 2004).

and protect Muslims of Bosnia and Kosovo underscores Europe's attitude towards Muslims living on its shores. In European minds, the above examples only reinforce the idea that Muslims and Islam are incompatible with secularism.

It is hard to believe that the current clash between Islam and the West and the injustices committed by Europeans towards their own Muslim populace has escaped the notice of Turkish leaders. If Gul is serious about Turkey occupying a new position in the Muslim world then the very least he can do is to stand firm against Europe's oppression of its Muslim populace. This can be achieved by Turkey demanding a significant improvement in their circumstances as a precursor to any talks between Turkey and the EU. Such a bold gesture would dramatically increase Turkey's standing in the Muslim world. Thereafter, Gul should dwell profoundly on Turkey's past in order to discover how the present Turkey can occupy a new position in Europe. He would quickly conclude that only in Islam and under the shade of the Caliphate did Turkey occupy a pre-eminent position amongst the nations of the world. Back then, the oppressed Europeans used to yearn for the justice of the Caliphate and longed to become a part of it. Did not the people of Constantinople implore Sultan Mohammed to liberate them from the tyranny of Constantine?

June 14, 2005

7

# America Exports Democracy Abroad, Cultivates Totalitarianism at Home

*"Those that can give up essential liberty to obtain a little temporary safety deserve neither liberty nor safety."*

*--Benjamin Franklin*

In the 8th of March 2005, President George Bush citing progress in Afghanistan, Iraq and Palestine said that democracy was beginning to spread across the Middle East and that "the authoritarian rule is the last gasp of a discredited past."

The Bush administration and its supporters have seized upon the events in the Middle East to give an upbeat assessment of democratic reform and America's standing in the region. Some have even gone far as making comparisons with the fall of the iron curtain, while others are pointing to a vindication of Bush's foreign policy since 9/11.

However, behind the rhetoric, Bush's vision of exporting democracy to the Middle East and other parts of the world falls way short of the very same democracy standard America routinely employs to dismiss election results, castigate despots, and put states on notice.

A central tenet of democracy requires people to choose legitimate representation in an environment that is impartial, free from local intimidation and foreign intervention. Bush was quick to apply this standard to Ukraine and more recently to Lebanon.

In the case of Ukraine, Bush contravened this standard, as evidence emerged that the US embassy was responsible for spearheading Yushchenko's "Orange Revolution".

In Lebanon, Washington's open incitement and support for the "Cedar Revolution" and its demand that forthcoming elections cannot be fair and free, unless Lebanon is completely free of Syrian occupation stinks of hypocrisy.

Were not the elections in Afghanistan, Iraq and Palestine held under American and Israeli occupation? Were not the candidates vetted by America? Was not the atmosphere prior to and on the day of the elections one of insecurity and fear? Were not the election results manipulated and the electoral process staged and managed? Clearly the answer to all of these questions is a defiant "yes". Hence the elections in these countries can only be described as unfair, illegal and imposed on the people.

But according to Bush's democracy yardstick the dodgy elections in Afghanistan, Iraq and Palestine were a resounding success. Even by third world standards such elections would have been declared null and void.

Likewise, Bush has failed to evaluate Pakistan, Egypt and Saudi Arabia against his benchmark for democracy. Musharraf's sham referendum in 2002, Mubarak's upcoming presidential façade and the Saudi municipal elections, which bars women from participating, can only be regarded as an indictment against democracy.

Rather than punishing these states for subverting democracy, Bush has rewarded them with billions of dollars in aid and offered muted criticisms in their defence. This was particularly evident, after Bush's inauguration address. The US State department scuttled to assure the rulers of Egypt, Pakistan and Saudi Arabia that they were not targets of his speech.

Ironically, Iran, which is comparatively more democratic than Egypt and Saudi Arabia put together, has been earmarked for regime change.

However, America is more concerned about securing Iran's huge oil and gas reserves than about nurturing democracy in Iran. In 1953, America worried about the nationalisation of Iranian oil removed the then elected Prime Minister, Dr. Mohammad Mossadegh and replaced him with the Shah – an absolute monarchist.

America's obsession with making bold claims about spreading democracy and liberty, while simultaneously propping up despotic regimes has a notorious history. On March 12 1947, President Truman said, "One of the primary objectives of the foreign policy of the United States is the creation of conditions in which we and other nations will be able to work out a way of life free from coercion…totalitarian regimes imposed on free peoples, by direct or indirect aggression, undermine the foundations of international peace and hence the security of the United States." [7]

Henceforth, America armed with the "Truman Doctrine" proceeded to sabotage democracy and freedom throughout the Muslim world in return for exploiting resources for her multinational corporations and safeguarding her strategic interests. America did this by supporting all manners of secular autocracies, monarchies and sheikhdoms.

Bush's vision for a democratic Muslim world is the same as the Truman Doctrine. In both, the exporting of democracy and liberty, as well as the support for dictatorships is totally subservient to American corporate interests.

America is not alone in promoting its corporate interests dressed up in Western values. Other Western powers most notably Britain, France and the EU compete with the US in trouncing these values. The banishment of slavery in the 19th century and drive to grant independence to colonies in the 20th century were solely motivated by rivalry between great powers to

---

[7] http://www.johndclare.net/cold_war8_TrumanDoctrine.htm

hold onto their precious resources. Exporting Western values was the least of their concerns.

Today, there is a bitter struggle between the EU and America over the resources of the Muslim world, in particular its energy reserves. Bush under the cover of freedom and democracy is seeking to remove those regimes that are either pro-European or look towards Europe for guidance and assistance. The EU-US conflict over oil and gas can be found in Muslim countries like Sudan, Morocco (Western Sahara issue), Iraq, Afghanistan, Iran, Libya, and the Gulf sheikhdoms.

Those minority of Muslims who are still enchanted by Western values need to realise that the Western powers are not interested in the liberation of the Muslim world. Nor are they interested in granting Muslims freedom and democracy.

These Muslims should take a quick look at the domestic affairs of Western countries and they will quickly learn that Western values are only a myth. The anti-terror laws in Britain, the Patriot Act in the US, the indefinite detention of Muslims in Guantanamo and Belmarsh (UK) and the humiliation of Muslim prisoners in Abu Ghraib, Bagram and Basra clearly belittle their values.

As for Westerners, they need to take a serious look at how their governments are using the war on terrorism as an excuse to enact draconian laws that are transforming their liberal societies into totalitarian ones.

Measures such as imprisonment without trial, internment of citizens, extra judicial torture, concentration of power in the hands of the executive, unelected government advisors, ministers over-ruling the judiciary, greater press restrictions, pre-packaged news stories, suppression of information and intrusion into personal privacy strike at the very heart of liberal democracies.

How soon America and Europe transform themselves into a fortress of totalitarianism depends upon whether Americans and Europeans value liberty and democracy above safety.

March 17, 2005

8

## UN Reforms to Legitimize Terror against Muslims

*"The United Nations system is flawed even in its foundation, and even in its motives, to those who can see through the veil and false declarations of love and peace from wealthy, powerful, conniving fear mongers who only want to always be in control over others."*

*--Ron McEntee*

The obsession of some Muslim countries on which countries should occupy a seat in the expanded UN Security Council is misdirected. Instead the focus should be on the proposed reforms and what it means for the Muslim world.

Besides the plan to expand the Security Council, the new reforms advocate the use of pre-emptive strikes and include an open-ended definition on terrorism. The proposals are meant to be debated by the General Assembly later this year, but so far the discussions have revolved around the expansion of the Security Council.

The inclusion of pre-emptive strikes and a loose definition on terrorism will enable Western powers to legally justify punitive actions against Muslim countries that pose a threat to their interests. The threat does not have to be real, only perceived. This will preserve the West's domination over Muslims lands within the ambit of international law.

Since its inception in 1945, the UN has been used by the great powers especially America to cement their hegemony all over the world. No people have suffered more at the hands of the UN then the Muslim *Ummah*. The West used the UN to carve up Muslim land such as the separation of

Bangladesh from Pakistan, dismemberment of Bosnia and the division of Indonesia.

Furthermore, the UN has been used by the West to plunge a dagger deep into the heart of the *Ummah* by creating Israel and supporting its existence by issuing resolutions in her favour.

The UN has also played the instrumental role in isolating Muslims from each other by imposing sanctions on Iraq, Libya, Sudan, Iran and Afghanistan. The UN has also been used by the West to justify the invasion of Somalia, and the occupation of Iraq and Afghanistan.

Given the UN's criminal record against the Muslim world, its hostile plans for the future and its inability to restrain American hegemony, it beggars belief why the rulers of the Muslim world blindly submit to the UN and hold it in such great esteem.

Any sane ruler with a modicum of common sense should have realized by now that severing ties with the UN would give them a better chance of fighting Western imperialism. Or else they will meet the same fate as Saddam Hussein who followed UN resolutions to the letter and caused the destruction of Iraq.

Today, the bitter irony is that while the rulers of the Muslim world pledge their loyalty to the UN, America realizes UN's limitations to fight Islam and still wants to pursue a unilateralist course to subdue the global Islamic revival.

The only source of protection from the aggression of Western powers and their instruments of terrorism such as the UN lie in the emergence of a powerful Islamic State. In actual fact it was the Ottoman Caliphate's march towards Europe that encouraged European nations to conclude the Treaty of Westphalia and international law was born.

The Ottoman Caliphate stood firm against international law with such resoluteness that for many years it was able to demand warring countries to sign up to peace treaties on its terms and without surrendering the *Ummah*'s resources or compromising Islamic values.

July 15, 2005

# 9

## America and Iran Out of Step with Democracy and Islam

*"Half the work that is done in this world is to make things appear what they are not."*

--*Elias Root Beadle*

Even before a single vote had been cast, America had already decided to dismiss the Iranian presidential election. Bush said, "Power is in the hands of an unelected few who have retained power through an electoral process that ignores the basic requirements of democracy."[8] After the election, America was quick to describe the electoral process as flawed and that Iran was out of step with moves towards democracy in the region.

Yet scrutiny of American actions in the region and beyond demonstrates that it is America that is out of step with democracy. One of the basic tenets of democracy is that elections must be held fairly and free from local or foreign interference.

However, this was not observed during the elections in Palestine, Iraq and Afghanistan. These elections were conducted under foreign occupation, insecurity was rampant, voters were too frightened to vote and the turnout was dubious to say the least. Despite this, America hailed the elections as a victory for democracy.

Furthermore, the selection of the leaders, the formulating of the constitutions and the convening of elections were all conducted under the

---

[8] Bush, W, George. "Middle East: Bush Criticises Iran's Election", BBC News, (June 16, 2005).

guardianship of America. America handpicked Abbas, Karzai and Jaffari to oversee the implementation of pro-American policies. In the case of Afghanistan and Iraq, America used the Loya Jirga and Iraqi Governing Council to enshrine American inspired canons that would ensure her dominance over the people of Afghanistan and Iraq.

Undeterred and unashamed, America still continues to interfere in the electoral process of many Muslim countries threatened by Islamists, America has taken the precautionary step of postponing the parliamentarian elections in Afghanistan and Palestine. In the case of Palestine, America ordered Abbas to amend election law, so as to prevent Hamas from winning a majority of the seats in the parliament.

America's unabashed support for the municipal elections in Saudi Arabia, the upcoming presidential elections in Egypt and her silence over the low turnout in the Lebanese election (the turnout was higher during Syrian occupation) stinks of hypocrisy and falls way short of the democracy standards that are taught in American high schools.

In comparison, the presidential elections in Iran are much more credible. Elections were conducted in relative safety with a 62% voter turnout. This was 2% higher than the 2004 US presidential election. There may have been irregularities as voiced by Rafsanjani but these pale into insignificance when compared to the farce of the 2000 US presidential race.

Rather than preaching to Muslim countries about the virtues of democracy, America should examine its own handiwork at subverting democracy in the region. Surely it is America that is out of step with democracy.

Those who argue that the election of Ahmadinejad will usher in a fundamentalist government are equally mistaken. Since the Iranian revolution, Iran has never been the bastion of Islam. A cursory study of Iran's constitution inspired by Ayatollah Khomeini shows that it is a secular autocratic state which limits the role of Islam in social, educational, economic, and foreign affairs. The few laws of Islam that are implemented are designed to mollify the Islamic sentiments of the people.

This gives Iran an Islamic appearance, similar to Saudi Arabia and Pakistan which also pretend to be Islamic. Professing Iran to be Islamic, while implementing non-Islamic rules makes the Iranian regime out of step with Islam.

Islam stipulates that Muslims must choose a ruler who will govern all aspects of their lives according to the rules derived from the Qur'ān and the Sunnah. This is accomplished by electing a Caliph and re-establishing the Caliphate State. The Caliphate guarantees legitimate representation for the *Ummah* as well as ensuring that sovereignty belongs to God.

June 27, 2005

**10**

# Iraq: Another Fake Islamic State in the Making

*"Cautious recognition of Islamic symbolism is the tried and true path of Muslim kings and dictators, and it would be naive to say definitely that they will not be able to sustain it over time."*

*--Noah Feldman*

The current deliberations over the Iraqi constitution have once again raised the spectre of Islam in the country's future. Some argue that Islam should be made the primary source of legislation. Others most notably the Kurds prefer Islam to be given the status of rites and ritual and oppose Islam's role in public life. Previously, under the mandate of Transitional Administrative Law (TAL) a compromise between the two sides was reached. It states Islam is the official religion and "a source of legislation," but also says the government may not enact a law "that contradicts those fixed principles of Islam that are the subject of consensus."

There are also disagreements over the naming of Iraq. Some leaders have proposed changing the country's official name to the "Islamic Republic of Iraq", a move opposed by Iraq's secularists. Whether Islam becomes the sole source of legislation for Iraq or the country is renamed Islamic Republic of Iraq the basic question still remains—what constitutes an Islamic state? Two dominant views pervade Muslim and non-Muslim thinking on the subject.

The first view endorses the perception that if the majority of the inhabitants of a particular country are Muslims than the country is classified as an Islamic state. This is a gross misrepresentation of reality. A clear majority in the US believes in Christianity but no one holds the view that America is governed by the bible and is therefore a Christian state.

More common but equally perverse is the second view. This view asserts that if some references are made to Islam in the constitution then the country can be called an Islamic state. Proponents of this opinion often cite examples from the constitutions of Muslim countries to lend credence to their arguments. For instance, Article II of the 1980 Egyptian constitution states that Islam is the religion of the state and "Islamic jurisprudence is the principal source of legislation". The 1992 Basic Law of Saudi Arabia states that the nation's constitution consists of the Qur'ān and the Sunnah (the actions and sayings of the Prophet Muhammad (SAW)). Article IV of the Iranian constitution states that "all civil, penal, financial, economic, administrative, cultural, military, political, and other laws and regulations must be based on Islamic criteria". And Article 227(1) of the Pakistani constitution reads, "All existing laws shall be brought in conformity with the injunctions of Islam as laid down in the Holy Qur'ān and Sunnah ... and no law shall be enacted which is repugnant to such injunctions."

If any casual observer, irrespective of their religious orientation was to scrutinise the basic law of these countries they would very quickly realise that Islam has no relationship whatsoever with such constitutions. For instance to become a leader of Saudi Arabia, Iran or Pakistan one has to be a Saudi, Iranian or Pakistani. This contravenes Islamic teaching, as Islam abhors nationalism and insists that those contesting for leadership have to be Muslim before they can be considered suitable.

In Islam, there are two basic tenets, which defines the Islamic state above all else namely sovereignty belongs to God and authority is with the people. Sovereignty to God means that God is the sole lawgiver and Islam must govern the temporal lives of Muslims and non-Muslims residing in the Islamic State. In the case of Muslims, their personal lives are to be governed by Islam and the state has no jurisdiction over the private affairs of its citizens. There are four main sources of Islamic law. Qur'ān, Sunnah, Ijma Sahaba (Consensus of the Prophet's companions) and Qiyas (Analogy based on divine reasons). The basic law of the state is derived from these sources only. Any other source be it customs, traditions, environment, history or man himself is considered invalid. All laws related to economic matters, social relationships, educational affairs, foreign policy and the like are derived from the aforementioned sources.

Likewise authority in Islam lies with the citizens of the Islamic state. Islam has clearly mandated that the people have the exclusive right to elect, account and dismiss the ruler if he openly implements non-Islamic laws. These rights are delegated to the ruler via the *Bay'ah* (pledge of allegiance given to the Caliph), which, in essence is a binding contract between the ruler and his subjects.

The usurping of authority by the ruler or his refusal to grant these rights is considered a flagrant violation of Islam. In the past there have been some occasions where the ruler has assumed the *Bay'ah* by force and the *Ummah* has remained silent. The misuse of the *Bay'ah* did not transform the Islamic state into a dictatorship or a theocracy as suggested by some historians. This is similar to misappropriation of votes in the 2000 US presidential race. The fact that the people did not challenge the outcome meant that the system of ruling in America continues to be democratic. Therefore the Islamic state is a unique state, unlike any other state in the world today.

This state is commonly known amongst the Muslims as the Khilafah and is often referred by non-Muslims as the Caliphate. The Caliphate is not a theocracy where God's chosen representative implements God's law upon the subjects. Nor is it a dictatorship or a monarchy where authority and law-making reside exclusively with the dictator or monarch. It shares some resemblance with democracy in that authority is exercised by the people to elect and account the ruler. But differs greatly from the democratic state, which bestows the power of law-making to parliament or congress as opposed to God. Despite these glaring differences, the West still continues to describe the Caliphate as a dictatorship, theocracy and a monarchy.

Some Western leaders have even gone at great lengths to portray the Caliphate as a totalitarian state. This claim borders on insincerity to say the least. In actual fact the label of totalitarianism is more applicable to Western states. If the passing of the PATRIOT ACT in the US and the endorsement of anti-terrorism legislation in Britain is not a hallmark of totalitarian states then what is?

In contrast, Islam forbids spying on its citizens and all those found guilty of a crime have to be tried before a court of law before they can be punished. As long as the West continues to place itself at the centre of nation building like in Afghanistan and Iraq, fake Islamic states will be born to join a long list of pseudo Islamic states. Such states do little to mollify the Islamic sentiments of the *Ummah*. Instead they prolong the misery of the *Ummah* and subject her to endless campaigns of foreign interference and exploitation. To avoid such pain and suffering the *Ummah* must pull all of her resources together and work towards a single project, which is the re-establishment of the Caliphate. Did not the Caliphate end the suffering of the Iraqis when Baghdad was ransacked by the Mongols in 1258?

August 20, 2005

# Part 2
# Western Masters and Agent Rulers

# 11

## Abdullah Sacrifices Saudi Arabia to Shore up Bush's Future

*"Never before in history has a president of the United States— and I'm really referring to both President Bushes—has had such a close relationship with another foreign power... we had a pact with Saudi Arabia in a relationship that's gone back 40 years... we get oil, we sell them weapons, and part of the pact was we didn't look too closely at what was really going on in Saudi Arabia."*

*--Craig Ugnar*

In April 25 2005, Crown Prince Abdullah visited George Bush to discuss a number of issues ranging from the Middle East peace process to fighting terrorism. However, the centrepiece of Abdullah's visit was to present President Bush with a fresh proposal to boost Saudi oil production that would go some way towards easing pressure on the price of crude oil.

The visit was carefully scripted to coincide with Bush's announcement of a new energy strategy to counter growing concerns amongst oil companies and ordinary Americans that the administration's oil policy was faltering and hurting the US economy.

Criticism from oil companies has been fuelled by the lack of progress made in securing Iraq's oil. Despite devoting $1.6 billion of Congressional aid to develop Iraqi oil infrastructure, Iraq is still producing 25 percent lower than levels in early 2003, before the US invasion to topple Saddam Hussein. The popular Iraqi insurgency has reduced the flow of oil to a trickle. The sabotage of a pipeline to Turkey has restricted exports from Iraq's northern fields, around Kirkuk, and violence has hampered efforts to modernize the larger southern fields. The result is that Iraq exported 1.43 million barrels of crude oil last month, down 30,000 barrels from March. This is nowhere near the 4 million barrels forecasted by some analysts in the aftermath of the war.

In addition, US oil executives have been further aggrieved by the neo-conservatives whom they blame for encouraging the insurgency through the privatization of Iraq's oil industry as opposed to its re-nationalization. The plan to nationalize Iraqi oil, which was put forward by the US oil industry, was superseded at the last minute by a neo-conservative plan to privatize Iraq's oil and destroy OPEC. In the ensuing chaos of the post Saddam era, the US oil companies were prevented from exploiting Iraq's oil fields thereby hindering their efforts to increase Iraqi oil supply. Failure to work with Iraq's oil fields was a huge blow to American oil companies. According to the United States Department of Energy the costs of bringing new production on line in Iraq are among the lowest in the world. As of yet only 15 of its 74 fields have been developed; known reserves are 112 billion barrels, but some predict it may turn out to exceed 300 billion barrels. With recovery rates of 50 per cent and reserves of 250 billion barrels, Iraqi oil could be worth more than $3 trillion.

On the domestic front, consumers have had to put up with soaring gas prices at the pump and blame Bush for much of America's energy woes. A recent Associated Press-AOL poll found the public giving the president low marks for his handling of energy problems, with 62 percent saying they disapproved. The democrats have seized on the poor approval ratings to drive home the point that the Bush administration has done next to nothing to rescue the beleaguered public from high oil prices. "Five years later, and Americans suffering under record-high gas prices are still waiting to see the president keep his promise to jawbone OPEC,"[9] said Senator John Kerry.

---

[9] "Bush, Saudi crown prince to discuss oil, terrorism", Gulf Times, (April 25, 2005).

The Bush administration faced with the growing tide of criticism has responded by removing influential neo-conservatives like Wolfowitz and Bolton away from policy making to policy execution. The administration has also asked the Saudi's to come up with a plan that dramatically increases its oil production capacity. The plan outlined by Saudi Oil Minister Ali Naimi before Abdullah's visit to Texas, proposes to spend $50 billion over a five–year period to increase Saudi production capacity to 12.5 million barrels per day by 2009 from the current 11 million limit. If necessary, Saudi Arabia says it will eventually develop a capacity of 15 million barrels a day. US National Security Adviser Stephen Hadley described the Saudi plan as a major breakthrough. He said, "What really came was a plan for increasing production through substantial investment — to the tune of about $50 billion over time. So it's a major initiative that they've undertaken."[10]

Notwithstanding this huge investment to supplement America's economy, the Saudi's also plan to give US energy companies a huge bonanza by inviting them to invest in Saudi Arabia's other energy sectors. Addressing an audience of American businessmen organized by the Saudi-American Business Council (SABC) at the Fairmont Hotel, Prince Abdullah announced his intention to host a conference of the International Energy Forum (IEF) in the last quarter of 2005. He said, "We invite you to continue to cooperate with us in the mining and gas sectors which offer a number of investment opportunities. There are many opportunities and success is guaranteed, God willing. You can choose direct investment or establish joint projects." Crown Prince Abdullah also plans to make it easier for American businessmen to take wealth out of the country by proposing to relax the laws protecting the fledging Saudi economy. Speaking about the economic reforms, Abdullah said, "We have enacted a clear and flexible taxation law, reorganized the financial market so that it matches international standards and have expedited the privatization process."

---

[10] "Hadley, Stephen. Press Briefing on the President's Meeting With the Crown Prince of Saudi Arabia", (2005).

Clearly the Americans will be the real beneficiaries of Abdullah's plan.

Firstly, the Saudi's will spend $50 billion to increase the production of crude oil only to flood the international oil market and have its price reduced. This will sharply diminish Saudi profits and significantly damage the country's economy. On the other hand, cheap crude oil will be a godsend to the American economy, which at present is reeling from high oil prices.

Secondly, the Saudi's will be paying American oil companies billions of dollars to carry out the necessary work to increase the capacity of oil production. It will neither result in transfer of technology nor create sufficient jobs to lessen Saudi Arabia's burgeoning unemployment figures. At present, the unemployment rate is at 20% (the real figure could be as high as 30%). But this figure could increase even further, given that the Saudi population is going to double from 20 million to 40 million by 2020. Hence the outlook for Saudi's seeking employment in the near future looks extremely bleak.

Thirdly, the privatization drive coupled with loose taxation laws will result in American ownership of some of Saudi Arabia's vital assets like the Saudi Telecom Company. In addition, under the pretext of providing better public services, the American multinationals will charge higher prices and generate huge profits, very little of which will be ploughed back into the Saudi economy. Most of it will be repatriated back to the US, whilst some of it will end up in the foreign accounts of Saudi princes.

Fourthly, though the bilateral trade between Saudi Arabia and the US has increased from a measly sum of $160 million in 1970 to $26 billion in 2004, the Saudi people during this period have become increasingly poor. In 1999, the per capita GDP was less than it was in 1965, before the massive rise in oil prices. So by inviting the Americans to invest in other energy reserves, Abdullah is signing away the future of the Saudi people to American slavery.

Not surprisingly, the Bush administration embraced Abdullah's plan and included it, as part of their revitalized energy strategy. This consists of turning military bases into oil refineries, exploring ways of tapping US oil reserves and exploring cleaner fuels.

Therefore, when Bush unveiled his rejuvenated energy policy, he succeeded in pushing down the price of crude oil. This explains the reason behind Abdullah's visit to Texas and was confirmed by National Security Adviser Stephen Headley who said, "The problem in the oil market now is a perception that there is inadequate capacity." Reassurance that can be given to the market on available supply, he said, should "have a downward pressure on the price."

Hadley's statement also alludes to the fickle nature of this reassurance. Much is dependent upon the Bush administration's ability to overcome resistance from environmentalists and other pressure groups who are opposed to the drilling for oil in places like Alaska and also to the conversion of existing military bases into oil refineries.

In this respect, Bush's energy strategy is a defensive one. Having failed in Iraq, the administration has been forced into exploring ways to boost the domestic output of US oil. With winter approaching and OPEC pumping oil to its maximum, the race is on in the White House to find ways to stymie the next crisis.

However, America's current predicament presents an ideal opportunity for the Saudi's to free their people from American hegemony. Had the House of Saud been sincere about this, they could have employed number of strategies to sever their dependency on the US.

The Saudi's could have cut the supply of crude oil, de-coupled it from the dollar and sold it in currency like the Euro or the Yaun (Chinese currency). This would force the world to quickly sell the dollar in return for the Saudi's preferred currency of exchange. A move like this would also force powers like Europe and especially China, a country that has sharp differences with the US to counter any US manoeuvres against Saudi Arabia.

The Saudi's could also barter some of their oil in exchange for technology and heavy industry thereby reducing dependency on foreign workers and creating new jobs. In this way the Saudi's could steer their economy towards a path of self–sufficiency and economic prosperity.

It is very unlikely that Abdullah and the House of Saud would opt for such radical ideas, as their very existence depends upon Anglo-American support.

These ideas can only be pursued in an environment that is free from Anglo-American surrogates who dominate the Saudi regime. Only the Caliphate can produce an environment where the Saudi's can enjoy political independence and economic sovereignty free from foreign control.

May 10, 2005

**12**

# Syria Aids American Hegemony Over Iraq

*"You can't make war in the Middle East without Egypt and you can't make peace without Syria."*

*--Henry A. Kissinger*

In October 26 2008, four US helicopters flew 8 kilometres into Syria from Iraq, and attacked a farm compound in Eastern Syria[11]. The operation led by US Special Forces killed eight people including four children and Al Qaida operative Abu Ghadiya. Immediately after the raid, the Syrian regime vehemently denounced the attack as a violation of its sovereignty and carried out a series of retaliatory measures in protest. This included the removal of Syrian troops from the Iraqi border, mobilization of crowds to vent anger against America, closure of the American school and the US cultural centre. Additionally, Al-Assad's regime demanded an official apology and compensation for the victims. However, beyond the fiery rhetoric, new details have emerged that suggest Syria's complicity in the attack.

On November 2 2008, the English newspaper, The Times revealed that Syria had given permission for the raid to go ahead and when the operation was bungled, Syria's notorious secret intelligence services flooded the region to clear up the mess and muzzle local villagers. The paper further disclosed that the farm area was a heaven for jihadi fighters who were free to train and move across the Iraqi border. Some spoke with thick Iraqi accents. The revelations are not new and confirm long standing suspicions that Syria is covertly assisting America to stabilize Iraq.

---

[11] "Syria: US Attack Kills 8 In Border Area", CBS News, (October 26, 2008).

After the fall of Saddam, many Iraqis fled Iraq and sought refuge in Syria. At present their numbers stand at approximately 1.5 million. Under American auspices, Syria set up militant training camps to recruit and train the Iraqi refugees into fighters with the explicit purpose of infiltrating the Iraqi resistance, providing real-time intelligence to US officials, and executing covert operations in Iraq, especially those that encourage sectarian discord. Syria also established checkpoints every 4 kilometres along the border that abuts Iraq. Through such endeavours the Syrian regime was able to monitor and keep track of jihadi fighters moving across the border. This arrangement resulted in the arrest of several thousand independent resistance fighters as well as the elimination of several high value targets— latest addition being Abu Ghadiya.

Subsequently, Syria was able to some extent pacify Iraq's western border and aid America's control over the area. To provide greater political legitimacy to Iraq's ailing pro-American government; Syria recently normalized diplomatic ties and sent its first ambassador to Baghdad in 26 years. Not surprisingly then, that in September Jalal Talabani, Iraq's president, told his master US President George Bush that Syria no longer posed a problem to Iraqi security. So if Syria posed no threat then why did the US conduct the raid?

It appears that the timing of the attack was meant to achieve three objectives. First, America was presented with valuable information to apprehend Abu Ghadiya. A few weeks before, several militants were captured in Baquba a base for Al-Qaida fighters in Iraq and information gained from them prompted the raid. Second, the removal of Syrian border troops is helping America pressurize the Iraqis to sign up to a new security pact that will keep US forces formally in Iraq till 2011. Third, America exploited the raid to announce its much expanded pre-emptive war doctrine.

On October 28 at the Carnegie Endowment for International Peace (CEIP), US Defence Secretary Robert Gates declared that "the US will hold any state, terrorist group, or other non-state actor or individual fully accountable for supporting or enabling terrorist efforts to obtain or use weapons of mass destruction." The cross-border raids against Syria and Pakistan from US forces stationed in Iraq and Afghanistan is a manifestation of this strand of thinking.

Syria's collusion with America is not just limited to Iraq but extends to Lebanon and Palestine. Damascus's support of pro-Syrian factions in Lebanon and Syria's peace overtures to Israel are designed to facilitate America's stranglehold over the region.

November 3, 2008

**13**

# American-Iranian Relations: Collusion or Collision?

*"They [Iranians] also provided considerable assistance to Operation Enduring Freedom. Tehran offered to allow American transport aircraft to stage from airfields in eastern Iran to assist operations in western Afghanistan. It agreed to perform search-and-rescue missions for downed American airmen who bailed over Iran...The Iranians weighed in with the Northern Alliance and helped convince it that Washington was deadly serious and that therefore the Northern Alliance should participate fully in the American war effort."*

*--Kenneth Pollack*

In 15 September 2008 the International Atomic Energy Agency reported that Iran had repeatedly blocked a UN investigation to probe allegations that it had tried to make nuclear weapons. The findings of the report were once again seized upon by Western powers to portray Iran as a pariah state and a menace to its neighbours. America, France, Britain and Israel have raised the spectre of a new set of sanctions to punish in their view Iran's intransigence over its peaceful nuclear programme.

White House spokesman Gordon Johndroe said, "We urge Iran to suspend its uranium enrichment and reprocessing activities or face further implementation of the existing United Nations Security Council sanctions and the possibility of new sanctions."[12] French Foreign Ministry spokesman Eric Chevallier said, "We have no other choice than to work in the days and weeks to come toward a new (UN) Security Council sanctions resolution"[13]. Israel's Prime Minister's Office spokesman Mark Regev said,

---

[12] Johndroe, Gordon. AFP, (2008).
[13] Chevallier, Eric. (2009)

"This is another clear signal that the Iranian regime is playing games with the international community with a policy of deception. ... It is now incumbent upon the international community to ratchet up the pressure on Teheran."[14]

Iran on the other hand defended its stance and rebuffed American claims about its peaceful nuclear programme. "We do not think there should be an open forum so America can bring up a new claim every day and pass it on to the agency, expecting Iran to address any claim," said Alaeddin Borujerdi, head of parliament's national security and foreign affairs commission.

Iran has every right to be angry. There is no tangible evidence that Iran has a nuclear weapons programme. A number of prestigious Western think tanks and intelligence agencies in the past have unequivocally stated that Iranian nuclear bomb is many years away.

Furthermore, the recent IAEA report stresses that at the very least Iran is 2 years away before it will possess enough uranium to make a bomb— even then the process is tedious to master and many observers predict it will take years.

Over the past 5 years, the bellicose nature of US-Iran relations have followed a well trodden trajectory, and the tiff over Iran's nuclear programme and the ascendency of Ahmadinejad has played a pivotal role.

That is to say fiery rhetoric employed by Washington and Tehran interwoven with covert collaboration between the two, has resulted in America consolidating its presence in the region. The pacifying of Iraq and Western Afghanistan, new security arrangements with the Gulf countries, impetus behind the deployment of US missile shield programme in Europe are some of the benefits accrued by US policy makers. Even now, Iranian

---

[14] Regev, Mark. "France Pushes for more Iran Sanctions", The Jerusalem Post, (September 16, 2008).

air force exercises, the Revolutionary Guards new responsibility to defend the Persian Gulf and US navy manoeuvres should be viewed within this context.

Increasingly, behind the scenes there are growing signs that US-Iranian relations are heading towards normalization. The presence of William Burns in the Geneva talks in July, the prospects of the establishment of a US diplomatic mission in Tehran and Obama's repeated mantra of engagement with Iran signal a warming of relations.

On Monday, five former US Secretaries of State among them Madeleine Albright, Colin Powell, Warren Christopher, Henry A. Kissinger and James A. Baker III called for greater engagement with Iran. The only sticking point for American policy makers is Israel's insistence on neutralizing Iran's imagined nuclear threat.

Hitherto, America has snubbed Israeli advances to attack Iran. America played down Israel's show of air power over the Mediterranean a few months ago, and has refused to sell the powerful GBU-29 bunker-busters bombs. Nonetheless, the decision to sell GBU-39 bomb a smaller version is America's way of assuaging Israel's concerns.

With the Bush administration embroiled in election fever, it is unlikely that the US will be at war with Iran. In fact the opposite is likely to happen—warming of ties between the US and Iran is on the cards.

September 21, 2008

14

# Musharraf's Bloodbath at the Masjid

*"Musharraf may be America's last hope in Pakistan, and if he fails, the fundamentalists would get hold of the Islamic bomb."*

*--Anthony Zinni*

The intensification of fighting between the students of Lal Masjid and the Pakistani army has left hundreds dead and many injured. This has prompted President Musharraf to issue the following provocative statement: "If they do not surrender so I am saying here today that they will be killed. They should not force us to use force. They should come out voluntarily; otherwise they will be killed..." Even before Musharraf's ultimatum, his government was swift to attribute the entire blame for the current crisis on Abdul Rashid Ghazi—the principal of the seminary. However, a close examination of the events preceding the standoff, suggests that the entire event was engineered by the Pakistani government.

For the past six months the Musharraf government has tolerated the behaviour of the students whenever they chose to challenge its writ. The accumulation of illegal arms, the abduction of Pakistani socialites and policemen, and the seizure of six Chinese women was met with muted criticism from government officials. Furthermore, these activities were not clandestine, and were planned and executed in full view of ISI's headquarters located in close proximity to the confines of the Lal Masjid. The frequent visit of ISI officials and government representatives negates government claims that it was exploring an amicable outcome— especially when measured against the ferocity of the Pakistani government's response to similar incidents in tribal agencies and elsewhere in Balochistan. So why has the Pakistani government waited so long to barricade the Masjid with military hardware fit for an overwhelming assault.

This question can only be answered in the broader context of the challenges facing Musharraf's rule. At present the Musharraf government has had to contend with both the secular opposition and Islamic forces calling for his removal. The secular forces championed by the Alliance for the Restoration of Democracy (ARD) and Chief Justice Iftikhar have gained momentum and have frustrated America's initiative to get Musharraf re-elected. To diffuse this threat, Musharraf under US auspices has held secret talks with certain leaders of the secular opposition and has deployed force against others. The deaths in Karachi are a manifestation of the latter approach. As far as negotiations are concerned, the US on Musharraf's behalf is already engaged in advanced talks with Benazir Bhutto with aim to break the back of the secular opposition and secure a second presidential term for Musharraf. This also explains Bhutto's recent ambiguous stance on the All Parties Conference (APC) in London[15], which she has shunned so far.

Whilst the Islamic opposition unhappy with Musharraf's pro-American policies and his neo-liberal attitudes have taken upon themselves to oust him from power. Some have resorted to militancy and others have engaged in protests to vent their anger. But the wellspring of their resentment is fuelled by the religious seminaries which America has identified for secularisation or closure. Unlike the secular opposition—where America was keen to compromise and broker a deal— the Islamic forces in the eyes of American policy makers must be secularised at gun point, and any resistance must be crushed. Hence the surrounding of Lal Masjid by the military in the absence of martial law, the humiliation of Abdul Aziz Ghazi on Pakistan television, the abrupt cancellation of talks, the media blackout

---

[15] "BB should attend APC in London, says Qazi",Pak Tribune,( June 28, 2007).

and the announcement of 'surrender or die' as a solution to the crisis is an ominous sign for the future of religious seminaries in Pakistan.

What transpired at Lal Masjid has all the hallmarks of becoming a template for Musharraf to deal with other religious schools and institutions— a recipe for civil war. Not to mention that the timing of the crisis suits Musharraf, as it deflects the public's attention away from the secular opposition and the government's disastrous response to the floods in Balochistan.

What is evident is that the utilisation of force by the government to deal with both secular and Islamic forces exposes the intellectual bankruptcy of Musharraf's mantra of enlightened moderation. Instead of employing thoughts to battle the ideas of the opposition, Musharraf has resorted to force. The same method has been repeated by Musharraf's allies—America, NATO and Israel— under the guise of 'battle of hearts and minds' and both have failed to crush the Islamic movements in Iraq, Afghanistan and Palestine. So what chance does Musharraf have?

July 9, 2007

# Part 3
# Fighting to Preserve Western Decadence

**15**

# Liberal Values Spawn Violent Crime

*"Society prepares the crime; the criminal commits it."*

*--Henry Thomas Buckle*

The killing of Pc Sharon Beshenivsky in Bradford[16], Briton spurred some to call for the arming of the British police force, while others demanded stiffer laws in curbing gun crime. Speaking on BBC Radio 4's Today programme, Tom McGhie the chairman of the West Yorkshire Police Federation called for a rethink on routinely arming officers.

The number of offences involving firearms in England and Wales has been increasing each year since 1997, according to the Home Office. Firearms incidents recorded by the police have nearly trebled in eight years. This is despite the government's efforts to curb violent crime involving guns. In 2003, the then Home Secretary David Blunkett introduced a host of measures which included a new gun amnesty, a five year prison sentence for illegal possession of firearms and greater protection to witnesses who testify in gun crime cases. The measures were in response to the brutal killing of two young girls in Birmingham. The initiatives did little to combat violent crime or address its root cause.

Over the past few months the British public has witnessed a large number of high profile crimes involving murders, stabbings, child abductions, rapes and robberies. Anyone turning on the television or listening to the radio will not fail to notice that a fair proportion of these

---

[16] "Horror and disbelief seize city", BBC News, (November 20, 2005).

crimes do not involve the use of firearms. There are countless incidents, where knives are the primary means of perpetrating violent crime and still ministers, politicians, social workers, and police officers choose to focus on gun control as a means of reducing violent crime.

This reactionary approach towards tackling crime is not only limited to violent offences, but extends to all forms of crime. Instead of solving the problem the current approach leads to more crime, extra legislation and further strain on the over populated prison system as well as a greater burden on the judiciary, a demoralised police force, a vulnerable public and a huge drain on resources estimated to be in the region of £60 billion.

A similar trend can be found in all other Western societies. In these societies the public is resigned to accept that crime is on the increase and very little can be done to reduce it. This does not need to be the case. Rather, what lies at the heart of the issue is the incorrect understanding in Western societies of crime and its causes; this has led to Western governments implementing ineffective solutions to combat crime.

Even the severity of the law does not deter people from committing crime. Thus for many years, Western governments have struggled to reduce the growing number of paedophiles, rapists, drug addicts, joy riders, burglars, fraudsters and the like - no matter how many laws they enact or how much time and money they spend on policing. The capitalist goal in life has greatly affected the public's attitude towards preventing crime. The public in capitalist societies are more concerned about preserving their ability to pursue sensual pleasure to the extent that they would not intervene to help other people enjoy their right to pursue pleasure, particularly if such intervention was associated with difficulty or danger.

Unless it is something that threatens their collective pursuit of enjoyment, the public rarely intervenes to stop crimes committed in front of them. This mind-set has moulded the public in Western societies to become apathetic towards crime, thereby allowing criminals to thrive amongst them. For instance if a thief ran out of a shop in a crowded shopping centre, the majority of the shoppers would be hesitant to give chase. If a group of people were attacking an individual on the bus, most people would remain quiet in their seats. If a pensioner was being mugged in the street, most people will ignore it.

The capitalist goal in life has also undermined the ability of capitalist states to fight crime. This is because the role of Western governments is to pass laws and implement policies which enable individuals to realise their optimal level of sensual fulfilment. All too often, the true benefactors are a small minority of people who are able to influence governments.

They pass laws that protect their right to pursue enjoyment at the expense of the vast majority of the people. In turn, this vast majority feel that these laws unfairly impinge on their right to pursue the capitalist goal and hence many resort to breaking the law. For instance, the majority of the British public abhors firearms, but fails to understand why the government has repeatedly taken no action against the media companies that glorify gun violence as the quickest way of attaining happiness through films, music, books and video games. Equally, in America, the public's demand to ban the selling of guns is met with government silence. In both cases, governments are more interested in allowing the media moguls and gun companies to maximise profits at the cost of the public.

The same argument applies to the redevelopment of deprived inner city areas, which governments and wealthy capitalists intentionally ignore as they are deemed to be commercially unprofitable. Understandably, people living in such areas will resort to crime. Even the punishment of criminals is based upon the capitalist goal; instead of designing punishments to deter potential criminals in society, punishments exist merely to restrict the convicted criminal's pursuit of pleasure. For example, the millionaire Geoffrey Archer was able to follow his lavish lifestyle, even though he is serving a custodial sentence. Therefore, at all levels of human behaviour the capitalist goal in life is the main driving force behind crime in Western societies.

On the other hand, Islam produces a society where crime is not the norm but an exception. This is because the Islamic goal in life is about seeking the pleasure of Allah (swt). It is through seeking the pleasure of Allah (swt) that a Muslim attains happiness.

Therefore Muslims are extremely careful when undertaking actions, large or small because they know that in the hereafter they will be held accountable for them. The outcome of which will be either paradise or hellfire determined by the Muslim's compliance to Allah (swt)'s commands and prohibitions in this life. This belief instils in Muslims a strong sense of *Taqwa* (fear of Allah (swt)), responsibility towards others and obedience to Islamic laws and authority. At an individual level this becomes a very powerful deterrent against crime, as one is constantly aware of the consequences of one's actions. Allah (swt) reminds us in the Qur'ān:

*"And We are nearer to him than his jugular vein."* [TMQ Qaf:16]

The manifestation of this self-policing would mean that unlike capitalist countries, the future Islamic state will not need to spend huge resources to fight crime, use large numbers of surveillance techniques to catch criminals or employ a large police force dedicated to crime prevention.

Similarly, the Islamic society's yearning to seek the pleasure of Allah (swt) will engender a collective mentality amongst the public where the preservation of society and Islamic laws will be regarded as more important than one's own interest. This is because for Muslims, the transgression of the commands and prohibitions of Allah (swt) by offenders is a sin that must be stopped. Islam has obliged Muslims to enjoin Mar'uf (good) and forbid Munkar (evil). The Prophet (SAW) said in a Hadith narrated by Abu Sa'id al Khudri:

"Whosoever sees a Munkar (an evil or wrong) let him change it by his hand, if he could not let it be by his tongue. If he could not let it be by his heart, and this is the weakest of Iman."                                    [Muslim]

In the case of non-Muslim citizens it will be the justice of Islam that will be the motivating factor for crime prevention. This will galvanise public opinion to become an effective deterrent against crime.

However, there will always be a minority that will choose to violate the laws imposed by Islam. For them, Islam has laid down a comprehensive punishment system, which is administered by the state. The punishments in Islam are not intended to restrict the offender, but are meant to dissuade others from carrying out crime. For instance concerning the thief, Allah (swt) says:

*"As to the thief, male or female, cut off his or her hand. It is the reward of their own deeds, an exemplary punishment from Allah (swt). Allah (swt) is All Mighty, All Wise."*

[TMQ Al-Maida:38]

In Islam the individual through his *Taqwa*, the public through their concern about the preservation of society and the state all act in unison to ensure that laws are implemented and that crime is minimised. Islamic history bears testimony to this fact. For example, when Imam Malik was appointed the judge of Madinah, he had to wait almost a year before he presided over his first case. Also the records of the courts that existed in the main cities in the Islamic State show that the types of cases dealt by courts were primarily social issues like divorce, inheritance and business related disputes. The number of cases involving murders, muggings, rapes and the like were nowhere near the figures that occur in Western societies today.

November 20, 2005

# 16

# Individualism in the West Contributes to Child Neglect

*"Most of the obstacles children face today are linked to the belief among adults that the prime duty of the individual is to make the most of their own life, rather than contribute to the good of others... excessive individualism is causing a range of problems for children including: high family break-up, teenage unkindness, commercial pressures towards premature sexualisation, unprincipled advertising, too much competition in education and acceptance of income inequality."*

*--UK Good Childhood Inquiry*

The ever-increasing reports of child neglect in the West clearly demonstrate that more and more parents are mistreating their children to pursue the fulfilment of their own needs. In Britain, the notorious case of a mother who repeatedly tortured her 17 month old baby to death, so that she could carry on with her own life is just the tip of the iceberg. When the body of the baby was examined he had 50 injuries including 8 broken ribs, a fractured spine and missing finger nails[17]. Preliminary findings suggest that social workers, police officials and health professionals failed to piece together the jigsaw of neglect in spite of several warning signs. Then there is the horrific story of 56 year old man from Sheffield who routinely raped his 2 daughters and fathered 9 children with them.

---

[17] "After 17 months of unimaginable cruelty, Baby P finally succumbed", The Times, (November 12, 2008).

According to the latest available figures from National Society for the Prevention of Cruelty to Children (NSPCC), there are 32,700 children on child protection registers in the UK. Every ten days in England and Wales, on average, one child is killed at the hands of their parent. The people most likely to die a violent death are babies under 1 year old, who are four times more likely to be killed than the average person in England and Wales. 16% of children experienced serious maltreatment by parents, of whom one third experienced more than one type of maltreatment. Over a quarter of all rapes recorded by the police are committed against children under 16 years of age. Nearly 79,000 children are currently looked after by local authorities in the UK[18]. It is fair to assume that the actual figure is much higher, as many children are either too scared to report abuse or simply do not know how to report it.

It is almost customary for governments to respond to cases of child neglect by launching public inquiries. In the past the outcome of such inquiries has led to either the social services playing a greater role in the prevention of the ill-treatment of children or new legislation aimed at offering children greater protection from abusive parents. All too often these inquiries fail to stem the growing tide of child abuse pervading British society. This has led some to call for tougher measures such as permanently taking children away from cruel parents or even stripping them of their right to reproduce. It is highly unlikely that the present government will make any headway in reducing the ill treatment of children. This is because the main cause behind child abuse is the unbridled individualism, which governments, sociologists and parents alike have repeatedly refused to acknowledge.

Individualism is an important pillar of Western Secularism and dominates many of the relationships that exist between people in Western societies. Individualism stipulates that people should put their interests first

---

[18] NSPCC Media Center

and foremost. This imbues in people a selfish mentality and encourages people to satisfy their own needs before the needs of others. Furthermore, individualism leads people to view responsibility as a burden and a hindrance towards the fulfilment of their selfish motives. Therefore, it is common to find people in the West, especially in the social sphere, entering and leaving relationships in order to avoid responsibility - all of which has a detrimental effect on society. Hence rampant fornication, abortions, single parent families, fathers avoiding child maintenance costs, mothers forsaking children to pursue careers, parents giving up children to foster homes and wanton child abuse are all symptoms of individualism.

Western governments are unable to deal with the effects of individualism and the harm it causes to society. This is because the role of the government is to guarantee individualism for its citizens and not to impose restrictions on people's individuality. Therefore, the primary concern of government is the welfare of the individual and not the family or wider society. For instance, when dealing with the issue of child abuse, Western governments view the child and its rights as separate to the rights of the mother and the rights of the father. Naturally any solutions arising from this type of thinking will focus more on preserving the individuality of the child, mother or father than protecting the family or society. In this way, the family and society bear no collective responsibility towards the mistreatment of children, since law and responsibility are solely applied at the level of the individual.

In Islam, the concept of individualism is limited to the relationship between man and God and the relationship of man with himself i.e. in the matters of worship, foodstuffs, clothing and morals. In relationships that involve people, individuals are permitted to satisfy their needs provided that they do not violate the rights of other individuals or transgress the limits imposed by Islam for the welfare of the society. In all types of relationships Muslims are required to seek the pleasure of God by conducting themselves according to laws prescribed by Islam. These laws when practiced produce a unique and distinct character for the human being, a character shaped by altruism and not selfishness. Islam promoted and raised high, not only the relationship between the parent and child, but also that of family and society.

Islam praised the family, the Messenger of Allah (SAW) said, *"Do marry the devoted and prolific women, for I will be proud of you before other nations on the Day of Judgement."* [Abu Dawood, at-Tirmidhi]. Islam forbade the killing and torturing of children. It is mentioned in the Qur'an:

*"Kill not your children for fear of want, We shall provide sustenance for them as well as for you."*

[TMQ Al-Isra:31]

Islam has forbidden the neglect of children and has made it obligatory for parents to provide food, clothing and shelter in addition to fulfilling the various other requirements of their children. The Messenger of Allah (SAW) said,

"It is enough sin for a person that he ignores those whom he is responsible for."                                                              [Abu Dawood]

Today, individualism threatens the social fabric of British society through the erosion of family values and violation of civil rights. Left unquestioned and unchecked, individualism will result in the fragmentation of both Muslim and non-Muslim communities. The Islamic attitude towards the family and society is much more responsible than the narcissistic outlook of secularism.

November 28, 2008

# 17

## Ethics in the West: Deciding Whether Cloning is Right or Wrong?

*"As soon as questions of will or decision or reason or choice of action arise, human science is at a loss."*

*--Noam Chomsky*

Cloning has rekindled the ongoing debate centred on ethical concerns, which scientists, pro-creationists, politicians and religious personalities are struggling to define in terms of right and wrong. Scientists, who favour cloning, argue that the tissue material from cloned embryos could lead to breakthroughs in the treatment of severe human diseases such as Parkinson's, Motor Neuron or Diabetes. On the other hand the Church and pro-life campaigners argue that the cloning of embryos constitutes life, and to terminate an embryo would be no different to terminating the life of any other human being. Western politicians are also deeply divided between the two views. In 2003, White House spokesman said that US President George Bush had found the news "deeply troubling", and added that the news underscored the need for legislation to ban all human cloning in the US. While other politicians most notably those with close ties with biotechnology firms are fervent supporters of human cloning. So who is right?

Many people in the West believe that science is fully capable of providing truths about human behaviour, which in turn can be used to govern people's lives. This view is erroneous as the scientific thought is a particular type of thought only suited to the study of material objects under laboratory conditions. Under these conditions no ethical truths are revealed or discovered. This is because material objects do not possess an inherent ethical attribute, which during experimentation manifests itself as right or wrong. Science can only provide explanation of how things function and cannot answer questions such as 'is it right?', or 'should this be allowed?'

The same argument applies to the so called scientific study of human behaviour. Human beings are not born with an ethical code, nor do human actions have an intrinsic ethical quality, which helps the scientist decide whether the action is right or wrong. For instance science can explain the process by which procreation occurs, but can it tell us whether it is right to have sexual relationships in or out of wedlock, between brother and sister or between an adult and a child? Those who choose to engage in incest or sexually abuse children are branded deviants and abhorred by society. The same was said about homosexual relationships, until recently, when public opinion was changed to make homosexuality acceptable as an idea. Scientist then suggested that some people were born with the inclination to prefer people of the same gender. If it were proven that people were born with a tendency to commit incest, sexually abuse children or murder would that in any way make it right? Would these actions be regarded as acceptable by society?

Science is unable to pass ethical judgements especially on human actions and can never provide a code of ethics for mankind. In reality, people live according to a specific viewpoint of life, which shapes their inclinations and tastes. This viewpoint of life emanates from a creed and gives rise to a specific system, which binds people together to produce a distinctive society. The creed coupled with its viewpoint of life produces a code of ethics responsible for governing society.

In Western societies it is the secular creed together with its view point on life based on benefit, which determines what is right and wrong. In practice the politicians who are the elected representatives of the people are given the responsibility of deciding what is right and wrong on behalf of society. Politicians may entertain scientific facts or arguments from other sources during the law making process, but ultimately the Western point of view i.e. benefit determines ethics. Therefore it is common to find Western politicians subscribing to those ethical views, which provide them and their sponsors with the greatest amount of benefit. Usually the sponsors of such views are powerful interest groups such as big businesses, wealthy industrialists and influential organisations. Often there is a clash between these powerful groups as each group competes by lobbying politicians to protect their interests. In such circumstances politicians seek a compromise verdict to appease these interest groups. Nevertheless, in both cases no serious attempt is made to seek the truth, the foremost concern of all parties is to safeguard their interests. For instance on the issue of human cloning Tony Blair's New Labour party, which has close links with biotech companies, is in favour of human cloning, while opposition groups such as the anti-abortion charity, Life, want a total ban on all forms of human cloning.

In the end, the government sought a middle ground and enacted legislation to support the cloning of human embryos[19], but outlawed the cloning of a human being. An ethical position which is definitely incorrect, as it fails to provide an answer to the original question.

A major flaw of Western way of life is that ethical standards constantly evolve and change around benefit. There is no absolute truth or falsehood, right or wrong. What is viewed as evil and abhorrent in a particular age is praised and raised high at different times. Take for example the issues of adultery, homosexuality, and children born out of wedlock or the taking of cannabis. All of these issues have been despised in the past, but now are accepted by society. Similarly, what is considered by people as wrong is regarded by other people who share the same values as right. For example,

---

[19] "Peers back cloning research", BBC News, (January 22, 2001).

the Europeans consider capital punishment to be barbaric whilst the Americans uphold it as a civilised form of punishment. This leads to people losing confidence in ethical standards and eventually society becomes morally bankrupt and declined.

In Islam truth and falsehood, right and wrong are clearly defined and do not change with age, places or people. The Islamic laws or ethical standards in Islam are fixed and do not revolve around benefit nor are subject to environmental influences. This is because the Islamic creed recognises God as the only sovereign and not man. God alone is the arbiter of what is right and what is wrong. This means that all actions undertaken by Muslims or all judgements pronounced by Muslims on things or events must comply with Islam.

Islam did not leave human beings without guidance in this life. On the contrary, Islam provides a complete and comprehensive way of life in the form of the Qur'ān and the Sunnah of the Messenger of Allah (SAW). The legal texts found in the Qur'ān and the Sunnah are more than capable of addressing all human problems. This is because the legal texts of Islam have an immense capacity to produce a multitude of solutions to problems encountered by human beings irrespective of diversity of the problem or its complexity. So what is Islam's view on cloning?

The aim of cloning in plants and animals is to improve quality and increase productivity, and to find a natural cure for many common human diseases, especially the acute ones, instead of using chemical drugs which have harmful side effects on mans health.

The improvement in the quality of plants and animals and the increase of productivity is not prohibited from a shari'i perspective, and it is among the things that are allowed. Also, the use of plants and animal cloning to cure human diseases, especially acute ones, is allowed in Islam. It is even recommended because seeking a cure for illness is recommended and manufacturing medicine for curing is recommended as well. Imam Ahmad narrates from Anas that the Messenger of Allah (SAW) said,

"Allah (swt) has created the illness and the cure. So seek a cure."

Therefore, it is allowed to use the cloning process to improve the quality of plants and to increase their productivity. It is also allowed to use the cloning process to improve the quality of cows, sheep, camels, horses, and other animals, in order to increase productivity of these animals and to increase their numbers, and to utilise this to cure many of the human diseases especially the acute ones.

This is the ruling concerning cloning plants and animals. As for cloning human beings, it is as follows:

For foetal cloning, the zygote is formed in the womb of a wife as a result of the husband's sperm and the wife's egg. That zygote is then divided into many cells, which can divide and grow. These cells are divided so that each cell becomes a foetus by itself, as a duplicate of the original zygote. Then, if they were to be implanted in the womb of a foreign woman or in the womb of the husband's second wife, these two forms of cloning would be prohibited (Haram) because this would result in mixing of kinship. Then, it would cause loss of kinship, and Islam has prohibited this.

If on the other hand, one or more of these zygotes were implanted in the wife's womb (who was the source of the original cell) then this form of cloning would be permitted (*Halal*). This is because it is a multiplying of the zygote, which existed in the wife's womb through a medical procedure to bring about identical twins. This is the rule concerning foetal cloning.

As for the cloning of humans, it could be done by taking a body cell from the male, extracting its nucleus, merging it with a female's egg after removing the egg's own nucleus. This male nucleus in a female egg would be transferred to a woman's womb to double and grow. Hence, it would become a foetus and then a baby, which is a duplicate of the original male from whose body the cell was taken. Also, cloning could be done among females only without a need for a male. This is done by taking a cell from the body of a female and extracting its nucleus in order to merge it with a female's egg. Then, the egg is transferred to a woman's womb after it is merged with the cell's nucleus, to grow and become a foetus and then a baby, which is a duplicate of the female from which the cell was taken. This is what happened with Dolly, the sheep, where the nucleus was taken from a sheep's breast cell. Then, the elements related to the breast were taken out from this nucleus and the nucleus was placed in a sheep's egg after removing its own nucleus. The cell was placed in the womb of a sheep to multiply and grow, and become a foetus. Dolly, the sheep, was born as an exact duplicate of the first sheep from which the cell was taken.

This cloning of humans, males or females, if done, would be a disaster for the world. This would be the case whether the aim was to improve quality, select the offspring which is smarter, stronger, braver, healthier, or more beautiful, or if the aim was to increase the number in order to increase the population or to make the state stronger. It is prohibited because of the following reasons:

1. The production of children in this manner is different from the natural way that Allah (swt) made humans to reproduce their offspring. Allah (swt) says,

*"And that He (Allah (swt)) created the pairs, male and female. From Nutfah (drops of semen - male and female discharges) when it is emitted."*

[TMQ An-Najm:45-46]

Allah (swt) also says,

*"Was he not a Nutfah (drops of semen) poured forth? Then he became a clot; then (Allah (swt)) shaped and fashioned (him) in due proportion. And made him in two sexes, male and female."*

[TMQ Al-Qiyamah:37-39]

2. The children who are born out of cloning females, without a male, have no fathers. In addition, they will not have mothers if the egg that was merged with the nucleus of the cell was placed in the womb of a female different from that female whose egg was used in the cloning process. This is the case because the female whose womb was used to implant the egg is no more than a place to house the egg. This will lead to the loss of that human, where he has no father and no mother. This contradicts the saying of Allah (swt),

*"O mankind! We have created you from a male and a female."*

[TMQ Al- Hujurat:13]

And also His (swt) saying,

*"Call them by the names of their fathers, that is more just in the sight of Allah (swt)."*

[TMQ Al-Ahzab:5]

3. Loss of kinship. Islam has obligated preserving affinity and maintaining it. Ibn Abbas said that the Messenger of Allah (SAW) said,

*"Whoever claims relationship by birth to other than his father or belonged to other than those he belongs to, then the curse of Allah (swt), the Angels, and all the people be upon him."*

(Narrated by Ibn Majah).

Abi 'Uthman an-Nahri said that he heard Sa'd and Abu Bakrah each of them saying that they had heard and understood from the Messenger of Allah (SAW) saying,

*"Anyone who makes a claim for somebody other than his father and he knows that he is not his father, then Paradise is forbidden for him."*     (Narrated by Ibn Majah).

Abu Hurayrah also narrated that he heard the Messenger of Allah (SAW) saying (when the verse of cursing was revealed),

"Any woman who introduced to some people an offspring that does not belong to them, then she has nothing to do with Allah (swt) and she will not enter Paradise; and any man who denies his son while looking at him, Allah (swt) will not reveal Himself to him and Allah (swt) will disgrace him in front of the first and last generations." [Narrated by Al-Darimi].

The cloning which aims at producing people who are outstanding in terms of their intelligence, strength, health, and beauty would mean choosing the people with characteristics among the males and the females regardless of if they were married couples or not. As a result, the cells would be taken from the males who had the required characteristics, and the eggs would be taken from selected women and implanted in selected women. This would lead to the kinship being lost and mixed.

4. The production of children through cloning prevents applying many of the shari'i rules, such as the rules of marriage, kinship, alimony, fatherhood, sonship, inheritance, custody, Maharim and 'Usbat (forbidden degrees of consanguinity) in addition to many other shari'i rules. The affinity would get mixed and would be lost. This goes against the natural way that Allah (swt) has created people, in terms of reproduction. Therefore, human cloning is prohibited (Haram) from a *shari'i* perpective and it is not allowed.

Allah (swt) said quoting the cursed Satan,

*"I will command them to change the creation of Allah (swt)."* [TMQ An-Nisa:119]

The creation of Allah (swt) is the nature (fitra) which Allah (swt) has created in people at birth, and the nature (fitra) of reproduction of humans from a male and a female through the fertilisation of the sperm of the male with the egg from the female. The law of Allah (swt) is that this process is to be done between a male and a female with a valid contract. It is not the nature (fitra) that reproduction and birth are achieved by cloning. This is in addition to the fact that this would happen between a male and a female who do not have a valid marriage contract that binds them.

Clearly, the 1400 year old legal texts of Islam present unambiguous answers to issues arising out of human cloning, which Western societies and science are unable to answer. Muslims should take every opportunity to highlight the inability of Secularism and science to make ethical judgements for society.

December 8, 2005

**18**

## America's Spy Scandal is Confirmation that it is a Totalitarian State

*"It's almost incomprehensible and more than tragic that this kind of adversarial relationship exists between the government and the people; where fear and distrust prevail and government policies and actions are tearing down the Constitutional foundations of this nation. And if this descent into the deepening darkness of totalitarianism is not somehow aborted, then America will become a living hell."*

*--Michael Payne*

With each passing day new revelations about the extent of US spying operations both at home and abroad are making headlines across the world. At home the National Security Agency (NSA) has been spying on millions of Americans by sweeping up metadata, and tapping data centres of leading American companies such as Google. Eric Schmidt, the CEO of Google attacked NSA practices and said, "It's really outrageous that the National Security Agency was looking between the Google data centres, ...The steps that the organization was willing to do without good judgment to pursue its mission and potentially violate people's privacy, it's not OK.[20]"

However, Schmidt's remarks do not absolve American companies from the brewing spy scandal. On the contrary, the existence of the notorious PRISM programme, which collects internet communication in collaboration with leading US tech companies such as Google, Yahoo and Microsoft, belittles Schmidt's remarks. Additionally, PRISM is the number one source of raw intelligence used for NSA's analytic reports, and it accounts for 91% of the NSA's Internet traffic acquired under Foreign

---

[20] "Google: NSA spying on data centers is 'outrageous'", Fox News, (November 04, 2013).

Intelligence Surveillance Act (FISA) section 702. This squarely places American tech companies at the forefront of the digital spying efforts.

The scale and magnitude of the spying operation led by NSA on foreign shores is simply mind boggling. For instance it is claimed that between December 10, 2012 and January 8, 2013 NSA spied on 70.3 million phone calls in France. In Spain, NSA secretly tracked 60 million phone calls in Spain in a single month. The agency has also spied on at least 35 foreign leaders and the most high profile victim is Angela Merkel whose phone was tapped for at least 10 years. Brazilian President Dilma Rousseff cancelled a visit to the US in protest, and a statement on behalf of Merkel said, "Among close friends and partners... there should be no such monitoring of the communications of a head of government.[21]" The statement also said that Mrs Merkel had told Mr Obama: "Such practices must be prevented immediately."

Leaving aside America's enemies, American citizens and America's allies abroad must be wondering what crimes they have committed to warrant such extensive intrusion into their privacy. The Obama government has sought to play down the outpouring of rage over NSA tactics by offering feeble justifications ranging from the prevention of terrorism to every country spies and America is no different. For instance, NSA's Director, General Keith Alexander, claimed the NSA surveillance had contributed to the prevention of 54 terror plots. But after media furore of over the claims, NSA's deputy Director admitted that only one terror plot was foiled due surveillance.

The fallout from America's spy programme has been immediate and far reaching. American technology giants such as Microsoft, Google, Verizon, AT&T are facing credibility issues after being caught red handed in aiding and abetting NSA, and the EU is reconsidering its intelligence cooperation

---

[21] "Merkel calls Obama about 'US spying on her phone'", BBC News, October 23, 2013).

with the US. Meanwhile Brazil, Russia, India and China (BRIC countries) are accelerating plans to complete the building of a new internet.

So clearly then the crisis for America is not limited to overturning its trust-deficit with allies and other countries. Rather, America the harbinger of freedom and democracy faces a much graver threat i.e. its behaviour is incompatible with the values it espouses. Already, some notable American personalities are raising their voices. For example, when Jimmy Carter was asked about Edward Snowden's exposure of Washington's secret global surveillance system, he said, "America does not have a functioning democracy at this point in time."

Unlike Western countries where spying has become a fundamental means of controlling the behaviour of citizens, Islam has specified clear rules about the Islamic state spying on its citizens. It is mentioned in the Qur'ān :

*"You who have iman! Avoid most suspicion. Indeed some suspicion is a crime. And do not spy and do not backbite one another. Would any of you like to eat his brother's dead flesh? No, you would hate it. And have Taqwa of Allah (swt). Allah (swt) is Ever-Returning, Most Merciful."*

[TMQ Hujurat:12].

In relation to this verse, Abdur Rahman ibn Awf (RA) reported during the reign of Umar bin Al Khattab (RA) be pleased with him) the second Caliph that he would patrol the city at night with Umar and on one occasion they were walking when the lamp of a household caught their attention. They approached it until they heard loud voices inside the door. Umar grabbed the hand of Abdur Rahman(RA) and he said, "Do you know whose house this is?" He said, "No." Umar said, "This is the house of Rabia ibn Umayyah ibn Khalaf and they are inside drinking wine right now! So what do you think?" Abdur Rahman said, "Indeed, I think we have done what Allah (swt) has prohibited for us. Allah (swt) the Exalted said: *"Do not spy"* [TMQ Hujurat:12] and we have spied on them." So Umar turned away and he left them alone.

The return of the Islamic Caliphate will set a new benchmark in governance and how people will live in peace and security. The citizens of the caliphate will live safe in the knowledge that the ruling authority is not allowed to spy on them, be it through physical means or via electronic surveillance. The protection of privacy in the Islamic Caliphate will stand in strong contrast to the West, where it is routinely abused and has become a form of persecution and distress for the people.

November 11, 2013

# Part 4
# Return of the Caliphate

**19**

# Europe's Constitutional Schisms Reveal Important Lessons for Muslims

*"The extinction of race consciousness as between Muslims is one of the outstanding achievements of Islam, and in the contemporary world there is, as it happens, a crying need for the propagation of this Islamic virtue."*
                                                                   *--Arnold Toynbee*

The crisis in the European Union (EU) over its constitution and economic budget has become a subject of great debate amongst Europeans. Non-Europeans too have taken a keen interest in the EU's predicament and have been eager to speculate on Europe's future. Some predict Europe's demise, while others view the current crisis as an opportunity to modernise and transform the EU into a world power that is able to challenge American global hegemony.

Opinions of most Muslim commentators fall into these two camps. However, there are some important lessons to be learnt from the present crisis, which has escaped the attention of many commentators. These can be summarised as follows:

## 1. Islamophobia - a permanent barrier between Europe and the Islamic world

The overwhelmingly decision by Dutch[22] and French[23] voters to reject the EU's constitution was in part fuelled by centuries old animosity towards the Islamic world. This is not the first time that Islamophobia has raised its ugly head, but it is the first time that ordinary Europeans have been given a chance to voice their fears of Islam via the ballot box.

---

[22] "Dutch Voters Reject European Union Charter", Fox News, (June 01, 2005).
[23] "French say firm 'No' to EU treaty", BBC News, (May 30, 2005 ).

The events of September 11, the bomb blasts in London and Madrid, and Turkey's desire to join the union has created a well of anti-Islamic feelings that permeates all sections of European society. Europe's premier media institutions and elitist politicians have exploited this sentiment to create a permanent wedge between Europe and the Islamic world.

Europeans fed on a daily diet of Islamophobia have taken every opportunity to spurn immigration from the Islamic world and reject Turkey's entry into the Union.

Even Britain and America that champion Turkey's entry, do so, because they believe it will stoke the flames of Islamophobia and bring an end to the Franco-German dream of a powerful Europe. Simply put the barrier of hate erected by Europe to ward off advances from Turkey and Maghreb countries has become insurmountable. It is foolhardy for the elite in these Muslim countries to continue efforts to make their countries part of a union that reviles Islam.

## 2. Nationalism resurgent in Europe but fades in the Muslim world

Once again Europe is confronted with its old adversary-nationalism, which for centuries has wreaked havoc on the continent. European nationalism suppressed for decades has been reawakened by the forces of globalisation and now threatens to destroy the very soul of the Union.

Today, Europeans are more worried about safeguarding their national identities than moving forward with a constitution that places greater emphasis on a European identity. Subsequently, the current problems faced by Europe, and the solutions advocated are no longer viewed from the perspective of a unified Europe, but through the prism of nationalism. The dispute over the budget is a classic example of European nationalism tearing apart the EU.

In contrast, nationalism which was exported to the Islamic world and used to 'divide and conquer' Muslims is in full retreat. Today the concept of *Ummah* has superseded nationalism and has become a unifying force for Muslims across the world. Muslims from Morocco to Indonesia are quickly discovering that they have more in common with the Islamic vision of brotherhood than their present identities defined by artificial borders.

The plight of Muslims in Palestine, Chechnya, Kashmir, Iraq and Afghanistan is no longer viewed as parochial problems, but as Islamic problems that must have an Islamic solution.

### 3. Political unity is a dream for Europe but a reality for Muslims

The EU experiment was a bold attempt by some European nations to put to rest centuries of division and warfare. This initiative was given further impetus, when the elites in France and Germany realised that American supremacy could not be challenged by them alone. Hence the concept of a European Super state was born.

But after 40 years of trying to create a post modern state, the EU has disintegrated into a collection of pre-modern states (nation states), where powerful states like England, France and Germany are at loggerheads over Europe's future.

This was a predictable outcome. The European continent has been plagued with cultural differences, religious schisms and intense rivalries between powerful states. European history clearly demonstrates that there is very little to unite Europeans except foreign threats.

In the 17th century the advance of the Ottoman army to the gates of Vienna briefly spurred European nations to put aside their differences-only to be resumed later. In the 20th century, the threats from the Soviet Union, and later from America's global hegemony forced Europe to coalesce in the form of a union.

More often than not, the coming together of European nations is a temporary affair and is used by some to recuperate after experiencing the ravages of war. But as soon as the external threat weakens, in this case America's position in the world, Europe defaults to a state of disunity.

However, the unification of Muslim world into a single entity is not a mere dream but a reality. For centuries, Muslims irrespective of differences in race, language, colour and geography remained part of a single political entity known as the Caliphate.

The present day nation states in the Islamic world are alien to Muslims. They do not have any precedence in Islamic history nor are they a product of Islamic jurisprudence. The nation state was forced upon the Muslims by Western powers to prevent the re-establishment of the Caliphate.

As such, the Muslim masses never really expressed their loyalty to these artificial states and had to be governed by tyranny. Now it's just a matter of time before these regimes of terror are toppled and a global Caliphate is established on their ruins.

The rulers of the Muslim world are not blind to these realities; rather they are opposed to them. These rulers continuously preach that Muslims can never be united and that the establishment of the Caliphate belongs to the realm of the past.

If by chance, they ever do suggest unity between Muslims then it is through Western inspired institutions like the OIC, Arab League, Gulf Cooperation Council (GCC) and the like.

Paradoxically these institutions and the nation-states that were manufactured to delay the political unity of Muslims have become the vehicles of change. Their impotence has encouraged Muslims worldwide to discard Europe and America as model states, and to redouble their efforts to re-establish the Caliphate.

July 9, 2005

**20**

# Middle East: America's Democracy Advance Puts Secularism into Retreat

*"65% want to unify all Islamic counties into a single Islamic state or Caliphate."*

*--WorldPublicOpinion.org*

N‌ot so long ago, President Bush announced his much coveted Greater Middle East Initiative as part of his global war on terrorism. The aim of the plan was to preserve the existing secular order across the region through the promotion of freedom and democracy. But in today's Middle Eastern societies, Bush's initiative is having just the opposite effect. Islamists throughout the region have shown unprecedented gains in recent elections and now pose a direct challenge to the dictatorships and monarchies that thrive under American patronage.

During Egypt's parliamentary elections in 2005, the Muslim Brotherhood secured 20%[24] of the seats. Had not Mubarak's regime resorted to intimidation in the second and third rounds of the balloting, the figure would have been much higher. But despite the regimes brutal tactics to suppress the Islamists, the Muslim Brotherhood employed the slogan 'Islam is the solution' and outperformed secular rivals in garnering greater support amongst Egypt's electorate. In the Iraqi parliamentary elections of 2005, the religious parties took the bulk of the Iraqi votes. Of 275 seats in the Council of Representatives, the Shia dominated United Iraqi Alliance won 128 seats. The alliance includes the Dawa Party led by Prime Minister

---

[24] "Egyptian Parliamentary Elections: CNN interviews Amr Hamzawy", Carnegie Endowment, (December 8, 2005).

Ibrahim al-Jaafari and the Supreme Council for the Islamic Revolution in Iraq, led by Abdul Aziz al-Hakim. The alliance fell 10 votes short of an absolute majority. The Sunni fundamentalists of the Iraqi Accord Front secured 44 seats, while Kurdish Islamists took 5 seats. Had not America and her surrogates interfered directly in the electoral process, the strength of the Islamists' vote would have completely marginalized the secularists. In any case, the Iraqi Council of Representatives will be dominated by representatives who have a strong religious disposition and are expected to throw out policies, which they deem to be overtly secular. The outcome of the Palestinian election scheduled for January 25 2006 will probably mimic the election results of Egypt and Iraq. Already pollsters are predicting a strong showing for Hamas, which is avidly anti-Israeli and has vowed its destruction. Hamas fielding 62 candidates is projected to take more than a third of the 132 seats available in the Palestinian Legislative Council. Threats from Israel to preclude the organisation from contesting the election and America's dislike of its hard-line stance have boosted the group's popularity. Apart from Fatah, the other secular party's cannot mount an effective challenge to the growing influence of Hamas and other Islamists. Fatah reeling from internal schisms and widely viewed as being corrupt will be the main looser.

The pattern of Islamists outshining secularists in elections is being repeated elsewhere in the Arab world. For instance in the Saudi municipal elections last year, Islamists won 6 of the 7 seats in Riyadh and swept the elections in Jeddah and Makkah. Candidates backed by Sunni Islamists also won control of the municipal councils in a number of towns in the Eastern Province. In the 2003 parliamentary election in Yemen, the Yemeni Reform Group (Islah), a combination of Islamist and tribal elements, won 46 of the 301 seats and now forms the opposition. That year, Islamists combined to win 17 of the 50 seats in the Kuwaiti parliament, where they form the dominant ideological bloc. In Jordan, Bahrain and Morocco too, Islamists have made gains often at the expense of secularists[25].

The ubiquitous presence of Islamists and the rapid decline of the secularists have altered the political landscape of the Arab world. Early indications suggest that this transformation is going to be permanent. According to the 2004 Zogby International-Sadat Chair poll, of those surveyed in Jordan, Saudi Arabia, and the UAE said the clergy should play a greater role in their political systems. Fifty percent of Egyptians polled said the clerics should not dictate the political system, but as many as 47 percent supported a greater role for them. So the political trend is clear; more democratic the Arab world gets, the more likely it is that Islamists will come to power[26].

Not only has Bush's democracy drive in the Middle East strengthened political Islam it has also failed to stymie the tide of militant Islam which grows more violent by the day. In April 2005, the US State Department decided to stop publishing an annual report on international terrorism after the government's top terrorism centre concluded that there were more terrorist attacks in 2004 than in any year since 1985, the first year the publication covered. Another casualty of this initiative has been the battle of hearts and minds. According to the 2005 Zogby poll on Arab attitudes towards America, 63% of Jordanians, 85 % of Egyptians, 89% of Saudis, 66% of Lebanese, and 69% of the people in UAE had an unfavourable opinion of America.

The collapse of Bush's plan to advance democracy in the Middle East has not escaped the attention of policy makers back home. A bitter dispute has broken out between supporters of Bush and the critics of his plan. The opponents of his plan argue that Bush is not doing enough to isolate the

---

[25] F. Gregory Gause III , "Can Democracy Stop Terrorism?", Foreign Affairs, (September/October 2005)
[26] ibid

Islamists and promote the moderates as part of the democracy push in the Middle East. They also maintain that Islamists, especially those that are vociferously anti-American cannot be trusted and must be excluded from the democracy experiment. Their view is based on the idea that the refusal of the Muslim world to accept Western values lies with the ideology of Islam. In their opinion the Islamic texts have to fundamentally change before the Arab world can be accepted by the West.

The supporters on the other hand advocate a more pragmatic approach. They believe that by co-opting Islamists in the democratic process, the Arab world can be moulded into a region that accepts Western values, is substantially less anti-American and willingly accepts American hegemony. Their belief rests on the premise that by keeping Islamists out of the democratic process will only breed resentment and violence against the West. They cite Turkey as the ideal model for the Arab world to follow. A major proponent of this view is the neoconservative Marc Gerecht who recently argued in an article entitled 'Devout Democracies' that self rule in the Muslim world will have a religious component and the West should not be afraid of this phenomena.

Whichever of the two views succeeds in guiding America's democracy experiment in the Middle East, it will have a negligible impact on curbing the rise of political Islam. This is because the people of the Middle East will never forget or forgive America's unstinting support for Israel, her unflinching support for the brutal Arab dictatorships, her exploitation of their natural resources, her imposition of capitalist solutions and values, and her determined efforts to wage wars against the people of Iraq and other Muslims. These painful realities are permanently etched on the minds of the Arabs and continuously urge the Arab populace to seek solace in political Islam.

The Middle East is the heart of the Islamic world and right now it is pulsating with political Islam that will inevitably lead to the re-emergence of the Caliphate. Promoting democracy or eschewing its implementation, substituting Islamic texts with secular interpretations, isolating Islamists and encouraging moderates, destroying regimes and replacing them with compliant US surrogates is not going to change the outcome. America's past relations with the Arabs has sealed her fate with the present Arabs. The time has come for US policy makers to think about the future – what type of relations does the US want with the Caliphate?

January 23, 2006

# 21

# 21st American Century is About to End

*"Much like the time leading up to World War I, coalitions and regional blocs could form to contest American supremacy. If one of these entities could consolidate its power quickly enough, a new bipolar world could emerge. Potentially, China, a pan-Arab coalition, or a unified European Union (EU) could become this new superpower."*

*--Robert DeYeso*

Barely six years have elapsed since President Bush took office and the much coveted 21st century belongs to America is about to come to an abrupt end. America's pre-eminence in four corners of the world is being challenged by friends and foes alike.

In America's own backyard— Latin America—Venezuelan President Hugo Chávez is spearheading a crusade to undermine US interests across the region. He has successfully garnered the support of the leaders of Cuba, Bolivia and Ecuador to propagate his cause. Together they have challenged American supremacy by embarking on a campaign to reclaim oil and gas fields from Western companies and put them directly under state control.

Across the Atlantic, Europe smitten by the Iraq war and deeply hostile to the unilateralist agenda of the Bush administration has at best offered nominal assistance. Rather, given the opportunity the Europeans—notably the French, the Germans and the British have behaved more as foes than American allies. French intransigence in Lebanon, Europe's refusal to commit significant troops to Iraq and Afghanistan, Britain's interference in Palestine, and French and British hostility towards a Darfur settlement have damaged America's standing in the world and eroded her legitimacy.

Russia and China subdued by twenty or so years of American power have reawakened to counter American inspired revolutions sweeping Central Asia. Uzbekistan returned to Moscow's sphere of influence, Kyrgyzstan and Belarus successfully thwarted US backed uprisings; America failed to press home the political gains made in Ukraine, and Georgia witnessed a severe backlash from Russia over its ties with Washington.

Furthermore, Kyrgyzstan and Tajikistan the minnow states of the Shanghai Cooperation Organization (SCO) have become emboldened enough to demand withdrawal of American bases. America's gains in this region almost stand to naught.

Worse still is that the war on terror has inadvertently solidified China's relationship with Russia—undoing years of American strategic planning to keep the two erstwhile enemies apart. The China-Russian alliance reinvigorated with economic growth and a common desire to see a bipolar world has spread its tentacles across the globe harming US interests.

Russia unfazed by American threats is equipping Venezuela and Iran with modern weaponry[27]. Chinese energy companies are signing oil deals in places that have traditionally been the preserve of American oil giants[28]. In the Middle East, both Russian and China have taken strong objection to America's position over Iran. On the Korean peninsula, Beijing's unfettered support for Pyongyang has exposed Washington's inability to prevent North Korea from becoming nuclear.

Throughout the Muslim world America's credibility has plummeted to an all-time low. The ferocity of the resistance in Iraq and Afghanistan has broken the back of the US army and forced President Bush to abandon his

---

[27] Mahdi Darius Nazemroaya, "Russia Arming Venezuela in Anticipation of an Expected U.S. Invasion?", Global Research, (January 8, 2010).

[28] Peter Brookes and Ji Hye Shin, "China's Influence in Africa: Implications for the United States", Heritage Foundation.

plans to advance democracy. Bush unable to extricate America from Iraq and Afghanistan has had to revert to the 'Truman Doctrine' and seek the help of secular autocracies like Syria, Iran and Pakistan. Instead of reshaping the Muslim world in America's image, the nefarious policies of the Bush administration has Islamised the region, politicized the Muslim masses to awaken from their spiritual slumber and galvanized the Muslim intelligentsia into a powerful force or political Islam— to sum up the last six years— it is suffice to say that America is precipitating the birth of the Caliphate.

After two decades of dominating world affairs, America finds itself at the mercy of her friends and enemies. Graham Fuller, former vice chairman of the National Intelligence Council, described America's predicament correctly when he wrote in the latest issue of the National Interest, "diverse countries have deployed a multiplicity of strategies and tactics designed to weaken, divert, alter, complicate, limit, delay or block the Bush agenda through death by a thousand cuts."

So what happens after America has fallen from its perch as the world's sole super power? Europe is too divided to take up the mantle of the leading state. Russia has yet to translate her economic strength into political capital to position herself as the pre-eminent power. Both China and India lack the political will and the experience to affect world politics. For the foreseeable future, both countries will be confined to their respective spheres of influence.

The country that wishes to supplant America must possess a huge population, abundant resources, a universal ideology and the political will to succeed. The most obvious candidate is the Muslim world under the Caliphate, which Bush has often spoken about.

December 4, 2006

22

# Why the West Has Lost the Ideological War against Muslims

*"The West won the world not by the superiority of its ideas or values or religion but rather by its superiority in applying organized violence. Westerners often forget this fact, non-Westerners never do."*

*--Samuel P. Huntington*

During his visit to Europe, George Bush emphasised to his European hosts that spreading freedom and democracy was the only way of defeating terrorism in the Middle East and the wider Muslim world. His remarks echo a familiar tenet of his presidency - freedom triumphing over terrorism.

But, by coining the struggle as freedom versus terrorism, the Bush administration has avoided answering some pertinent questions like - What is terrorism? Who are the terrorists? Who is the enemy in the eyes of Bush and his acolytes the neo-conservatives?

The 9/11 Commission (by no means the first) stressed that the term war on terrorism was misleading and recommended that it should be renamed to place greater ideological emphasis against Islam. In October 2001 US General Wesley Clark, said that the US war against terrorism "was a war over Islam" that would define Islam "as either a peaceful or militant" force in society[29]. Yet others have argued that it should be appropriately labelled war against political Islam.

Whatever differences exist amongst America's political elite over the naming of the war there are few to be found amongst ordinary Americans. Thanks to the Islamophobic corporate media, most Americans irrespective of their political orientation view the war on terror as a fight against Islam.

The same milieu exits in Europe. The lack of boldness on part of Europe's political class to confront Bush on these questions together with the Islamophobic media has convinced ordinary Europeans that their new enemy is Islam and Muslims who live in their midst.

Before 9/11 Muslims long held the view that American intervention in their lands is part of the ongoing struggle between Islam and the West. The aftermath of 9/11 only served to reinforce this view. Today an overwhelming majority of Muslims believe unequivocally that the war on terrorism is a war against Islam and Muslims.

Hence, behind Bush's charade of fighting terrorism the clash between Islam and the West is well and truly under way. This struggle is being fought at several levels. The most important of all is the ideological struggle. The winner of this battle will decide whether the future belongs to Islam or Western secular liberalism.

So the question that now arises is who is winning the battle of ideas? The answer is that the West lost the ideological war against Islam long ago. This is due to the following reasons:

1. The West has spent the last two hundred years combating Islamic thoughts in the hope of dissuading Muslims from Islam. This campaign

---

[29] "Wesley K. Clarke speaking on BBC World's Hardtalk Programme", BBC, (October 29, 2001).

began with the orientalists who studied Islam and attacked its beliefs and rules.

For instance they attacked the divinity of the Qur'ān, jihad, polygamy, the Islamic punishment system and the Caliphate. But despite this organised effort to alienate Muslims from Islam, the West is facing a resurgent Islam both at home and abroad.

In the West, Islam is the fastest growing religion both amongst immigrants and the indigenous community. Between 1989 and 1998 the Islamic population in Europe grew by over 100 percent, to 14 million (approximately 2 percent of the population), according to United Nations statistics.[30] "Within the next 20 years the number of British converts will equal or overtake the immigrant Muslim community that brought the faith here", says Rose Kendrick the author of a textbook guide to the Koran[31]. America is not immune from this phenomenon. One expert estimates that 25,000 people a year become Muslims in the US; some clerics say they have seen conversion rates quadruple since Sept. 11[32].

Conversion figures aside, the attitudes of Muslims living in the West towards secular liberalism is equally damning. A recent ICM poll surveying Muslim attitudes in Britain published the following results: 81% view freedom of speech as a means of insulting Islam, 61% support the Sharia, 88% want Islam in schools, and 60% do not think they need to integrate.

If this is the outlook of Muslims in one of the main citadels of enlightenment then one can only guess the stance of Muslim world towards secular liberal values. Suffice to say that the West has failed to convince the Muslim masses that Western culture is better than Islam.

---

[30] "Muslims in Europe", The Economist, (October 18, 2001),
[31] "The Spread of a World Creed", The Times, (November 9, 1993).
[32] "Islam Attracts Converts by the Thousands", The New York Times, (October 22, 2001).

2.  In the past the West employed the services of modernists such as Rifa'a At-Tahtawi (1801-1873), Jamal Ad-Din Al-Afghani (1838-1897), Muhammad Abduh (1849-1905), Taha Hussein (1889,1973), Rashid Rida (1865-1935) and Syed Ahmad Khan (1817-1898) to spear head their campaign of introducing Western culture under the guise of Islam. The impact of these reformists has not only been nullified but also reversed.

    Today's modernists find themselves in a precarious situation. They are despised by Muslims and are seen as instruments of the cultural imperialism undertaking the West's bidding to defame Islam.

    In Western eyes they are viewed as being too Islamic and are no longer entrusted with the responsibility of turning Muslims away from Islam. America's decision to revoke Tariq Ramadan's visa and the media outrage at Al-Qardawi's visit to the UK epitomises the West's mistrust of modernists. On the whole they are discredited and have become irrelevant in the battle of ideas between the West and Islam.

3.  The biggest blow dealt by the West against the Islamic world came on March 3rd, 1924, when Britain through her stooge Mustafa Kamal destroyed the Caliphate. Lord Curzon speaking in the House of Commons said, "The point at issue is that Turkey has been destroyed and shall never rise again, because we have destroyed her spiritual power: the Caliphate and Islam." Subsequently, the European powers carved up the Islamic lands between them, establishing direct colonial rule over the Muslim people.

    The Muslim masses for the first time were exposed to Western solutions ranging from economic solutions which plundered their wealth to an educational syllabus which disconnected them from their history, reduced Islam to a mere set of rituals and taught them how to think like Westerners.

Moreover, Islam was effaced from temporal life only to be replaced by a secular rule. Later the West granted pseudo independence to the Muslim countries they had invented and appointed loyal servants to safeguard Western interests and to rule over Muslim people on their behalf.

If the West had thought that eight years of subjugation to secularism would have been enough to deter the Muslim masses from political Islam then they were gravely mistaken. The ferocity and direction of today's Islamic revival has seized the attention of Western leaders. Vladimir Putin, Tony Blair and Donald Rumsfeld have joined a long chorus of Western leaders in 2004 warning about the dangers of a resurgent Caliphate. This was aptly summed up by Kissinger who said,"…what we call terrorism in the United States, but which is really the uprising of radical Islam against the secular world, and against the democratic world, on behalf of re-establishing a sort of Caliphate [33]".

4. There is an inherent flaw in the ideology of secularism, which has led to its predictable rejection by the Muslim world. This is because secularism insists on restricting the role of Islam in society to personal worship only. Political decisions about running the society are left to human beings. This directly contradicts the doctrine of Muslims, which considers politics an indivisible part of Islam i.e. to Muslims Islam is politics. Bernard Lewis gave a similar assessment and said, "The absence of native secularism in Islam and the wide spread rejection of an imported secularism inspired by Christian example, may be attributed to certain profound differences of belief and experience in the two religious cultures [34]".

Furthermore, secularism always leaves a spiritual void, especially when human beings are confronted by problems, which they are unable

---

[33]Kissinger, Henry, Hindustan Times, (November 2004).
[34] Lewis, Bernard, What Went Wrong?, (2003).

to solve. Separating God from temporal matters only accentuates this feeling. It is this intellectual weakness that has contributed to the dramatic rise of political Islam under the secular autocratic rule, which pervades much of the Muslim world.

The West should take heed from the inability of communism to dissuade Muslims from Islam. Communism a far deeper ideology than secularism also failed to convince the Muslim masses of materialism and man-made laws.

5. The duplicity of the West in promoting Western values across the Muslim world has greatly undermined its credibility. Especially, after September 11, when Western doubles standards reached new heights. It was the episode of Abu Ghraib that revealed the true extent of the Western hypocrisy and hatred towards Muslims.

Western ideas such as freedom, democracy, human rights were given a devastating blow not by Muslims, but by America the so-called defender of liberty. Even the agent rulers in the Muslim world were left gasping and could not shield America from the evil crimes she had committed.

In one swoop, America by its own handiwork had permanently damaged its standing in the Muslim world and had gravely weakened the very ideas that represent the cornerstone of Western civilisation. So much so, that many non-Muslims are questioning the validity of these ideas and the deceitful role played by their governments abroad.

Hence for the very first time, Western governments are faced with the challenge of convincing their own citizens why these values have to be curbed at home, while they are forcibly thrust upon the Muslim world. Perhaps Westerners should seek solace in the words of Oscar Wilde who said, "Democracy means simply the bludgeoning of the people by the people for the people."

These are some of the reasons, which have contributed to the Muslim world's rejection of Western culture and its secular liberal philosophy.

The stark reality facing Western governments today is that the Muslim *Ummah* has won the battle of ideas. The chapter of ideological struggle between the Muslim *Ummah* and the West is more or less closed. But the chapter of political struggle between the *Ummah* and the West is still open- albeit for limited period. This is because the West and their surrogates have no political legitimacy left in the Muslim world. These surrogates only survive because of dogged support from Western powers.

Therefore the West and their puppets stand alone in coercing the *Ummah* to accept Western values. While the *Ummah* stands firm rejecting Western culture and calling for the return of a global Islamic state. The two positions are irreconcilable and polarisation in viewpoints between the regimes and its people cannot continue indefinitely.

It is only a matter of time before Muslims overthrow the secular order, which has been unjustly imposed upon them. Sensing the failure of its surrogates to contain political Islam, the West under the pretext of fighting terrorism has sought to re-occupy the Muslim lands in a desperate bid to reinforce its values and to safeguard its material interests.

West's behaviour towards the Muslim world can be likened to that of a failed schoolteacher. A failed schoolteacher is a person who continues to beat his pupils in the vain hope of imbuing them with the values of the school. Instead, the teacher not only loses control of the class but also brings down the very establishment he is trying to protect.

Indeed Westerners have got far less to fear from the Islamists and more to fear from their own governments who in the name of freedom and democracy are slowly but surely ebbing away at the very foundations of their civilisation.

March 1, 2005

## 23

# CIA's 20:20 Vision for the Future Caliphate is Short Sighted

*"They talk about wanting to re-establish what you could refer to as the Seventh Century Caliphate. This was the world as it was organized 1,200, 1,300 years, in effect, when Islam or Islamic people controlled everything from Portugal and Spain in the West; all through the Mediterranean to North Africa; all of North Africa; the Middle East; up into the Balkans; the Central Asian republics; the southern tip of Russia; a good swath of India; and on around to modern day Indonesia. In one sense from Bali and Jakarta on one end, to Madrid on the other."*

*--Former US Vice President Cheney*

I n December 2004, The National Intelligence Council of the CIA predicted that in the year 2020 a new Caliphate would emerge on the world stage. The findings were published in a 123-page report titled "Mapping the Global Future". The aim of the report is to prepare the next Bush administration for challenges that lie ahead by projecting current trends that may pose a threat to US interest. The report is presented to the US president, members of Congress, cabinet members and key officials involved in policymaking.

What is striking about the report is that it is full of references about political Islam and the various challenges it poses to US interests in the foreseeable future. There is even a fictional scenario depicting the emergence of Caliphate state in 2020 and its impact on the international situation.

However, the report is predicated on assumptions which undermine the validity of the report in various parts, especially the section on the

Caliphate. Below is a critique of some of the arguments postulated in the fictional scenario: -

The report asserts that the strength of the new Caliphate will be borne out of the efforts of a global Islamic movement taking power. While it may be true that a global Islamic movement may instigate civil disobedience or initiate a coup to bring about the Caliphate, its strength and longevity is dependent upon something entirely different.

Intellectual conviction in a common set of values amongst the citizens of a state is the measure of the state's strength and not the movement, which founded the state. The Soviet Union collapsed not because it was deficient in technology, but because its people abandoned communism and the communist party was powerless to convince them otherwise.

An accurate appraisal of the convictions of the Muslim masses for the resumption of the Islamic way of life through the re-establishment of the Caliphate is the single most important factor in determining whether the Caliphate will succeed or fail in the 21st century. This is more important than technology and resources, both of which can be quickly gained as long as the Caliphate is able to defend itself and base its progress exclusively on the Islamic ideology.

Whenever Islamic movements are taken as the sole gauge for estimating the extent of Islamic revival in Muslim countries, a skewed picture will always emerge. The CIA is not alone in employing this false standard. The practice is wide spread and has tainted the analysis of respected think tanks and the writings of some notable commentators such as Francis Fukuyama and Samuel P. Huntington.

This flaw is not the result of their malice towards Islam, but is due to their adherence to the philosophy of individualism, which has marred their understanding of society and reduced it to a collection of individuals.

A proper understanding of society reveals that it is composed of individuals, which are bonded together by common thoughts and emotions, and live under a specific system. The degree of support amongst people towards the existing system of governance or for an alternative system of ruling can only be ascertained through the evaluation of these common thoughts and emotions.

The attachment to individualism has led the West to grossly underestimate the penetration of Islamic thoughts and sentiments in the Muslim countries, and also to miscalculate the wide spread support for the re-establishment of the Caliphate.

Another point of contention in the report is the claim that the emergence of the Caliphate will not cause the regimes in Muslim countries to collapse one after the other – the domino effect.

Again this understanding is derived from an incorrect understanding of society. A cursory study of the Muslim world shows that there exists strong polarisation in viewpoints between the regimes and the people they govern. Before the collapse of the Baath regime, Saddam an atheist was delivering speeches laced with Islamic terms. He did this, because he realised that the people were no longer motivated by Baathism, secularism or Arabism and only responded to Islam. Similarly, when Musharraf sided with America's war against Afghanistan he had to quote lengthy passages from life of the Messenger of Allah (SAW) to justify his stance.

The conflict between maintaining the secular order and preventing political Islam from assuming power is a daily occurrence in much of the Muslim world. The regimes in the Muslim world are viewed as the custodians of Western interests and antagonistic towards Islam. Muslims simply loathed these regimes and are eager to extinguish their existence. The only reason these regimes survive is because of the dogged support from Western governments.

Today, the Islamic *Ummah* stands on the cusp of a monumental change, just as the Warsaw pact countries stood some 18 years ago. The iron curtain came down because people had changed their viewpoint from communism to capitalism. Likewise the Muslim *Ummah* has abandoned both communism and capitalism, and is waiting for the emergence of the Caliphate, which will cause these regimes to collapse in spectacular fashion, only to be absorbed by the Caliphate.

Finally the report claims that Muslims would find the temptations of Western materialism too much to bear, causing them to flee the shores of the new Caliphate. This view is obviously founded on the prevalent Western notion that the Caliphate is the antithesis to modernisation. Another factor that enhances this perception amongst Westerners is the current exodus of Muslims from the Islamic world to the West.

Nothing could be further from the truth. First, the Caliphate that Muslims want to establish is the rightly guided Caliphate, which was at the zenith of human civilisation. A historical fact widely recognised by several eminent experts on Islam—most notably Bernard Lewis.

Second, the mass migration of Muslims to the West is a consequence of Western foreign policy ventures in the Muslim world and not because of Muslim infatuation with Western values. Most migrants, if not all are either economic migrants or political asylum seekers escaping the tyranny of regimes often supported by Western governments.

Even those Muslims, who have settled in the West, have yet to embrace secular values for fear of corrupting their Islam. The recent endeavour by Europe to coerce its Muslim population to adopt Western values speaks volumes for Europe's obsession with secularising Muslims and runs counter to the stereotyped image projected by the Western media that Muslim countries are pleading to be Westernised.

The typecasting of Muslims is based on the erroneous understanding of anti-Western feeling that pervades the Muslim world. Often in Western circles, anti-Western sentiments are equated with the total rejection of Western civilisation and attributed to the fundamentalist camp.

To make matters worse, the desire amongst Muslims to own Western goods are interpreted as a craving for the Western way of life. Westerners often classify those who display admiration for Western goods into the moderate camp.

To pigeonhole Muslims into the two camps based on such interpretations is wrong. This is because the anti-Western rhetoric found amongst Muslims is a denunciation of Western culture and not of Western goods. Likewise, the expression for the admiration for Western products is an acknowledgement of the superior quality of the goods and is not an affirmation for the wholesale acceptance of Western culture.

For the first time in many years, the Muslim world has undergone a radical transformation in reconciling which aspects of the Western way of life can be accepted or rejected with Islam. Muslims today accept Western goods such as DVDs, Satellites Dishes, and TVs only because such items do not contradict their Islamic viewpoint. On the other hand Western concepts such as freedom, democracy and individualism are discarded because are deemed to contradict Islam.

Previously, the Muslim world was torn between two factions i.e. the modernists who wanted to adopt everything from the West and the traditionalists who were keen to rebuff all aspects of Western civilisation. This mentality stifled progress and allowed the West to establish their hegemony over Muslim lands.

Today, it is not Muslims who are holding themselves back from human advancement and meeting the demands of the 21st century, but rather it is the West that chooses to suppress these developments and insists on imposing its values upon the Muslim masses in connivance with the regimes of the Muslim world.

This attitude has not only contributed to the West's misunderstanding of Islam, but has encouraged the West to define an inequitable relationship with the Muslim world. Furthermore, the mind-set has prompted the West to shun everything to do with Islam. West's occupation of Iraq and Afghanistan has already highlighted the abuse of the Muslim people, the pillage of their land and denigration of Islam.

If this attitude is not reversed then the West will find itself in a precarious position on two fronts. First, the Caliphate will be a strong, progressive state charting a new destiny for the Muslim people after liberating them from the political, military and economic hegemony of the West. The West weakened by this abrupt loss of control will struggle to maintain its dominance in world affairs. Secondly, the Caliphate will swiftly harness the synergy between Islam and science, thereby surpassing the West in terms of inventions, technologies and new scientific discoveries. Given the West's negative attitudes towards all things Islamic, it will find itself closing the doors to knowledge and shielding its people from progress and challenges of 21st century.

January 23, 2005

## 24

# Obama the Crusading Knight and the Muslim World

*"Let me say this as clearly as I can...The United States is not and never will be at war with Islam."*

*--US President Barrack Obama*

In October 9 2009, US President Barack Obama was awarded Nobel Peace Prize for astounding services in the name of world peace. In its statement, the Nobel Committee said he had "created a new climate in international politics.... Only very rarely has a person to the same extent as Obama captured the world's attention and given its people hope for a better future."[35] It continued, "His diplomacy is founded in the concept that those who are to lead the world must do so on the basis of values and attitudes that are shared by the majority of the world's population."[36] Usually awards are conferred upon people when they have accomplished something tangible and not for mere pledges to achieve meaningful results. In Obama's case, he has neither achieved peace nor has he undertaken efforts to establish the foundations for world peace. On the contrary, he is a warmonger and a crusader who is spearheading America's war against Islam and the Muslim world.

No sooner had Obama received the prize for peace he convened his war council to discuss how best to wage war in Afghanistan. "The president had a robust conversation about the security and political challenges in Afghanistan and the options for building a strategic approach going forward"[37] an administration official told AFP. One of the measures

---

[35] The Norwegian Nobel Committee, Oslo, (October 9, 2009).
[36] ibid
[37] White House Administration, (October 10, 2009).

Obama will endorse is to increase the number of US soldiers deployed in Afghanistan. This will be on top of the huge number of private security contractors that already work for the Pentagon and are responsible for much of the mayhem and the slaughter of innocent Afghan civilians.

Obama's war council is also deliberating options to expand America's war in Pakistan. American officials are openly debating whether to launch missile attacks on Quetta—Balochistan largest city. If the nod is given this will mark a new phase in America's war against Pakistan and means that fortification of the US embassy in Islamabad—one of the largest in the Muslim world— will be used as the nerve centre to plan and orchestrate the killing of Muslims. Additionally, America has mandated two private US security firms Blackwater and InterRisk to hound and terrorize Pakistanis.

In Iraq, Obama's so called draw down policy masks a similar sinister plan that relies heavily on private security contractors to strengthen America's military presence in the country and to compensate for the withdrawal of US troops. The private security contractors operate with complete impunity, spilling Muslim blood and humiliating ordinary Iraqis.

According to new statistics released by the Pentagon this year, there has been a 23% increase in the number of private security contractors working for the Department of Defence in Iraq in the second quarter of 2009 . The figure for the same period in Afghanistan is a 29% increase. Overall, contractors (armed and unarmed) now make up approximately 50% of the "total force in Centcom AOR [Area of Responsibility]." This means there are a 242,657 contractors working on these two US wars under the leadership of commander in chief Barack Obama. This exceeds the present number of forces in Iraq and Afghanistan which amounts to 132,610 and 68,197 respectively.

Under Obama's watch the civil war in Somalia is mushrooming at an alarming rate. The war is fuelled by Washington through the supply of US arms and weapons to the beleaguered US puppet government of Sharif Ahmed. Last month, Obama gave the signal to his military to directly intervene in Somalia and conduct air strikes against militants—very much reminiscent of America's invasion of Somalia in 1993.

Against Iran, Obama is not advocating peace, but urging crippling sanctions that will surely hurt ordinary Iranians and incubate resentment against America for decades to come. Likewise Obama's continued support for autocratic rulers of the Muslim world has convinced many Muslims that Obama is no different to his predecessor George Bush.

However, nowhere is Obama's failure to deliver peace more pronounced than Palestine. As a prelude to his inauguration, Obama displayed resolute determination not to condemn Israeli savagery in Gaza. In fact, Obama's refusal to censure Israel over war crimes has ushered in a new standard that pays pittance to the value of Muslim life, blood and honour. In office, Obama's indifference to the Jewish state's intransigence to halt settlements has shot down all efforts to commence pseudo peace talks.

Evidently, Obama's peace endeavours equate to making pieces of Muslim countries through war and bloodshed. The political climate Obama has presided over is one of intimidation and tyranny. The values Obama espouses are based on deceit and injustice. By awarding the Nobel Peace Prize to Obama, the Nobel committee has avowed that waging war against Muslims and Islam under the guise of peace is a noble action. Obama may have captured the hearts of the Nobel committee, but amongst Muslims and much of the world, Obama epitomizes an imperialistic empire that is an enemy of humanity and world peace.

October 10, 2009

25

# Pakistan's Leadership Vacuum Precipitates the Caliphate

*"Pakistan: The Most Dangerous Place on Earth."*

*--Newsweek Magazine*

After almost eight years of military rule, Pakistan faces a myriad of challenges that threaten its very existence. American threats of unilateral action in the tribal area, an Indian backed insurrection in Balochistan, a dramatic increase in suicide blasts, and the economy in tatters are some of Pakistan's woes. But perhaps, the most significant issue is the leadership vacuum that pervades all segments of society. A manifestation of this void is the antics of the current coalition government, which over the past six months has struggled to define its purpose and chalk out a concrete program to confront these challenges. Politicians are not the only culprits. Military top brass, bureaucratic big-wigs, industrialists and civic leaders are just as guilty. Put it another way, all have either abdicated responsibility or simply buried their heads in the sand. The only thing common amongst the nation's leaders is the beseechment of foreign powers.

Politicians unashamed of courting American and British officials frequently plan and execute trips to Dubai, London and Washington for even the smallest of issues. A large proportion of them, openly desire servitude to Western powers and shamelessly promote their interests. Then there are the pseudo-Islamist politicians, whose contributions to date include none other than adding corruption to the political landscape, legitimizing the abhorrent actions of the rulers and destroying the confidence of the public in political Islam.

The behaviour of the military top brass is equally callous. Both Musharraf and Kayani like their fraudulent predecessors have moved heaven and earth to secure Amerixcan interests in Pakistan. The incarceration of Abdul Qadeer Khan, the abandonment of the Kashmiri people, the massacre at Lal Masjid and the slaughter of Muslims in Waziristan, Bajaur and Hangu are some of their noteworthy accomplishments.

The business community and industrialists are not immune from this critique. History bears testimony that they are content to be bedfellows with any government – civilian or military – long as the tax bill is kept to a minimum and they are granted immunity from loan defaults. When the achievements of the business community is measured in terms of transfer of technology and contribution to the nation's self-sufficiency they score naught. In sum – Pakistan's leadership since its inception in 1947 has repeatedly failed to emancipate Pakistan from the intellectual, political and economic subjugation of colonialist powers.

The root cause of Pakistan's leadership predicament can be attributed to a single factor—namely the economic and political system left behind by the British—later modified by the US. This system has meticulously cultivated a plethora of civilian and military leaders who were defeated, corrupt and infatuated with the West. In their eagerness to serve Western powers—Western solutions were relentlessly borrowed and applied to all walks of Pakistani life. The cut and paste mentality was bound to fail, as the adopted solutions were disconnected from the problems of Pakistan and opposed to the beliefs and cultural values coveted by the people. Subsequently, Pakistan witnessed years of turmoil and polarization which has reached a tumultuous climax today.

The only salvation for Pakistan is for a new dynamic Islamic leadership to take the reigns of power and reverse Pakistan's decline. This leadership must be radically different from the past and cannot be an existing player in the nation's corrupt systems and institutions. It must possess an acute sensation of the problems of Pakistan and an ideological vision that reflects the beliefs and values of the people. It must eschew violence, but be bold enough to lead the masses to a comprehensive revolt against the present secular order and raze all vestiges of Western domination. The West has already described this political trend as the movement to re-establish the Caliphate.

The end to the leadership crisis is dependent upon how quickly the people of Pakistan wake up from their slumber and embrace this phenomenon.

March 8, 2008

# Part 5
# Struggle for the future of the Arab world

# 26

# Arab Revolution: Democracy or Islamic Theocracy in the Making

*"Islam is bound to play a larger role in government in the Arab world than elsewhere. Most Muslims do not believe in the separation of religion and state, as America and France do, and have not lost their enthusiasm for religion, as many Christian Democrats in Europe have."*

*--The Economist*

The wave of revolt sweeping the Arab world has divided commentators and political pundits alike. Some speculate that this will lead to the democratization of the Arab world and are eager to make comparisons with the demise of the Iron curtain in 1989. Indeed, such commentators cite parallels between the Arab world and the collapse of the communist rule in Poland, Hungary, Czechoslovakia, East Germany, Romania, the Baltic republics of the Soviet Union etc to bolster their arguments. They also point to the chants of democracy and freedom amongst the protestors to augment their case. Then there are those analysts that find similarities between the Arab revolution and the Iranian revolution of 1979. They portend that the Arab world is on a path towards an Iranian style system of government and a threat to the West[38] and Israel. Such analysts buttress their views by signalling out anti-Western slogans and calls for the implementation of *Shar'iah*. Both assessments in many ways are misleading—at best they are simply fictitious.

---

[38] The term West does not mean a set of countries based on geographical location. Rather, it implies a group of countries that share a specific set of values rooted in the birth of secularism in the 1700s e.g. Europe, America, Canada, Australia etc.

In the fall of the Iron Curtain, nations abandoned 'godless socialism' and embraced free market capitalism. Eastern European countries shifted from Russia's sphere of influence to American colonization. The super power struggle between the Soviets and the Americans ended with Russia's defeat and the ascendency of the lone super power America. Charles Krauthammer, a famous American columnist, coined the term 'the unipolar moment' to describe America's newfound position in the world.

In contrast, the domino effect that is toppling autocratic leaders across the Arab world has not ended free market capitalism, nor has it ousted the world's lone super power. Tunisia, Libya, and Egypt remain staunchly secular, their solutions are capitalistic in nature and the countries are firmly in the grip of Britain and America. Furthermore, the geopolitical struggle is confined between Europe and America over who controls the hydrocarbons and other riches of the Arab world. If change does materialize, then this will merely be the elimination of European hegemony—especially British control—over countries like Morocco, Algeria, Tunisia, Libya, Yemen and the Gulf countries. Additionally, the face of the ruling system and apparatus will undergo some modifications to make America's rule more palatable to the people and stymie further uprisings.

Equating the Arab revolution with the Iranian one is equally flawed. The fall of the Shah and the arrival of Khomeini only switched the rule in Iran from British hands to America hands. Capitalism still flourishes and is peppered with Islamic dressing, which to most observers is misconstrued as a form of theocracy. The fact of the matter is that Iran is a secular regime with some facets of democracy and staunchly operates within the ambit of American foreign policy. Again, the bouts of uprising that Iran experiences is not seeking an end to capitalism, American hegemony or for that matter an end to Western patronage. This is the only similarity between the present rebellions in the Arab world and the Iranian revolution.

If valuable lessons have to be learnt then there are two noteworthy observations. First, the slogans of freedom and democracy amongst the Arab populace, which the Western media is keen to portray in a favourable light, do not necessarily equate to the West's understanding of freedom and democracy. Rather, to the vast majority of protestors, freedom is associated with freedom from tyranny and not freedom from the laws of Islam. Likewise, democracy is likened to the right of the people to elect their own rulers and is not equated with law making and legislation.

Second, it is quite evident that almost all revolutions in societies that covet change -irrespective of ideological orientations-require domestic partners that can tangibly deliver change and ensure genuine independence from Western interference. These partners are the powerful armies of the Arab and Muslim countries. General Rachid Ammar of Tunisia and General Chief of Staff Lieutenant General Sami Hafiz of Egypt could have easily catapulted the revolutions towards real and meaningful change. Instead, they betrayed the pure feelings of their people and chose to stand by the West. Therefore, in such cases the regimes that were responsible for years of despotism and aggression have remained in place and are ever more perceived to be safeguarding the interests of the West.

In fact, it is the last point that is attracting the attention of many Arabs and encouraging them to liken their situation today with the establishment of the first Islamic state in Madina. Then, the Arab Muslims sought the help of powerful Arab tribes[39] of Madina to establish the Islamic state, and today more and more are seeking to emulate this. Hence the real danger for the West is that the Arab revolution may neither produce

---

[39] The Messenger of Allah الله عليه و سلم sought nusrah (material power) from several tribes before Al Aws and Al Khajraj gave him the material support to establish the first Islamic state in Madina. The equivalents today, are the armies in Arab countries, which many people have recognised during the revolution as the only means to bring permanent change for Islam.

democracy or an Iranian style government, but a system of Islamic ruling based on the Islamic state of Madina.

September 20, 2011

27

# Remaking the Arab World in the West's Image

*"[We need an] Arab facade ruled and administered under British guidance and controlled by a native Muhammedan and, as far as possible, by an Arab staff.... There should be no actual incorporation of the conquered territory in the dominions of the conqueror, but the absorption may be veiled by such constitutional fictions as a protectorate, a sphere of influence, a buffer state and so on."*

*--Lord Curzon*

In the early part of the twentieth century, Britain was at the forefront of Western efforts in moulding the Arab world much to the liking of the officers of the British Empire. Almost a century later, nothing has changed. This week, Western powers met in Paris to seal Libya's fate. The scramble for Libya's oil and gold has begun. Abdeljalil Mayouf, an executive at Libyan rebel oil firm Agoco told Reuters, "We don't have a problem with Western countries like the Italians, French and UK companies. But we may have some political issues with Russia, China and Brazil."

The West has embarked upon a new campaign, not just to remake Libya, but the entire Arab world, in its image. America is leading a pack of colonial powers in this endeavour, and is spearheading efforts to either dissect some Arab countries or subtly instigate regime change in others to preserve America's primacy in the region.

The incessant Western media coverage about the promotion of freedom and democracy in the Arab World conceals the real motives of Western powers, which are to groom pro-Western elites that will facilitate Western multinationals to control the Arab world's oil supply, natural gas reserves, mineral resources, and energy security, as well as maintain security pacts with Israel.

The campaign started with the separation of oil rich Southern Sudan earlier this year. The secession of South Sudan under America's tutelage has already spurred Christians in Nigeria and Coptic Christians in Egypt to demand independence. The aspirations of the current Coptic leaders were lucidly captured by a Jewish Journalist Oded Yinon in 1982. In his paper, "A strategy for Israel in the nineteen-eighties", he stated: 'Egypt is divided and torn apart into many foci of authority. If Egypt falls apart, countries like Libya, Sudan or even the more distant states will not continue to exist in their present form and will join the downfall and dissolution of Egypt. The vision of a Christian Coptic state in Upper Egypt, alongside a number of weak states, with very localized power and without a centralized government as to date, is the key to a historical development which was only setback by the peace agreement, but which seems inevitable in the long run.'

The idea of creating a sacred Coptic state within the contours of Egypt is similar to the one advocated by US Lieutenant-Colonel Ralph Peters concerning Mecca and Madina. In June 2006, Peters published a map of the "New Middle East" in the June edition of the US Armed Forces Journal. The journal depicted, amongst other mutilated Muslim countries, the "Islamic Sacred State", which consists of Mecca and Madina, segregated from the rest of Saudi Arabia.

Earlier, various US officials had played upon sectarian and ethnic differences and called for the creation of a super *Shi'a* state that stretches from Lebanon to Pakistan. The idea behind such a creation is to shift the control of oil away from Sunni domination and into *Shi'a* hands, for the Americans regard the *Shi'a* as much more trustworthy in the management of their colonial interests.

Indeed, the American occupation in Iraq is viewed by some Middle Eastern leaders, as the first step towards *Shi'a* domination of the whole region. In an article entitled "Iraq, Jordan See Threat To Election From Iran" published by the Washington Post on November 8, 2004, King Abdullah warned: 'If pro-Iran parties or politicians dominate the new Iraqi government a new "crescent" of dominant *Shi'a* movements or governments stretching from Iran into Iraq, Syria and Lebanon could emerge, alter the traditional balance of power between the two main Islamic sects and pose new challenges to US interests and allies.'

He further went on to state that Iran was the main beneficiary from the chaos in Iraq. Ever since the *Shi'a*'s rose to power in Iraq, King Abdullah has oft repeated that America's occupation of Iraq is bolstering *Shi'a* power across the region.

The Arab revolt that started in Tunisia and spread to several Arab countries was manipulated by America to move closer to its goal of creating a new Greater Middle East, where old European powers have marginal influence. The dismissal of Zine El Abidine Ben Ali was not a random event. Rather, it was a synthesis of rampant corruption incubated by 23 years of Western patronage and fused with dire economic conditions, made worse by the global financial crisis and bloodsucking International Monetary Fund (IMF structural programs. America is eagerly awaiting similar turmoil to manifest itself in Algeria, Jordan, and the Gulf countries, so that she can engineer regimes that pledge greater loyalty to her hegemony, at the expense of Britain and France. As for Egypt, America defused the uprising by disposing of her loyal agent Mubarak like a soiled tissue and handing the power to the army to rule Egypt on her behalf. The passing of American freight via the Suez waterway and Egypt's pact with Israel remains intact much to the dismay of the Egyptian public.

Today, American officials have resurrected outdated plans to devour the Arab world that were once deemed too ambitious to accomplish and too dangerous to talk about in public. In January 2011, US Secretary of State

Hillary Clinton could not hide her glee and used the events in Tunisia to fire a salvo at the pro-European Arab leaders. She said, "In too many places, in too many ways, the region's foundations are sinking into the sand. The new and dynamic Middle East ... needs firmer ground if it is to take root and grow everywhere. While some countries have made great strides in governance, in many others, people have grown tired of corrupt institutions and a stagnant political order. Those who cling to the status quo may be able to hold back the full impact of their countries' problems for a little while, but not forever. If leaders don't offer a positive vision and give young people meaningful ways to contribute, others will fill the vacuum."

The term employed by successive American administrations to describe the plight of the Arab World, such as "sinking in the sand", "arc of crisis", "balkanization", or "Greater Middle Eastern Initiative", was done in an attempt to move away from the Sykes–Picot Agreement of 1916, which protected old Europe's supremacy and interests, a colonial legacy which still persist today—albeit in parts. The war in Iraq in 2003 was a desperate bid by Bush and his cabal of neoconservatives to refashion the Middle East through force.

However, the current popular revolts in the Arab world—some of which have been instigated by America through US-funded NGOs and civic institutions—presents the US with another chance to capture the Arab prize without sharing it with Britain and France. Since 1945, the US has been trying to exert total control over this prize. The US State Department, in 1945 stated that the Middle East was "a stupendous source of strategic power, and one of the greatest material prizes in world history."

But successive American governments were forced to share the spoils with Britain. For instance, Daniel Yergin, in his book "The Prize: The Epic Quest for Oil, Money, and Power", described the then relationship between Roosevelt and the British: 'Roosevelt received him [British ambassador Lord Halifax] that very evening at the White House. Their discussion focused on the Middle East. Trying to allay Halifax's apprehension and irritation, Roosevelt showed the ambassador a rough sketch he had made of the Middle East. Persian oil, he told the ambassador, is yours. We share the oil of Iraq and Kuwait. As for Saudi Arabian oil, it is ours'.

Iraq, Libya, Syria, and Yemen are just another battle in a long war that has ensued between America and Europe for the control of the Arab world. Nonetheless, despite America's differences with Europe, each possesses a single purpose when conducting relations with the Muslim World—divide, rule, and conquer. This is the beckoning call now reverberating in the Western capitals. The only salvation for the Arab world from neo-colonialism is to seek something similar to what George Washington did for America in the eighteenth century and what Mao did to China in the twentieth century: Both had provided resolute leadership on alternative ideologies—secular liberalism and socialism, respectively, to be precise—and successfully liberated their people from the shackles of the old colonial powers.

But that was then. The Arab world does not require secular liberalism or socialism for liberation, as both are alien to the cultural heritage of the Arab people and an anathema to their Islamic beliefs. The Arab world possesses Islam as a common political ideology, but lacks a leader like Washington or Mao to unify and emancipate it from the domination of Western powers.

The Arab masses need to rally around a leader[40] that is sincere to their interests only, and opposes Western interference. This can only happen if the Arab masses and their newfound leadership adheres to the tried and

---

[40] It is important to understand that this leader cannot be imported from the West, like so many leaders today that are supplanted by Western powers to look after their interests. Rather, the leader will emerge naturally from the masses and rule over them via the office of the Khaleefah, and the system of ruling will be based on the Qur'ān, Sunnah, Ijma Al-Sahaba and Qiyas.

tested vision of the Khilafah[41], which for centuries unified Arab and Muslim lands under a single system of ruling and protected the interests of its people.

September 3, 2011

---

[41] The Khilafah is a common leadership for all the Muslims in the world. Its role is to establish the laws of the Islamic Shariah and to carry the Dawah of Islam to the world. It is also known as the Imamah, and is referred to in English as the Caliphate. In this book, I have used the term Khilafah.

28

# The Arab Mind Awakens from Decades of Slumber

*"It is important to remember that the initiative has returned to the Arab people, initiative that has been absent for more than a century. Foreign powers and their agents have played a central role in drawing a bleak picture promoting the idea that solutions and change can only come from abroad, and that any change that does not take place in partnership with the external other - the one promoting modernization - is change that is lacking and uneven. This is accompanied by a corruption of change, and its transformation into a process that, in its ends, contradicts the aspirations of Arab societies."*

*--Mahjoob Zweiri*

As the world debates the various merits of the Arab revolt—whether the revolution will produce an alternative political landscape or not—very little has been said about the Arab mind-set. Yes, the Arab people have lost their former fear of the despotic regimes, but this is an accurate description of their psychological state, not their mindset. The thinking process of the Arabs has undergone a massive transformative change and is rapidly reaching a level of intellectual maturity that is likely to yield an outcome contrary to Western expectations.

Consider the euphoria that greeted the banishment of Ben Ali from Tunisia, or the incarceration of Hosni Mubarak in Egypt. Initially, the Arabs concluded that this would finally lead towards a permanent change from the present day autocratic systems with their draconian laws. Instead, and within a space of only a few months, the Egyptians learnt that the regime not only survived, but was given a new lease of life through a military coup. The peace treaty with the Jewish state, despised by the majority of the Egyptians, remained firmly intact. The military, once the stalwart of the revolution, went from heroes to traitors overnight. Torture, imprisonment without trial, abductions by security forces, extra judicial killings, and sectarian strife, all prevalent under Mubarak, returned to haunt Egyptians with renewed vigour. Western protégés groomed in exile and presented as viable alternatives to the status quo were quickly repudiated by the masses. Islamists, once coveted by the faithful, are now ridiculed for sounding more secular than the secularists! Even the public enthusiasm for constitutional reforms and the presidential election has faded.

The Tunisian experience is almost identical. Looking further afield, the same can be said for Morocco, Algeria, Libya, Jordan, Syria and some of the GCC countries. The narrative before and after the revolt, remains unchanged for many Arabs. For them, the Arab world is ruled by pro-Western elites who are more interested in the preservation of Western colonial interests than the liberation of Arab masses from tyranny.

Right now, it seems as though any Western attempt to orchestrate political change in Arab countries is instantly rejected and thrown back. The dormant Arab mind is now awake, and is fast producing results that are diametrically opposed to the West's longevity and primacy in the Middle East. The learning curve, which encompasses the sensation of the reality, contemplation and judgment, is no longer as steep for the Arab masses as it once was. So how have Arab minds changed?

It can be argued that over the past ninety odd years, the breadth and depth of problems faced by Arabs have grown in both magnitude and scope: The destruction of the Khilafah in 1924, Western occupation of Muslim lands, the establishment of the Jewish state in 1948, the successive Gulf wars, the war on terror and the physical reoccupation of Arab lands, have all left indelible impressions on Arab minds. These deep-seated feelings of humiliation, indignity, and violation of Islamic values spurred many Arabs to think profoundly about these feelings. However, the West, through Arab exiles and her surrogates in the Arab world fed the masses a diet of Western thoughts to confuse and shield the Arabs from arriving at the correct judgment about the events that befell them. Subsequently, the thinking process or thinking cycle—feelings about the problems that in turn require connectivity and contemplation, which is then followed by judgment—was either broken, or skewed, in the favour of Western interpretations.

This resulted in intellectual paralysis and stagnation of Arab societies. Severed from their natural feelings, the Arabs were unable to generate home-grown solutions to the problems they faced, and were forced to import Western solutions and ideas. Thus, the thinking process was temporarily disrupted. What compounded greatly the situation, was the adoption of Western solutions. Such solutions rarely solved problems, rather they further exacerbated and prolonged them, as they were often 'copied and pasted' without any real understanding of their origins and motives. This made the helpless Arabs more reliant on the West for their ever increasing portfolio of problems.

In this way, the West was able to keep its intellectual stranglehold upon the Arabs and the wider Muslim world for many years. Only a few Muslims managed to punctuate the West's intellectual dominance and expose the inconsistencies of its ideology. However, the majority remained in stasis, and plummeted into the abyss of gloom and despair.

Today, this no longer appears to be the situation. The Arab thinking process is no longer fragmented and disconnected from its surroundings. On the contrary, it is vibrant, in touch with its environment, and takes solace from its rich Islamic heritage. The time taken to truly understand events is visibly shorter and the judgments more often than not are rooted in Islamic thoughts. Western thoughts and views are now routinely discarded. In its place, a new constellation of Islamic concepts and values have sprung up. The concept of Khilafah, Jihad[42], Islamic politics[43],

---

[42] Jihad has a very specific meaning and should not be confused with the orientalist meaning to strive against oneself. On the contrary, jihad is about fighting in the way of Allah (SWT) to make Islam supreme.

[43] The term here should not be confused with the Machiavellian politics practiced in the West. In Islam politics is about looking after the affairs of the people.

*Ummah*[44], unity and *Shar'iah* is so prevalent now, that it is common to see these terms included as part of West's lexicon to interpret the events in the Muslim world.

July 19, 2011

---

[44] *Ummah* means people who share the Islamic belief. In other words *Ummah* or Muslim nation is a single entity that is not separated by borders.

# 29

## Libya: Another Western Crusade Turns Sour

*"For the West, whose ties to Arab dictators once gave it great clout in the Middle East, events in the region have spun way out of control."*

*--The Economist*

Once again the allied crusader forces have manufactured false pretexts, under the fig leaf of international law, to invade another Muslim country for the sole purpose of securing Libya's valuable oil resources. As with Iraq and Afghanistan before it, it is obvious to any sane person with a modicum of common sense that such wars are not about protecting civilians, finding weapons of mass destructions or removing brutal dictators coveted by the West for decades— rather it's all about oil security.

As the crusader forces pummel Gaddafi's obsolete hardware and ravage the country through indiscriminate bombing, resulting in hundreds of civilian causalities—one cannot ignore the fact that only a few months ago, Gaddafi and his family were portrayed by the West as reformed modernizers with a gleam of democratic credentials. In Britain, Gaddafi and his family mixed with the aristocracy and hobnobbed with the likes of Nat Rothschild, who, through his friend Lord Mandelson, a confidant of ex-Prime Minister Tony Blair, helped engineer Libya's rehabilitation in the so called comity of nations. As part of this assistance, Britain's former Prime Minister Tony Blair[45] also exercised great freedom over the Libyan Investment Authority, which at the last count had $70 billion of plundered money belonging to the Libyan people. Yet none of these intertwined commercial interests between Britain and their agent, Gaddafi, prevented the former from turning against their surrogate for the last forty-one years.

---

[45] For further information read the article by R. Spencer, H. Blake and J. Swaine, "Tony Blair visited Libya to lobby for JP Morgan", The Telegraph, (September 18, 2011).

Sensing the cataclysmic nature of protests across Libya, the UK was quick to abandon Gaddafi and expunge any vestiges of cooperation between the two countries. William Hague, the UK Foreign Secretary, scurried to announce Gaddafi's exit to Venezuela and that the UK was looking to a post-Gaddafi era. Nonetheless, the enigmatic Gaddafi, whom the British identified at Sandhurst and then nurtured and protected for four decades, dug in his heels and decided to fight his masters. Outraged by Gaddafi's defiance, the British mobilized Western countries and the UN to use force to remove him from power—the unofficial goal of military intervention.

The story is reminiscent of the lives of several other brutal dictators that the colonial powers brought to power and armed to the teeth. They watched as their protégés oppressed the *Ummah*, and when the time came, ditched them like disposal tissues. Saddam, Suharto, Musharraf, Mubarak, and Ben Ali are just some of the names that come to immediate recollection.

The West's unrepentant treachery is not limited to their agents—it is far worse in both scope and magnitude when applied to the Muslim world. For the past eighty odd years, the West has ignored the plight of the Muslim masses, denied them the same values they espouse for their own citizens, and turned a blind eye to the tyranny of the Arab and Muslim rulers. The callousness of Western duplicity has reached new heights in the history of. Where is the West's moral compass and human rights standards when Israel slaughters Palestinians at will, Russia covers up the killing fields in Chechnya, India desecrates the daily lives of the Kashmiris, and China routinely carries out extra-judicial killings of Muslims in East Turkestan? The crimes of these states are not less than those committed by Gaddafi, but the West remains muzzled in its criticism. Then there is the bitter tyranny of the Saudi and Syrian regimes against their own people, the savagery of the Bahraini monarchy, and the cruelty of the Yemeni government. The West has hitherto chosen not take any punitive measures against these regimes and has played down military intervention. This selective application of Western values has left an ineffaceable impression on the Muslim masses about the West's true intentions.

Nevertheless, despite the West's colonial suppression of Muslim masses and years of propping-up dictatorial regimes, a silver lining is fast emerging that makes uncomfortable reading for both the West and their agent despots. In a recent poll, the University of Maryland surveyed Muslims in Indonesia, Egypt, Pakistan, and Morocco, and found that 77% agree to unify all Islamic countries into a single Islamic state. The quest for the return of the Khilafah is no more a dream, but a reality that is shaping the contours of current thinking regarding alternative political systems for both Muslims and non-Muslims alike. In an IBD/TIPP poll, 61% of Americans were reported to believe that the establishment of the Khilafah is likely in the next 10 years.

The West, through its own handiwork, has already lost the Muslim masses, and now the inner power circles of other loyal agents to Western powers must be teetering on who to support. The choice is a simple one— the very same colonial powers that someday will intervene and hound them out of power or the *Ummah* and re-establishment of the Khilafah that will make them heroes overnight. If I were a general, I know who I would be supporting.

October 2, 2011

## 30

# Role of Foreign Hands in Egypt's Revolution

*"President Mubarak and military leaders view our military assistance program as the cornerstone of our mil-mil relationship and consider the USD 1.3 billion in annual FMF as "untouchable compensation" for making and maintaining peace with Israel. The tangible benefits to our mil-mil relationship are clear: Egypt remains at peace with Israel, and the US military enjoys priority access to the Suez Canal and Egyptian airspace. We believe, however, that our relationship can accomplish much more. Over the last year, we have engaged MOD leaders on developing shared strategic objectives to address current and emerging threats, including border security, counter terrorism, civil defence, and peacekeeping. Our efforts thus far have met with limited success."*

*--US Embassy Cables (Egypt's importance to US)*

There has been much debate about whether the Egyptian revolution sweeping the Arab world is indigenous, or orchestrated by foreign powers. Egyptians are not immune to this debate, and it is worth considering the various factors that have contributed to the uprising against Mubarak's regime:

A. First and foremost is that since 1958, Egypt has been under emergency law (Law Number 162), under which political parties were banned except those sanctioned by the state and the police and security forces were granted extended powers. They used these powers to prohibit protests, jail and torture opposition figures without due process, pry into the private lives of the Egyptian people, and create an atmosphere of fear, and tyranny to oppress the masses.

When Mubarak acceded to the Egyptian Presidency on 14th of October 1981, after the assassination of President Anwar El-Sadat, the oppression of the Egyptian people intensified and grew more draconian by the day. Mubarak and his acolytes sought to crush any vestiges of opposition, especially those from amongst the Islamic parties. His regime routinely jailed, tortured and killed those who spoke out against his rule. This continued until fear and terror permeated all sections of Egyptian society and the ordinary people became afraid even to speak to each other in private lest they attract the ears of the notorious security forces. Amnesty International stated in its 2010 report on Egypt: "The government continued to use state of emergency powers to detain peaceful critics and opponents as well as people suspected of security offences or involvement in terrorism. Some were held under administrative detention orders; others were sentenced to prison terms after unfair trials before military courts. Torture and other ill-treatment remained widespread in police cells; security police detention centres and prisons, and in most cases were committed with impunity. The rights to freedom of expression, association and assembly were curtailed; journalists and bloggers were among those detained or prosecuted. Hundreds of families residing in Cairo's "unsafe areas" were forcibly evicted; some were left homeless, others were relocated but without security of tenure. At least 19 people seeking to cross into Israel were shot dead by border guards, apparently while posing no threat. At least 269 people were sentenced to death, and at least five were executed." What emboldened Mubarak and his cronies to excel in the repression and plunder of their people was the silence of their master America. Successive US administrations ignored the plight of the Egyptian masses and continued to lavish praise on Mubarak's regime. On odd occasions, US officials would punctuate the status quo with some demands for reducing the terror of Mubarak's rule, but this was often ignored and soon forgotten. As far as Egypt and the Arab world were concerned, America's behaviour was rooted and indeed governed by the support for dictatorships and monarchies as a bulwark against political Islam.

B. Mubarak and his inner circle showed no affinity for the people and worked tirelessly to steal from the masses and enrich themselves and their families. According to the UN, 20% of Egyptians live on less than a $1 a day, yet Egypt ranks fourth in the Arab world in terms of the number of billionaires it has.[46] The stark gap between rich and poor was further fuelled by rampant corruption and nepotism. In January 2010, a report by the Al Ahram Centre for Strategic Studies, titled "The Role of Regulatory Bodies in Promoting Transparency and Combating Corruption", showed that a high portion of Egyptians believe that the recent rise in commodity prices is a manifestation of systemic corruption. The study noted that 28.5% of Egyptians believe that this was the sole reason for the rise in prices and that it exacerbated the widening gap between rich and poor, creating a lack of discipline in government and fostering ill-treatment of citizens.

International organizations have suggested that political interference by Mubarak's government and its close ties to business interests have contributed to widespread corruption. On 20th of March 2010, Omnia Hussien, program coordinator at the Berlin-based Transparency International said that there is political interference in the work of anti-corruption agencies, lack of effective "whistle-blowing mechanisms" and access to information, "coupled with excessive limitations on civil society freedoms and the media." Possible conflicts of interest involving government appointments and close ties between politicians and business are "an issue of concern".

C. The dramatic increase in the price of essential commodities in 2007, and the subsequent collapse of the global financial system in 2008, had a huge impact on Egyptian living standards. Not only the poor and destitute were affected, but the middles class, once relatively safe from declining living standards, was plunged into extreme poverty. According to Al Ahram Centre for Strategic Studies , 66% of the population described the economic situation in Egypt as bad, and 71% believed that the situation was better three years ago i.e. just before the onset of the food crisis. The contraction of the Egyptian economy as result of the global financial crisis has had an adverse affect on tourism and other sectors, and this has given

---

[46] "The widening gap between rich and poor in the Arab world", The Qatar Peninsula, (October 20, 2010).

rise to mass unemployment, especially amongst the youth, which is reported to be as high as 22%. The figure was published by Egypt's Central Agency for Public Mobilization and Statistics and based its findings on interviewing youth ranging between the ages of 18 and 29. The study also noted that the Egyptian youth represented 24.2 percent of the population in 2009.

D. The Tunisian uprising had a profound effect on the psychology of Arabs across the region. For the first time in decades, ordinary people across the Middle East felt that they could stand up against their tyrannical regimes governed by despots. This change in mindset was immediately visible in Egypt as thousands poured onto the streets of Cairo, Suez and Alexandria demanding the ousting of Mubarak and hoping for a similar outcome as that of their Tunisian brethren.

E. However, the aforementioned reasons were not enough on their own to push the Egyptians out on the streets, the Egyptians needed some encouragement, and this came from America. For some time now, America has been clandestinely working behind the scenes and exploring a number of ways to change Mubarak's regime in a manner that appeases the demands of the Egyptian people for greater political rights, reduction in corruption and simultaneously continues to safeguard her interests in the region. It is an open secret that America funded and supported a number of dissident groups to foment a rebellion against the Mubarak regime, which the world is witnessing today. For instance, according to Wiki Leaks and extracts from it reproduced by an English newspaper, The Daily Telegraph,[47] the American Embassy in Cairo helped a young dissident attend a US-sponsored summit for activists in New York, while working to keep his identity secret from Egyptian state police. The Newspaper further reported: 'In a secret diplomatic dispatch, sent on December 30, 2008, Margaret Scobey, the US Ambassador to Cairo, recorded that opposition

---

[47] T. Ross,M. Moore and S. Swimford, "Egypt protests: America's secret backing for rebel leaders behind uprising", The Telegraph, (January 28, 2011).

groups had allegedly drawn up secret plans for "regime change" to take place before presidential elections, scheduled for September 2011. The memo, which Ambassador Scobey sent to the US Secretary of State in Washington DC, was marked "confidential" and headed: "April 6 activist on his US visit and regime change in Egypt." It said the activist claimed "several opposition forces" had "agreed to support an unwritten plan for a transition to a parliamentary democracy, involving a weakened presidency and an empowered prime minister and parliament, before the scheduled 2011 presidential elections". The embassy's source said the plan was "so sensitive it cannot be written down". The protests in Egypt are being driven by the April 6 youth movement, a group on Facebook that has attracted mainly young and educated members opposed to Mr Mubarak. The group has about 70,000 members and uses social networking sites to orchestrate protests and report on their activities. The documents released by WikiLeaks reveal US Embassy officials were in regular contact with the activist throughout 2008 and 2009, considering him one of their most reliable sources for information about human rights abuses'.

Additionally, there are reports by Wiki Leaks that the US was active in the funding of the pro-democracy movement in Egypt as early as 2006. According to a December 6, 2007, cable posted online by Norway's paper of reference Aftenposten, the United States Agency for International Development (USAID) planned to dedicate 66.5 million dollars in 2008 and 75 million in 2009 to Egyptian programmes promoting democracy and good governance. The paper went on to state that the United States has thus directly contributed to "building up the forces that oppose the President" - Mubarak. The paper also reproduced requests from the Egyptian government imploring the US to stop the funding of movements. For instance, Egyptian Minister of International Cooperation Fayza Aboulnaga had sent a letter to the embassy requesting that USAID stop financing 10 of the organisations "on the grounds that (they) have not been properly registered as NGOs" according to a third cable dated February 28, 2008.

As for the current political situation in Egypt, the US is carefully managing the transition of the regime under Mubarak to one which is more palatable to the people and does not undermine her interests in the region and the wider Muslim world. America is prudently pressing Mubarak to introduce changes to the current political system in the full knowledge that the appointees Omar Suleiman as Vice President and Ahmad Shafiq as the new Prime Minister are both loyal to her. For instance, Suleiman has been the director of the Egyptian General Intelligence Services since 1993 and has played a pivotal role in executing American policy with regards Israel. As for Shafiq, he has served as the commander of the Egyptian Air force and is a close ally of Mubarak. Both men have strong ties to the Egyptian military, which is a recipient of US military aid, training and grooming. Mubarak also appointed a new cabinet, which was dominated by figures connected to the regime.

The appointments are just the first step in America's plan to undertake constitutional reform, produce a stable government that is perceived by the people to be 'more representative of their interests' in the run up to the presidential elections. US Secretary of State, Hillary Clinton, described the changes as preliminary; she said, "We are only at the beginning of what is unfolding in Egypt."[48] She also alluded to a post Mubarak scenario where the government will be more open and inclusive, and this will take place gradually and in a structured way. She said, "We have been very clear that we want to see a transition to democracy. And we want to see the kind of steps taken to bring that about. We want to see an orderly transition."[49] Hence, it is quite obvious that the US will fashion a government that consists of people both new and old that are loyal to her. As for the Egyptian army, it is loyal to America and it has played an instrumental role in ensuring that the transition takes place in an orderly fashion and that the

[48] S. Komarow, "Clinton Urges Egypt's President Mubarak to Hold 'Free and Fair Elections'", Bloomberg, (January 31, 2011).
[49] "Secretary of State Hillary Clinton, Speaker of the House John Boehner Talk Egypt Crisis", Fox news, (January 30, 2011).

uprising is not hijacked by unscrupulous elements loyal to other foreign powers, namely, Britain and Europe. The Chief of Army Staff Lt. Gen. Sami Annan is staunchly American and he is in close coordination with the US in managing the transition.

Given that the US has instigated and paid some of the opposition, especially the April 6th youth movement, it has also secured the key posts in government, therefore, at present is having the upper hand in seeing this transition through. The next step would be to create stable conditions and press for the 2011 presidential election. It is expected that during this process America will make further concessions to public demands by replacing some of the old guard with different faces. This will continue until America feels she has mollified the people. However, America and her agent will use force if they perceive themselves to be losing control. They have already allowed mobs to run amok in the streets of Egypt in a bid to sap the people's morale. All of this means that fundamentally the Egyptian regime would have not changed since 1952; i.e. since the appearance of Gamal Abdel Nasser.

Moreover, America may also permit the Muslim brotherhood to play some role in the future political makeup. However, this will merely be used as a ploy to meet the demands of the public and more importantly, use it as a tool to pressurize Israel to overcome its obstinacy towards the Palestinians. At present, the Jewish state is extremely anxious about the events in Egypt and what may become of their peace treaty with the country. They also feel that America is compromising Israeli security.

This is more evident in a recent comment in the daily Jewish paper Maariv, entitled "A Bullet in the Back from Uncle Sam". It accused Obama and his Secretary of State, Hillary Clinton, of pursuing a naive, smug and insular diplomacy heedless of the risks. It said, "To fuel the mob raging in the streets of Egypt and to demand the head of the person who five minutes ago was the bold ally of the president ... an almost lone voice of sanity in a

Middle East? The politically correct diplomacy of American presidents throughout the generations ... is painfully naive." The peace treaty signed by Anwar Sadat and guarded by Mubarak has provided Israel with 31 years of stability along its border with Egypt. No doubt the US will use the uncertainty of the viability of the peace treaty in the coming months to press the Jewish state to conclude peace with the Palestinians.

## Implications for the region

The situation in Egypt also implies that other Arab regimes will share a similar fate in the not too distant future. Through this process America will try and open up pro-British regimes such as those in Tunisia, Algeria, Morocco, Libya, Jordan and the Gulf countries and bring them under its sphere of influence. The countries in Maghreb are particularly important to US policy makers as they are major supplier of hydrocarbons and a transit route to ship gas and oil to Europe. With these countries under its control, the US will be able to apply greater pressure on Europe at a time when Europe is embroiled in bitter disputes with the US ranging from economic issues and trade wars to differences over foreign policy connected to North Atlantic Treaty Organisation (NATO) and Afghanistan.

For Syria and Iran, America will change the regime in these countries to make them more open and inclusive. America is hoping that the new regimes that emerge from this transition will resemble Turkey with its strong army guaranteeing a pseudo democracy. However, the result may turn out to be another Iraq or at best a precarious Lebanon, as the fragmented opposition vies in each country to assert itself.

Nevertheless, America is fully cognizant that even these changes will not dampen the *Ummah*'s quest for Islam, and at best America can delay the re-establishment of the Khilafah, but its return is inevitable—even sooner than most people think.

January 31, 2011

# 31

# Egypt Must Be Reclaimed for Islam

*"Nearly two-thirds of Egyptians want Shar'iah and end of peace with Israel."*

*--Pew Global Attitudes Project*

I t has taken around six months for the deposed tyrant Hosni Mubarak to finally appear in court to face 'justice' before the nation. The Egyptian state-run media—an obedient tongue of the military junta—greeted Mubarak's court appearance with extraordinary headlines: "Mubarak in the cage ... Now the revolution has succeeded," blurted Al-Akhbar and "Mubarak and his regime present in the grip of justice," wrote the Al-Ahram. Egyptians, who for many years have lived under the tyranny of Mubarak's rule, were captivated by his presence in court and most Egyptians felt that Mubarak deserved to be executed for his heinous crimes. According to a recent online poll conducted by the company YouGov, 60% of Egyptians wanted him executed.

This is understandable, as ordinary Egyptians have a long litany of complaints that speak volumes against the despot. Routine torture, false imprisonment and extra judicial killing of political opponents are among many crimes that top the list. Furthermore, the nation could barely conceal its disgust when it emerged that after Mubarak's removal the wretched dictator had amassed an enormous personal fortune estimated to be in the region of $70 billion— all at the expense of his people who lived in squalor and abject poverty.

The public show casing of the trial is no accident, but a desperate attempt by his erstwhile friends in the military to save their own skins and extend protection to America's waning hegemony over Egypt. At first, the military pretended to be the 'guardians of the revolution', but in the months that followed, Egyptians came to realise that the military had supplanted

Mubarak— through a bloodless coup— only to continue with the same draconian laws and pro-American policies that were the hallmark of the Mubarak era.

In fact, America has been extremely active in orchestrating changes on the ground to deflect the momentum of the revolution and accommodate the Islamic aspirations of the millions of Egyptians. The latter is America's real concern. In April 2011, a Pew poll highlighted that 60% of the population wanted Islamic law. In fact, so deeply ingrained is the desire for Islam amongst Egyptians that Egypt's widely circulated newspaper Al-Ahram continues to carry its increasingly pro-Islamic editorials; on the 8th of August 2011 it read 'shar'iah state would preserve life, justice'. None of this bodes well for the longevity of America's control over Egyptian affairs.

Unsurprisingly then, American officials have been tampering with the ongoing constitutional reforms, preparations for the upcoming parliamentary and presidential elections, aid to civilian groups and the recent deployment of the Egyptian army in North Sinai to prevent unwarranted disruption of gas supply to the Jewish State. Additionally, America, through its agency USAID, has hitherto this year channelled $65 million towards nurturing civil institutions and civilian groups to champion pro-American reforms.[50]

Egyptians, who have thrown away the shackles of fear, laid bare their chests in front of security forces and berated the military junta's ties with America have quickly become threats to Washington's strategists. The Egyptian public is incensed by this blatant American interference to shape the new political landscape. This has forced the army to take a strong stance against them. The military has waded into the debate by describing the recipients of these US funds as activists funded by foreigners. However, this puts the Supreme Council of the Armed Forces (SCAF) that is presiding over Egypt in an ugly predicament. The United States has given

---

[50] "Middle East-Country-Egypt", USAID.

Egypt an average of $2 billion annually since 1979, much of it military aid, according to the Congressional Research Service. The combined total makes Egypt the second largest recipient of US aid after Israel. In 2010, $1.3 billion went to strengthen Egyptian forces versus $250 million in economic aid. Egypt also receives hundreds of millions of dollars' worth of excess military hardware annually from the Pentagon.

In other words, ordinary Egyptians are not only able see through the hypocrisy of SCAF, but more significantly are growing more anti-American and are venting their fury at SCAF through daily demonstrations. Furthermore, the military is undermining its own credibility as an honest broker ahead of the upcoming elections by snuggling up to Washington. The recent visit of Major General Mohamed El-Assar to Washington only serves to underscore in the eyes of Egyptians that the scope and magnitude of the military's ties with America is not in the interest of the nation. The stench of this relationship is no longer bearable for many, but in the near term the nexus between SCAF and America is expected to survive.

What allows the US and her surrogate (SCAF) to continue to have an upper hand over Egyptians is that the opposition is divided, and to some degree, leaderless to. Indeed, there is the Muslim Brotherhood, Mohamed El Baradei, Amr Musa and others. But these so-called leaders are becoming increasingly unappealing to the Egyptian masses because of their close associations with foreign powers and their ever-shifting opinions on the role of Islam in society. Within this context, it important for the Egyptian masses to coalesce around a common agenda that helps them distinguish between those leaders that can really liberate Egypt from the clutches of colonialism and those leaders who covet to use Islam to ensure the continuity of American hegemony.

Below are some demands that should be put forward to those who aspire to be the leaders of Egypt, so as to understand their vision and ideological orientation.

1. *Shar'iah* must replace all forms of criminal and civilian law. Economics, ruling, and foreign relations must be governed in accordance with Islamic law.

2. All foreign embassies, particularly those of America, Britain and France should be closed, and their personnel asked to leave the country immediately. All diplomatic ties with these countries must be terminated.

3. The Egyptian army must renounce US military aid and sever its links with the American army. All US army personnel and those of other Western powers should be escorted out of the country.

4. Egypt must forsake all forms of economic assistance from Western institutions such as the IMF and the World Bank (WB), as well as, the lending institution associated with the European Union (EU).

5. Billions of dollars usurped by Mubarak and his acolytes must be placed in a trust, and disbursed according to *Shar'iah* rules for the benefit of the Egyptian people.

6. Egypt should actively block from using the Suez Canal those Western powers that are in an active state of war with the Muslim world.

7. Egypt must revoke its treaty with Israel, cut all diplomatic ties, stop the sale of gas and treat the Jewish state as the enemy of Muslims. Furthermore, Egypt should take all measures to liberate Palestine from the Zionist occupation.

8. Egypt must initiate steps to break down the artificial colonial borders with Sudan and Libya, and unify with these countries to form a single Islamic state.

9. Egypt must treat the Christians as Dhimmis (non-Muslim citizen(s) of the Khilafah), and extend all forms of protection to safeguard their religion, property and wealth.

These demands can be used as a criterion to measure the sincerity to Islam of those who aspire to lead the nation. If they deviate even an inch then they are not worthy of leading the Muslim nation. If they adhere to these demands, then the people should rally around them. As the Egyptians have already sacrificed much, their pure blood spilt and even some becoming martyrs. But during this sacred month of Ramadan when the doors of Jannah (paradise) are open and Allah (swt)'s mercy is in abundance, you need to increase your efforts and excel in your sacrifice, and campaign tirelessly for the above demands to be met. Allah (swt) reminds us in the Qur'ān:

*"Say: If it be that your fathers, your sons, your brothers, your mates, or your kindred; the wealth that ye have gained; the commerce in which ye fear a decline: or the dwellings in which ye delight - are dearer to you than Allah (swt), or His Apostle, or the striving in His cause;- then wait until Allah (swt) brings about His decision: and Allah (swt) guides not the rebellious."*

[TMQ Taubah:24].

Remember your rich Islamic history and how your forefathers stood firm for Allah (swt)'s cause in the face of great adversity, without flinching an inch and refusing to compromise their Islam. Allah (swt) says:

*"Oh you who have Iman. If you help Allah (swt), Allah (swt) will help you; and establish your feet firmly."*

[TMQ Muhammed:7].

Remember there is no life better then the life under the Islamic system, which can only be implemented through the re-establishment of Khilafah.

And only then total submission and obedience to Allah (swt) will be complete.


August 15, 2011

32

# Army Leadership Betrays the Hope of Muslims in Egypt

*"The military's unwillingness to cede power and allow a genuinely democratic government has been clear for months. Yet the United States has continued to support the council."*

*--Sara Khorshid*

Revolution for many Egyptians, once a beacon of hope and promise, has now transformed into a full scale nightmare. The military, previously regarded as the custodians of the popular uprising that toppled former President Hosni Mubarak, are now viewed with intense suspicion and contempt. The indiscriminate killing of the Coptic Christians at the hands of the military is just the tip of the iceberg in a catalogue of complaints against Egypt's remaining junta.

Other complaints include a delay in drafting the 'new' constitution, making the parliament subservient to the military, allowing former Mubarak cronies to stand for parliamentary elections and refusing to remove Egypt's emergency laws. In addition, the military rulers have also indicated that they will postpone the election of the president. "We will keep the power until we have a president," Major General Mahmoud Hegazy said.[51] These measures clearly underscore that the military does not see itself playing an interim role in governing. Instead, the military brass is endeavouring to extend its stay in power.

Missing, to, is American criticism. This was overtly prevalent in the days that led to Mubarak's dismissal from power, but now it appears to be muted. In an interview with the Associated Press, Secretary of State Hillary Rodham Clinton said, "the United States would continue to pressure long-

---

[51] D. Kirkpatrick, "Egypt's Military Expands Power, Raising Alarms", New York Times, (October 14, 2011).

time leaders to leave power in Syria, Yemen and ensure chaos is averted in Egypt, where demonstrators have succeeded in ousting an autocrat. But she cautioned against overly optimistic forecasts for how quickly each country could make its break with the past." Hence, America's wish is to prevent the liberation of the Egyptian and other Arab people from tyranny until the conditions are right to bring in another compliant government that will safeguard her interests.

The sole reason for the abrupt slow down towards civilian rule, is that both America and Egypt's military rulers are afraid of political Islam. Before the revolution, Egyptians showed strong support for Islamic values. A Pew Poll suggested that 77% of Egyptians believe that thieves should have their hands cut off, 82% believed that adulterers should be stoned and 84% subscribe to the view that apostates should be killed. Furthermore, after the ouster of Mubarak, the majority of Egyptians viewed the Islamic State as being indispensable for implementing these *Shar'iah* rules. In May 2011, Al-Ahram reported that 60% of Egyptians wanted to establish an Islamic state. Only 4% of the respondents suggested that a secular system in Egypt would indeed be desirable, while 3% said military rule was suitable for the future of their country.

It is very clear that America does not want a civilian government until the threat of political Islam is either eliminated, or sufficiently diluted and secularized. America is fully aware that the first option is futile, but she recognizes that there still exist individuals and groups that are eager to sell their *Deen*[52] in exchange for power.

Such people are eager to respond to America's beckoning call to become their agents, and indeed they have purchased error instead of guidance. Allah (swt) says:

---

[52] Deen is defined in Islam as a complete way of life. The term should not be equated with religion or understood as a limited to the spiritual side of Islam. Deen encompasses both the spiritual and the temporal spheres of life.

*"They are the ones who buy Error in place of Guidance and Torment in place of Forgiveness. Ah! what boldness (They show) for the Fire!."*

[TMQ Al-Baqara:175]

Cultivating such people to assume power is taking time and hence the US has instructed the Supreme Council of the Armed Forces (SCAF) to delay the elections until suitable agents dressed in Islamic garb are groomed under US auspices to take power.

The army leadership, rather than opposing American interference, is gladly accepted this task, and is prepared to spill blood, abduct people and repress any form of dissent.

Oh Muslims, the only thing that stands in your way and the return of Islam is the army leadership. And in sum, they do not amount to more than a handful of people, who have abandoned Allah (swt), His Messenger and the Muslims in preference for safeguarding America's hegemony and the security of the Zionist state. They look upon them as their friends and helpers, whilst they pour scorn over you. They embrace the enemies of Islam in clear violation of Allah (swt)'s word:

*"Oh you who have Iman! Do not take the Jews and the Christians as protecting Awliyaa (friends, allies)! Each of them are protecting Awliyaa (friends, allies) within their own. And the one amongst you who turns to them as protecting allies, then he is one of them. And truly, Allah (swt) does not guide the wrongdoing people."*

[TMQ Al-Maida:51]

They are closed to reason and dialogue, and are blind to the reality of their master America. Look how easily she disposed of her comrade Mubarak who had served her for many years. Yet despite this, they are willing to put their trust in America ahead of their trust in Allah (swt) and they see no shame in betraying your yearning for Islam.

*"Oh you who have believed, do not betray Allah (swt) and the Messenger or betray your trusts while you know [the consequence]."*

[TMQ Al-Anfal:27]

Moreover, they think they are clever by pretending to look after your affairs and your *Deen*, but they refer to *Taghoot* (non-Islam).

Allah (swt) says:

*"Have you seen those who claim to believe in the revelation revealed to you and the revelation revealed earlier? They seek the ruling of Taghoot (non-Islam) although they have been ordered to disbelieve in it."*

[TMQ An-Nisa:60]

Oh Muslims of Egypt! Remember your duty to uphold Allah (swt)'s *Deen* in all circumstances. You must work with your brothers in the army to uproot the army leadership and re-establish the Khilafah. Only then can your aspirations for peace, justice and the full implementation of Islam be realised. Know that Allah (swt) has power over all things.

October 22, 2011

## 33

## Egypt's Farcical Presidential Election Makes a Mockery of the Sacrifices of the Revolution and Strengthens America's Control Over Egypt !

*"There's broad consensus between the Brotherhood and military leaders on the need to accommodate the military's longstanding political and economic interest...But the devil's in the details; I don't think the two sides have reached agreement on specifics."*

*--Hesham Sallam*

Almost eighteen months after the downfall of Mubarak, America through her loyal agents in the Supreme Council of the Armed Forces (SCAF) has effectively scuttled the Egyptian revolution and disarmed the Muslim brotherhood. By doing so, the US has successfully managed to keep the regime intact minus a few missing faces. This is similar to the much coveted Yemeni model, where the West was able to keep Saleh's regime in power without him. In the present Egyptian regime, the only outward casualty of any prominence is Mubarak. Set against this background the claims of a Morsi victory in the presidential elections by supporters of the Muslim brotherhood not only sound increasingly hollow but are extremely naïve indeed.

Over the past year or so, SCAF, a vestige of the Nasserite period, has adroitly hoodwinked the Egyptian people and tamed the divided opposition to retain absolute control over Egyptian affairs and continue with America's hegemony in the region. The nomination of Shafiq's candidature to the presidency, acquittal of Mubarak's sons, and the declaration by the Supreme Court to dissolve parliament are just some of the glaring measures enacted by the army generals to ensure that SCAF retains its grip on power. But perhaps the most daring of all political manoeuvres instigated by SCAF was its decree to limit the powers of the president.

Such an act bestows upon the army general full control over all civilian and legislative matters. In summary, it is a carte blanche to write the country's constitution in the army's image. SCAF is free to appoint assembly members, to write the constitution, to interfere in the drafting of the articles and veto any proposed canons that are deemed against the interests of the army generals.

SCAF could not have mustered the courage to take such a bold military coup against the Egyptian people if it was not for the antics of the Islamic opposition. The Islamic opposition never spoke with one voice and repeatedly contradicted itself by trying to please the West, the army, the Egyptian Muslims and the rest. The Islamic parties were unable to express unambiguous opinions on Egypt's relations with America and Israel, the role of *Shar'iah* in society, the system of ruling and the treatment of non-Muslims. In their quest to appease the West they forgot to fear Allah (swt) and sought to assuage the apprehensions of His creation. Allah (swt) says:

*"Oh you who have Iman! Fear Allah (swt) as He should be feared and die not except as Muslims."*

[TMQ Al-Imran:102]

*"Oh you who have Iman! Keep your duty to Allah (swt) and fear Him, and always speak the truth. He will direct you to do righteous deeds and will forgive you your sins. And whosoever obeys Allah (swt) and His Messenger, has indeed achieved a great achievement."*

[TMQ Al-Ahzaab:70-71]

In their desire to appear more liberal to the West, the Islamic opposition lost the confidence of ordinary Egyptians, many of whom increasingly saw hypocrisy in their actions and began to turn away from them. Ordinary

Muslims were not the only ones who were disappointed. The rank and file of these movements, especially the young, challenged the stance adopted by their leaders. They found it very difficult to digest Islam's domination by *Taghoot* (non-Islam). Allah (swt) says:

*"Have you seen those who claim to believe in the revelation revealed to you and the revelation revealed earlier? They seek the ruling of Taghoot (non-Islam) although they have been ordered to disbelieve in it."*

[An-Nisa: 60]

However, what made matters worse for the Islamic opposition was their blind adherence to the democratic election process while remaining silent on the actions of SCAF. Islamic parties in Egypt must understand that it is impossible to bring Islam through either participation or negotiations with the systems of non-Islam. Our modern history is replete with examples where Islamic parties have failed miserably to bring about Islam through engagement with non-Islamic systems. The dismissal of the Islamic Salvation Front (FIS) in Algeria in 1991 and the exploitation of the Mutahiddah Majlis-i-Amal (MMA) by Musharraf in 2002 are two such striking examples.

The only way for the Muslims of Egypt to escape from the tyranny of the West and the rule of their agents is through the re-establishment of the Islamic state. Islamic parties must join forces with the Muslims of Egypt and collaborate with sincere officers in the Egyptian army to re-establish the *Khilafah Rashida* by giving *Bay'ah* (pledge of allegiance) to the Khalifah who will rule according to the Qur'ān and Sunnah.

*"Verily, Allah (swt) will help those who help His (cause)."*

[TMQ Al-Hajj:40]

June 24, 2012

**34**

# Morsi Follows Mubarak to Revive the Peace Process and Safeguard the Jewish State

*"These are important tidings. But whoever talks about peace and stability must understand that it cannot just be vague and hypothetical. Therefore, we hope to see President Morsi receiving official Israeli representatives, we want to see him giving interviews to Israeli media and we want to see him in Jerusalem."*

*--Avigdor Lieberman*

Uproar and commotion has erupted in Egypt over revelations that President Morsi has sent a communiqué confirming Egypt's commitment to peaceful ties with the Jewish state. In the letter sent to Shimon Peres, President of the Jewish State, Morsi states: "I am looking forward to exerting our best efforts to get the Middle East Peace Process back to its right track in order to achieve security and stability for all peoples of the region, including the (sic) Israeli people."

Despite vociferous denials by Morsi's representatives, the letter appears to be genuine. The English newspaper The Guardian reported that Peres' office said the president's aides received the official communiqué on July 31st, 2012, from the Egyptian ambassador to the Jewish state, both by registered mail and by fax from the Egyptian embassy in Tel Aviv. Furthermore, the paper stated that the fax number which appeared on the faxed letter was registered to the Egyptian embassy in Tel Aviv.

The appearance of the letter is not an extraordinary occurrence, rather it is a manifestation of Morsi's pledge to respect Egypt's international agreements, which includes the peace accords with Israel. The presence of the Egyptian embassy in the heartland of the Jewish state underscores Morsi's intention to have harmonious relations with the Jews.

The timing of the letter comes hot on the heels of visits to Cairo by Palestinian leaders— President Mahmoud Abbas and Hamas's political chief, Khalid Meshal. After his meeting with Morsi, Abbas told reporters: "the doors of the political process with Israel are shut."[53] Notwithstanding the close ties between Morsi's brotherhood and Hamas, no new offers were made to Meshal to ease the miserable plight of Palestinians in Gaza. In fact, Morsi reaffirmed that he would not pick sides between the divided Palestinian leadership. He said, "We have said before that we stand at equal distance from all Palestinian factions. We support and aid them and are always happy to help in reconciliation."[54]

These statements clearly point towards the fact that Morsi, under Tantawi's auspices, has been tasked by America to reconcile the differences between the Palestinian leadership and kick start the Middle East peace process, which is designed to safeguard the security of the Jewish state. So both Morsi and Tantawi are working together and picking up the pieces left behind during Mubarak's ouster to unify the Palestinian factions and re-launch the peace process. Speaking on the collaboration between Morsi and Tantawi for common goals, US Defence Secretary Panetta said, "It's my view that President Morsi and Field Marshal Tantawi have a very good working relationship and are working together for the same ends."[55] In return, America is offering Tantawi and Morsi $1.3 billion in aid to commit high treason against the *Ummah* and continue working with America and the Jewish state.

Do not Morsi and Tantawi heed the words of Allah (swt) that explicitly warn about taking allies that are sworn enemies of the Muslim *Ummah*? Allah (swt) says:

---

[53] "Egypt's president meets Palestinian counterpart", The Guardian, (July 18, 2012).
[54] *Ibid.*
[55] M. Rabechault, "Pentagon chief meets Egypt's new Islamist president", AFP, (July 31, 2012).

*"The Jews and the Christians will never be pleased with you until you follow their religion. Say, Allah (swt)'s guidance is the true guidance."*

[TMQ Al-Baqara:120]

*"You who have Iman! Do not take the Jews and Christians as your Awliyaa (friends, allies); they are the Awliyaa (friends, allies) of one another. Any of you who takes them as Awliyaa (friends, allies) is one of them. Allah (swt) does not guide wrongdoing people."*

[TMQ Al-Maidah:51]

The Muslims of Egypt must stand firm against the plans of the disbelieving American state to provide security and peace to the Jewish state. They must reject every proposal taken by Morsi and Tantawi that either strengthens America's hegemony over them or places Egypt's resources in the defence of the Jewish state.

The Muslims of Egypt must ensure that the resources of the country are placed in the defence of Islam and the Muslim *Ummah* only. And that every last morsel of these resources is used in the liberation of Palestine! This can only be achieved by the Muslims of Egypt uniting with their brothers in the armed forces to re-establish the Khilafah state and permanently lift the state of siege and fear perpetrated by the Jewish state against the Palestinian people.

August 6, 2012

## 35

# Morsi's Government Aims to Shackle Egypt to Disgraceful IMF Conditions

*"The IMF disguises its harsh and treacherous acts against the poor in Egypt or elsewhere as economic reforms. The irony is that loans from the IMF and WB always lead to social and economic uprisings. As far as Egypt is concerned, ex-President Hosni Mubarak paid the tragic price for the IMF's help. He was ignominiously toppled by a revolution that called for 'freedom, social justice and cheap bread'."*

*--Mohssen Arishie*

L ast week, Morsi's government officially begged the IMF for a $4.9 billion loan and the Prime Minister, Hesham Qandil, described the 5 year loan to be paid back with 1.1% rate as a good deal for the country. The Prime Minister appeared live on Egypt's state television in a desperate bid to justify the loan, while neglecting to explain its benefits to the people, as he knows very well that the IMF is an international vampire that sucks the blood of the people, strengthens the economy of the Western powers and props up rulers allied to the West. Instead, he chose to emphasize that Egypt would somehow have the upper hand over the IMF in how the money is to be spent. He said, "It is Egypt that will mainly have the authority when it comes to how these funds will be spent."[56]

However, he was unable to conceal the truth and in his follow on statement, he contradicted himself and exposed one of the IMF's stipulated conditions, which is to force Morsi's government to cut spending related to looking after the affairs of the Egyptian people. He said, "It is an

---

[56] B. Daragahi "Egypt formally requests $4.8bn IMF loan", Financial Times, (August 22, 2012).

Egyptian programme that will work on cutting and spending and adopting certain other measures."[57]

Fearing a backlash, Qandil intentionally chose not to elaborate on the other draconian measures. It is well known that such measures include: tax increases, price hikes on essential items, and further loans from other institutions. All of which will make the people suffer immensely and add to their misery. In fact, the Financial Times confirmed these measures. On August 22, 2012, the paper stated: "The IMF wants Egypt to outline plans to reduce its budget deficit by bolstering revenues and trimming the costly public sector, including fuel and food subsidies. Egypt must also secure financing from other lending institutions as part of the loan terms."

Qandil ended his live broadcast by spelling out, in unequivocal terms, how Egypt and her people would become hostage to the IMF's humiliating conditions over the next five years. He said, "Both parties have to agree on certain terms and conditions, and these terms and conditions will be binding to the country that signs this loan."[58]

So in a matter of 20 days, since taking office, Qandil has dashed the hopes of the Egyptian people who were expecting much relief from decades of economic repression under Mubarak's rule. Additionally, Qandil has gravely undermined Egypt's economic sovereignty by affirming the continuation of the IMF's wide spread interference in the country's economy, just as it acted with impunity during Mubarak's era. It is forbidden to give Colonial powers and their international financial institutions authority to interfere in the establishment of economic policy and its subsequent execution. Allah (swt) says:

*"And never will Allah (swt) allow the disbelievers to have a way over the believers."*
[TMQ An-Nisa:141]

---

[57] *Ibid.*
[58] *Ibid.*

Besides, Egypt is not in need of any loans or economic assistance. We ask Morsi and Qandil, what happened to the $70 billion that Mubarak and his family usurped from the people? Why is it that Morsi's regime remains quiet on the recovery of the plundered loot that rightfully belongs to the Egyptian people, but extends its begging bowl to be filled by humiliating IMF loans?

Whilst the treachery of Morsi's regime is becoming clearer to the people, the voices of support for Morsi's collaboration with the IMF from Islamic groups are truly disappointing. The Vice President of the Salafi Dawah group, Yasser Borhamy, attempted to legalize the riba[59] on IMF loans. He said that the interest on the loan Egypt is set to receive from the IMF does not involve usury, since the interest on the loan is only 1.1 percent, paid in the form of administrative fees, and the loan could be considered a grant. Previously, Yousry Hammad, spokesperson for the Salafi Nour Party, had stated that the interest on the IMF loan is not prohibited because it constitutes administrative fees. We ask Borhamy and Hammad why they are attempting to describe riba (not matter how minuscule it may be) as halal when Allah (swt) and His Messenger (SAW) have declared it haram. Allah (swt) says:

*"Oh those who have Iman, fear Allah (swt) and give up what still remains of the riba (interest) if you are believers. But if you do not, then listen to the declaration of war from Allah (swt) and His Messenger."*

[TMQ Al-Baqara:278-279]

---

[59] Riba (interest) is categorically forbidden in Islam and is regarded as a major sin. The messenger of Allah الله عليه و سلم said in his farewell sermon: "God has forbidden you to take riba, therefore all riba obligation shall henceforth be waived. Your capital, however, is yours to keep. You will neither inflict nor suffer inequity. God has judged that there shall be no riba and that all the riba due to `Abbas ibn `Abd al Muttalib shall henceforth be waived."

Abdullah ibn Mas'ud narrates that the Messenger of Allah (SAW) cursed the one who accepted usury, the one who paid it, the witness to it, and the one who recorded it.         (Sunan Abu Dawud: Book 22, Number 3327)

Oh Muslims of Egypt! Within the first 70 days of Morsi's rule, you have witnessed the true extent of his support for America's hegemony in Egypt, as well as his disregard for Islamic rules. The ugly achievements of his regime are: reaffirmation of peace with the Jewish state and enhanced security for the Jews through the demolition of tunnels providing vital supplies to Gaza, injection of fresh military blood to protect American interests from the continued revolts of Egyptians, appointment of a Christian women as a confidant, subjugation of the country to disgraceful IMF conditions and the legalization of riba.

Oh Muslims of Egypt! You will never enjoy economic prosperity as long as you remain silent about the non-Islamic laws that are openly implemented and justified in the name of Islam. Allah (swt) says:

*"And whoever turns away from My remembrance - indeed, he will have a depressed life, and We will gather him on the Day of Resurrection blind."*

[TMQ TaHa:124]

Oh Muslims of Egypt! Your only salvation lies in the absolute rejection of Morsi's regime and his pro-American reforms. To do this, you must redouble your efforts to re-establish the rightly guided Khilafah and immediately return the land of *Kinana* to its rightful state.

Only in the Khilafah state will you be able enjoy true economic prosperity through the use of money based on the gold standard, in the share of the public properties managed by the state on your behalf, and the protection of your ownership through Islamic contracts.

September 2, 2012

# 36

# Egypt's President Morsi is the New American Agent in the Region

*"Down with Morsi, America's agent."*

*--Chant from protesters at Cairo's Tahrir Square (*Bloomberg)

Ever since assuming the office of the Presidency, Morsi has worked resolutely to portray himself as a moderate Islamist working independent of American influence for the betterment of Egypt and the region. But beneath the veneer of Islamic rhetoric surrounding his domestic and foreign policy actions, Morsi is no better than his predecessor Mubarak— the former custodian of American interests in the region.

On the domestic front Morsi can claim that the opposition has not permitted his government enough time to push through reforms that will address the Egypt's battered economy, restore law and order, and improve the lives of the ordinary Egyptian people. This is despite the fact that such reforms is formulated under the auspices of IMF stipulations for Egypt's government to revise its economic agenda in order to qualify for the $4.8 billion loan. IMF spokesman Gerry Rice said, "We understand the Egyptian authorities have been working on revising their economic program. And once this step is completed, we will discuss the timing of a possible mission to Cairo to assess the revised program." The delay has prompted America's rating agency Moody to downgrade Egypt's credit worthiness. Thus America's economic enslavement of Egypt continues via the IMF and Moody regardless of the claims made by Morsi's government of following a sovereign economic policy.

On the foreign policy front Morsi cannot conceal his pro-American credentials behind the wall of protestors. Morsi's foreign policy is distinctively American and in many ways is more than Mubarak's era. Consider his treatment of Palestinians living in Gaza. On February 13th 2013, Egypt without warning flooded Gaza tunnels that are a life blood to the Palestinians living in concentration camp like conditions in Gaza, which for all intents and purposes is controlled by the cowardly Jewish state. The tunnels bring in everything from food and medicine to cement and iron, providing up to 75 percent of the goods to a population of 1.6 million people.

An Egyptian security official in the Sinai told Reuters: "We are using water to close the tunnels by raising water from one of the wells." Hamas has been reluctant to criticize Morsi in public, but Gazan's are more outspoken about the Hamas's naivety and Morsi's brutality. "Egyptian measures against tunnels have worsened since the election of Morsi. Our Hamas brothers thought he would open up Gaza. I guess they were wrong," said a tunnel owner, who identified himself only as Ayed, fearing reprisal. "Perhaps 150 or 200 tunnels have been shut since the Sinai attack. This is the Morsi era," he added.

So Morsi's government has exploited the attacks on Egyptian forces in Sinai in August 2012 to drive a ruthless campaign to close as many tunnels as possible and bolster the security of the Jewish state ahead of the much anticipated resumption of the dormant peace process. With Palestinian unity talks planned in the days ahead, Netanyahu weakened by the recent elections and Obama scheduled to visit the Jewish state in March 2013, Washington is keen to create the right atmosphere to give a vital push for peace between the Arabs and the Jewish state. Central to the commencement of peace talks is the security of the Jewish state, and Morsi like his predecessor is doing his utmost to meet American and Jewish expectations. Nonetheless, the timing of the recent operation is intended to mollify Jewish criticism of America's delivery of four F16 aircraft to the Egyptian air force.

Likewise, Morsi's close ties with Iran to find a political solution to the crisis in Syria that preserves remnants of Assad's regime bears the hallmark of America's intended solution. America has been working tirelessly with Iran, Turkey, Egypt, Gulf countries as well as with the EU and Russia to protect Assad's regime in some form through a variety of initiatives the latest being the Brahimi Plan. This will ensure the continuation of her hegemony over the Levant. Within this context Morsi visited Tehran in September 2012 and spoke of Iran as a pivotal stakeholder in finding a solution to the Syrian crisis. He said, "[Iran] a main player in the region that could have an active and supportive role in solving the Syrian problem… I don't see the presence of Iran in this quartet (Turkey, Egypt, Iran and Saudi Arabia) as a problem, but is a part of solving the problem." This also explains why Morsi a few days ago warmly greeted Ahmadinejad the butcher of the Syrian people. His treatment of the Iranian president attracted the ire of some of Morsi's close supporters such as Dawah Salafiyya which issued a statement: "Egypt is committed to the protection of all Sunni nations." Hence within a space of a few months Morsi has manage to surpass Mubarak and do what his predecessor failed to do i.e. forge a working relationship with Iran to safeguard America's interests in the Levant.

America is mightily pleased with the domestic and foreign policy actions undertaken by Morsi's government. On February 3rd 2013 US Ambassador to Egypt Anne Patterson said, "We look to Egypt to continue to serve as a force for peace, security and leadership as the Middle East proceeds with its challenging yet essential journey towards democracy."

There are important lessons for Egyptians to learn from Morsi's rule. First, by simply calling for the ouster of a brutal dictator only to be replaced by someone who overtly expresses his faith in Islam is a folly of enormous proportions and will not change the plight of the people. Second, the real cause of misery for Egyptians is the current system through which America continues to colonize the country. Unless the system is eradicated from its roots people will continue to suffer under America's colonial policies implemented by her loyalists in the present regime—be they Islamists or liberals.

Third, the only alternative to the present decadent system is the Islamic *Shar'iah*, and not Western liberal democracy as advocated by the short-sighted liberals. Western liberal democracy along with capitalism is dying and even people in the West are eagerly looking for an alternative system. But for Islamic *Shar'iah* to succeed it has to be implemented holistically not in a piece meal fashion as championed by Muslim brotherhood and its supporters.

Fourthly, the only practical way to realise the implementation of the *Shar'iah* in domestic and foreign policy areas is through the re-establishment of the Khilafah. Only the Khilafah can guarantee an independent economic and foreign policy free from Western interference.

February 20, 2013

## 37

# Bahrain: Rise of the *Shi'a* Crescent

*"Bahrain is the first of the Arab world's monarchies to experience major unrest in what is becoming a region-wide upheaval - and with good reason. The Khalifah family and ruling elite, who are Sunni, preside over a population that is 70 percent Shi'a..."*

*--Washington Post*

On March 26th, 2011, *Shi'a* protestors in Bahrain gathered in defiance of a 3 month ban imposed by King Hammad, and on the same day, *Shi'a* protesters in Qatif, Saudi Arabia, demanded the withdrawal of Saudi troops from Bahrain. Commenting on the current situation in Bahrain, Iraq's Prime Minister, Nuri al-Maliki, warned that the intervention in *Shi'a*-majority Bahrain by the Gulf kingdom's Sunni neighbours risked a sectarian war in the region. So is Maliki's portentous warning real or mere fiery rhetoric? In order to understand the unfolding political turmoil in Bahrain, the following must be considered:

1.       In the early nineteenth century, the British Empire faced severe hurdles in safeguarding their trade routes spanning from London via the Persian Gulf to India. Bahrain, along with some other countries (Qatar, UAE and Oman) that today are part of the Gulf Co-operation Council (GCC) was involved in attacking British naval vessels and trade ships. In 1820 the British deployed 'gun-boat diplomacy' against Bahrain and other territories in a bid to stem attacks against the East Indian Company trade routes. Against this backdrop the sly English colonial officers of the East Indian Company and other officials of the British government succeeded in overpowering Bahrain.

In May 1861, the colonial officer Sir Lewis Pelly signed an agreement with Sheikh Mohammad, and later with his brother Sheikh Ali, that placed

Bahrain under British rule and protection. The treaty stipulated that the ruler of Bahrain could not dispose of his territory except to the British. Furthermore, the treaty also specified that the ruler could not enter into relationships with a foreign country without the permission of the British government. In return, the British offered the rulers of Bahrain protection from aggression by sea or land. This treaty formed the basis of British colonization and hegemony over Bahrain, which still continues today, despite its so called independence from Britain in 1971.The discovery of oil in 1932, brought rapid modernization to Bahrain. Colonial relations with the United Kingdom grew closer, as evidenced by the British Royal Navy moving its entire Middle Eastern command from Bushehr in Iran to Bahrain by 1935. The British used Bahrain as a seaport to station their naval vessels to patrol the waters of the Persian Gulf.

2.      The period before Bahrain's independence coincided with Britain's waning influence in the Persian Gulf region and the ascendency of the US. Britain and her surrogates in the Gulf could no longer spurn American dominance of the Gulf and ceded control of strategic assets such as oil to American companies and seaports to the US Navy. Under the auspices of the British agent, Sheikh Isa the first ruler of pseudo-independent Bahrain signed an agreement, which permitted the US to rent naval and military facilities at Bahrain's seaports that was vacated by the British. This included piers, radio transmitters, warehouses, and other facilities left by the British.[60] Today, Bahrain is home to the US Navy's fifth fleet. The Fifth Fleet's area of responsibility includes the Indian Ocean and Arabian Gulf (the US uses the term "Arabian Gulf" instead of "Persian Gulf").[61]

3.      Despite Bahrain's declaration of independence, the British still continued to control the important affairs of the state, such as internal security through the deployment of British advisors. One of the most notorious British advisors was Ian Henderson, a former Colonial advisor in

---

[60] http://www.globalsecurity.org/military/facility/manama.htm.
[61] *Ibid.*

Kenya. He was placed in charge of the Director General of the Public Security Directorate (DGPSD), Criminal Investigations Directorate (CID) and the State Security Directorate (SSD) from 1996 to 1998 before becoming an advisor in the interior ministry in 2000[62]. Henderson's brutal role caught the attention of Amnesty International, which stated that 'Henderson's CID and SSD have for many years been responsible for gross human rights violations.' Methods at the security service HQ included pulling off finger nails, using dogs to attack prisoners and sexual abuse.[63] Henderson's ugly role in suppression of Bahrainis came as no surprise. And as far as the British were concerned, it was merely a continuation of the 1861 agreement. But this time, it was protection of British interests from Iran and the US. The US, via its surrogates in Iran, manipulated the *Shi'a*'s (*Shi'a*s form 70% of the population) in Bahrain to cause occasional problems for the British and her agents in Bahrain. Under the present King Hammad's rule, Britain tried to further strengthen its presence in the tiny emirate, especially over domestic security. This overlapped with the aftermath of the destruction of Iraq in 2003 and the rise of Iran. Eager to suppress domestic opposition—in particular *Shi'a* rebellions—the UK encouraged the sale of crowd controlling devices to Bahrain during the past decade. In 2010, equipment approved for export included tear gas and crowd control ammunition, equipment for the use of aircraft cannons, assault rifles, shotguns, sniper rifles and sub-machine guns. No requests for licenses were refused.[64] It is important to note that during the later years of the Shah's rule in Iran, Iranian claims over Bahrain were conveniently put on the back burner by the British. However, the pro-American Iranian revolution brought Iranian territorial claims over Bahrain to the fore and

---

[62] Mark Curtis, Web of deceit Britain's real role in the world, (2003).

[63] Amnesty International welcomes investigation into Henderson's role in torture in Bahrain, January 7 2000; "Anti torture groups object to visit by Bahrain's emir", Independent, (November 24, 1999).

[64] "UK arms sales to Middle East include tear gas and crowd control ammunition to Bahrain and Libya", Campaign against arms trade,(February 17, 2011).

have ever since defined relations between the two countries. For instance, in the summer of 2007, Hossein Shariatmadari, an advisor to Iran's supreme leader Grand Ayatollah Ali Khamenei, and editor of the Iranian newspaper, Kayan, called for Bahrain to be incorporated into Iran as its 14th province.

4.    In a bid to pacify unrest amongst Bahrainis, especially the *Shi'a*s, King Hammad undertook several political reforms such as parliamentary elections. Nonetheless, most of the reforms were cosmetic and the King still yields absolute control. In November 2006, the *Shi'a* opposition won 40% of the vote in a general election and a *Shi'a* Muslim, Jawad bin Salem al-Oraied, was named as a deputy Prime Minister. However, this was not enough to assuage the concerns of the restless *Shi'a* population. Indications of worsening relations between the monarchy and its *Shi'a* population came to a head in 2010, when 20 *Shi'a* opposition leaders were accused of plotting to overthrow the monarchy.

5.    Another interesting point to note is that in the run up to the handing over of Hong Kong to the Chinese in 1999, Bahrain, Qatar and the UAE gained greater significance by becoming a financial hub for British financiers and banks, and later served as a replacement for Hong Kong. The growth in the financial capabilities of these centres in recent years underscores this point.

**Present situation in Bahrain**

The Arab revolt that started in Tunisia and then spread to Egypt quickly found its way to Bahrain, which became one of the first GCC countries to be affected by large-scale protests. Initially, the opposition, consisting both of Sunni and *Shi'a*, called for greater political reforms and occupied Pearl Square. The Bahraini security forces reacted harshly and several protestors died. Subsequently, the opposition, consisting of people and groups such as the main *Shi'a* party al-Wefaq, presented their demands to the government. These included the release of all political prisoners; an impartial investigation into the deaths of protesters, a more moderate line from state-owned media, the resignation of the government and the formation of a new "national salvation" government, the introduction of a constitutional monarchy, and electoral reform. The King, however, only met some of the demands and released a number of political prisoners as a conciliatory gesture. For example, a prominent *Shi'a* opposition figure, Hassan Mushaima, was allowed to return from exile after the government dropped charges against him. However, the reluctance of King Hammad to meet the demands of the protestors, combined with his latest offer of national dialogue, were not enough to pacify the protestors. They quickly began to call for the removal of the monarchy. On March 8th, 2011, three *Shi'a* groups, the Wafa, Haq and Freedom Movement, formed the "Coalition for a Bahraini Republic", which called for the abolishment of the monarchy and the establishment of a democratic republic of Bahrain.[65] Sensing a hardening of the royal family's attitudes towards the protestors, US Secretary of Defence Robert Gates visited Bahrain on March 12th, 2011, and met King Hammad bin Isa al-Khalifa and Crown Prince Sheik Salman bin Hammad al-Khalifa in a bid to persuade the ruling family to speedily bring internal reform. He said, "I told both the king and the crown prince that across the region I did not believe there could be a return to the status quo and—that there was change, and it could be led, or it could be imposed," he said. "Obviously, leading reform—and being responsive—is the way we would like to see this move forward."[66] He also used the threat of Iran to ensure that the baby steps undertaken so far by the King were quickly accelerated. He said, "There is clear evidence that as the process is protracted, particularly in Bahrain, that the Iranians are looking for ways to exploit it and create problems...Under the circumstances, and with the impulse behind the political and economic grievances across the region...baby steps probably would not be sufficient to meet the need, that real reform would be necessary." It is clear from these statements that the

---

[65] "Hard line Shi'a groups demand republic in Bahrain", Montreal Gazette, (March 8, 2011).
[66] "Media Availability with Secretary Gates en route to Andrews Air Force Base from Manama, Bahrain", US Department of Defence News Transcripts, (March 12, 2011).

US was keen for the reforms to be implemented and for the Bahraini *Shi'a*s to have a much greater say in the political destiny of the country. King Hammad did not heed America's warning and on March 14th Saudi Arabia along with other GCC countries sent in soldiers to buttress King Hammad's efforts to put down the uprising and prevent a similar *Shi'a* uprising taking place in Saudi Arabia and other gulf states with *Shi'a* populations.. Bahraini opposition groups, including the largest *Shi'a* party Wefaq, said the move was an attack on defenceless citizens: "We consider the entry of any soldier or military machinery into the Kingdom of Bahrain's air, sea or land territories as a blatant occupation."

The Saudi intervention is a clear signal that Britain through its agents in the GCC will not allow a radical transformation of the region to take place. Indeed, the US sees an opportunity in the current *Shi'a* uprisings in Bahrain and Saudi Arabia to give greater political control to the *Shi'a* population at the expense of the Sunni leadership, which remains loyal to Britain. Furthermore, by allowing the *Shi'a*s to come to power in Iraq, America is confident that a similar process can be initiated in Bahrain (70 % *Shi'a*), Qatar (10% *Shi'a*) , Eastern Saudi Arabia (15% *Shi'a*), UAE(10% *Shi'a*) and Kuwait (40% *Shi'a*), where *Shi'a*s either are in the majority or make up a significant minority.

It is a longstanding wish of the US to create a 'shi'a Crescent' stretching from Lebanon, Southern Iraq, Iran, the Gulf, to Yemen  and placing the hydrocarbons and other strategic assets in the hands of a *Shi'a* elite that will owe its existence to the Americans and will be ever grateful. How the US manages the process of changing the current political landscape in the gulf will determine the extent to which there will be war along sectarian and religious fault lines.

March 26, 2011

## 38

# America Exploits Russian and Chinese Intransigence to Buy Assad Precious Time to Crush the Revolution

*"Paradoxically, Syria's strategic importance also helps to explain the lack of attention it is getting. Interested parties – the US, Israel, other Arab regimes, etc – would much prefer that the problem went away. Some of them recognise that Syria will have to change eventually but they are fearful of the possible outcome and don't really want any more uncertainties just at the moment. While they probably won't do much to prolong Bashar's stay in power, they won't try to tip him over the edge either – at least, not at this stage."*

*--Brian Whitaker*

On the 4th of February, Russia and China vetoed the UN Security Council resolution calling for Syrian President Bashar al-Assad to step down. The double veto attracted the ire of America, Europe and the Arab League. US Ambassador to UN, Susan Rice said that the United States was disgusted by the vetoes. She said, "For months this council has been held hostage by a couple of members. These members stand behind empty arguments and individual interests while delaying and seeking to strip bare any text that would pressure Assad to change his actions. Any further bloodshed that flows will be on their hands."[67] UK Foreign Secretary William Hague said, "It's clear, given what happened, that Russia and China will be held responsible for this terrible situation. I think it's a great mistake on the part of Russia and China to do this. It will have consequences for their influence in the Middle East."[68] The Arab League Chief, Nabil Elaraby, said that Russia and China had lost diplomatic credit

---

[67] M. Besheer, "Russia, China Veto UN Resolution on Syria", Voice of America, (February 3, 2012).
[68] "Hague attacks China and Russia over UN Syria veto", The BBC, (February 5, 2012).

in the Arab world by vetoing a UN resolution on Syria and may have sent a message to Damascus that it had a free hand to crack down on protests. For their parts, both Russia and China defended their actions and blamed the West for drafting a resolution that encouraged regime change.

In the light of these statements, can it be said that Russia and China want Assad to switch sides, and America realizing this is now seeking international legitimacy for the removal of Assad's regime and supplanting it with another surrogate government? Consider the following points:

A. The major powers in the world, namely Europe, America and Russia, as well as those that aspire to become a major power, such as China, undertake political actions based on national interests. These interests can be material, commercial, financial, strategic etc. In today's, world the major powers put their interests ahead of their principles and values. This leaves a noticeable trail of inconsistency in the foreign relations of these major powers with other countries. For instance American foreign policy during the Arab uprising is riddled with contradictory messages and actions. This thinking is aptly summed up by the following quote: "Great powers behave inconsistently—even hypocritically—depending on their interests. That's not unusual; it's part of the job description. In fact, in responding to the forces of change and repression loosed throughout the Arab world, flexibility is more important than ideological rigidity. The last thing America needs is a doctrine or ideological template to govern how it responds to fast-breaking changes in a dozen Arab countries, all of which are strikingly different in their respective circumstances."

B. Major Powers routinely conceal the attainment of their interests in a language that is made palatable for both the domestic and the foreign audiences. The aim is always to minimize undue opposition towards the attainment of the interest; hence, the political action is frequently shrouded in humanitarian overtones. In the case of Syria, the major powers have justified their respective stances in the name of the Syrian people. The same was done when the West invaded Afghanistan, Iraq, and Libya or imposed sanctions on Iran. Therefore, it is important to understand the motives of major powers behind their political actions and not be misled by the rhetoric.

C.   Out of the four powers involved in managing the Syrian crisis, namely: Russia, America, Europe and China—it is of great importance to understand Russian and American interests. As for China and Europe, they closely follow Russia and America respectively.

## Russian interests

Russia has a myriad of interests in Syria and they vary in scope and the degree of importance to the Kremlin.

1. Russia has huge commercial interests in Syria. Its firms have a substantial presence in the Syrian infrastructure, energy and tourism industries with exports to Syria worth $1.1 billion in 2010 and investment in the country valued at $19.4 billion in 2009. The Russian gas company Stroytransgaz is engaged in projects worth $1.1 billion, has 80 Russian staff on the ground in Syria. It is building a natural gas processing plant 200 kilometres east of Homs in the Al-Raqqa region and is involved in technical support for the Arab Gas Pipeline and another natural gas processing plant in the centre of the country. Another Russian energy company, Tatneft, began pumping Syrian oil last year and in January vowed to spend $12.8m drilling wells near the Iraqi border.[69]

---

[69] "Billions of Dollars of Russian Business Suffers Along With Syria", The Moscow Times, (February 02, 2011).

2.   Russia also has strong military interests in Syria, especially to use the country as a naval base. Syria signed an agreement to allow Russia to modernize port facilities at Tartous and Latakia, to provide the Russian navy with Mediterranean berthing. This gives Russia its only access to the Mediterranean Sea. No fewer than 50 Russian naval officers are reported to be deployed in Tartous to maintain and supply ships in the Mediterranean. In September 2008, it was agreed that Tartous should be developed into a full naval base and the first stage of development and modernization will be completed in 2012. As a naval base, it could serve as a base for guided-missile cruisers and even aircraft carriers. Moscow is acutely aware that if Assad's regime is toppled, its weapons sales and naval base could be jeopardized[70].

3.   Russia is eager to thwart America and NATO interventions in Arab countries such as Libya and Syria. Back in August 2011, Russian Foreign Minister Lavrov said, "Russia will do everything it can to prevent a Libyan scenario happening in Syria."[71] The reason for Russia's vehement opposition to intervention is that she fears that in the future NATO may use the Libyan intervention model to interfere militarily in the post Soviet space such as Central Asia and the Caucasus. Moreover, Russia is apprehensive that NATO could be eventually used to interfere directly in Russia's internal affairs, such as Chechnya. That is why Russia has deployed its warships off Syrian waters. Admiral Viktor Kravchenko, former Chief of Naval Staff, said that by deploying the warships, Moscow was sending a message to the US and Europe. He said, "Having any military force other than NATO(*sic*)'s is very useful for the region because it will prevent the outbreak of armed conflict."[72] While warding off the NATO threat is important, it is not the most significant threat to Russian interests. In the

---

[70] Hugo Odiogor, "Understanding Russia's interest in Syria's conflict", Vanguard, (November 21, 2011).
[71] S. Park, "Russia's Diplomacy During the Syria Crisis", Centre for Strategic & International Studies, (August 01, 2011).
[72] V. Radyuhin, "Russia sends flotilla to Syria", The Hindu, (November 30, 2011).

view of the Kremlin, to prevent the return of Islam to the forefront of Syrian politics is the biggest threat. Russia is already smitten by its Afghan defeat and the revival of Islam in Afghanistan, Central Asia and the Caucasus. She cannot afford to let another country in close proximity to it, slip away from secular autocracy and be transformed into a bastion of radical Islam. Russia is also acutely aware of America's previous and current attempts to use radical Islam to destabilize Russia's territorial integrity.

The threat of NATO intervention and the return of Islam to Syria's political landscape are part of Russia's strategic interests in Syria, and are regarded as more important than either commercial or military interests.

## Chinese interests

As for China, she has similar interests to Russia; however, the perceived threat from Assad's fall will be more acutely felt in Moscow than Beijing. China is very much aware of the dangers of NATO intervention, and how in the Libyan aftermath, the new transitional government moved against Chinese commercial interests. Beijing is concerned that a similar fate would transpire if Assad's regime were to fall.

Furthermore, China is facing growing unrest in many of its provinces due to the global economic crisis, and fears that if the West's desire to intervene is left unchecked, then NATO or its equivalent could be deployed to interfere in China's internal affairs.

Like Russia, China regards the rise of Islamic fundamentalism in countries that are in close proximity to its borders as a major strategic threat. She fears that this will further encourage its Muslim population in Xinjiang to revolt against the state.

The convergence of the threat from NATO intervention and the resurgence of Islam in the Muslim world have brought China and Russia closer together over the issue of Syria and the longevity of Assad's rule. Out of the 8 vetoes China has employed as a permanent member of the UN Security Council, two have been used for vetoing resolutions pertaining to Syria over the past six months. This implies that for the first time, Western powers are forced to deal with Russia and China together, as their strategic interests have merged. Previously, they only had to contend with Russia, and China usually abstained. It also means that the UNSC has developed permanent fault lines and on future issues pertaining to the Muslim world unanimity will be difficult to say the least.

**American interests**

Since the rise of Hafez Al –Assad in 1971, Syria has been firmly placed in the American camp and is playing an important role in safeguarding America's strategic interests in the Levant. These include:

1.     America has used Syria to either placate Israel via the War of 1973, or to pressurize Israel on numerous occasions to negotiate with Palestine through the provision of support to Hamas and Hezbollah.

2.     Syria has repeatedly served American interests in Lebanon, by occupying the country and marginalizing the influence of Europe. This continued until the assassination of Rafik Hariri in 2005, after which Syria was forced to pull out. However, Syria still plays an important role in administering Lebanon's political scene on behalf of the US, and ensuring that Europe does not get the upper hand.

3.     Syria played an important role in identifying and infiltrating Islamic fighters crossing into Iraq to fight US forces. The clandestine cooperation between the US and Syria helped America to subdue the Iraqi resistance from 2006 onwards.

4.     More recently, Syria has been part of America's strategic plan to create a *Shi'a* crescent power that stretches from Lebanon all the way to Yemen. This would allow the US to control the Middle Eastern oil, and the politics

of the Levant as well as Hejaz by exercising its influence through *Shi'a* proxies, especially Iran.

5.       Syria is also important to Iran, as it allows Tehran to spread its influence and power in the Levant. It is through this nexuses that American has been able to project its power in the Levant and control politics of the region. A weaker Syria would also mean a weaker Iran. Ali Banuazizi, a political-science professor at Boston College and a co-director of its Middle Eastern and Islamic Studies Program, said, "To put it bluntly, if Iran is a threat, then one way to weaken that threat would be to weaken Syria and to help the anti-Assad movement in Syria."[73]

For American policy makers a stable Syria is of paramount importance to safeguard America's strategic interests and is the principal reason why America is able to control the Palestinian conflict, the politics of Lebanon, minimize the influence of the pro-British Jordanian regime, give stability to Iraq and provide an important outlet for Iran to project *Shi'a* power. Because of this, America is content for Syria to engage in commercial and military relations with Russia, China and Europe.

To ensure the stability of Syria, America has been extremely reluctant to take strong action against the 11 month old uprising against Assad's rule. The chief reason behind this is that America sees no viable alternative to Assad and his Alawite ruling clan. The Syrian opposition is deeply divided and it will take some time to forge a consensus before the US can remove Assad and replace it with a government that is loyal to her interests. Furthermore, the increasing ferocity of the protests against Assad's regime coincides with stern international sanctions against Iran, thereby weakening America's ability to create a *Shi'a* crescent. In the light of this, the US has sought to buy time for Assad to crush the Syrian uprising, as well as pursue efforts to build a credible opposition. Hence, the imposition of sanctions

---

[73] Rick Gladstone, "Crisis in Syria could affect Iran", New York Times, (February 5, 2012).

against Syria, the deployment of Arab league monitors, and taking the issue to the UNSC are efforts designed to buy time for America to keep the two options going.

## European (led by Britain and France) interests

As for Europe, she overtly follows America's lead, but covertly executes her personal agenda of destabilizing pro-American countries and this includes Syria and Iran. Europe, led by Britain and France, is eager for Assad to fall, as both European powers believe that this will boost their influence and curtail American hegemony. Therefore, Europe rushed to impose severe sanctions on Syria, which are in many ways much tougher than those implemented by the US. For instance the EU put 13 Syrian officials on a sanctions list on May 10, 2011, including the President's brother Maher Al-Assad, who commands the elite Republican Guard. In May 2011, President Assad himself was added to the list, and the EU has since added more names and institutions accused of helping the regime. Those on the list have had their assets in the EU frozen, and are banned from travelling to the EU. The EU has also placed an arms embargo on Syria and in September 2011 it banned imports of Syrian oil. This has an enormous impact on the Syrian economy. Oil revenues account for around 20% of Syrian GDP. Before the EU ban, 90% of oil exports went to the EU, mainly to Germany, Italy and France.[74]

In addition to sanctions, Europe is eager to provide arms to the so-called Free Syrian Army (FSA). Pro-British governments such as Saudi Arabia and Qatar are providing military assistance to the FSA. Europe looks to undermine almost every initiative that America executes through her surrogates. For instance, the withdrawal of GCC monitors from Syria by

---

[74] "Q&A: Syria sanctions", BBC News, (November 27, 2011).

the pro-British GCC countries was a severe blow to the Arab League initiative sponsored by the US.[75]

It is quite evident that Europe is eager to sacrifice its commercial interests to bring down Assad's regime in return for a stake in managing Syria's strategic interests. This is what the English newspaper the Guardian had to say about Britain's current role in Syria: "The more Britain helps in the removal of Assad, the greater the stake it will have once he has left the country..." [76]

## In conclusion

America is using delaying tactics to buy precious time for either Assad's regime to crush the Syrian uprising or for the Syrian opposition to come together under America's tutelage and assume power. Furthermore, the delaying tactics are used to sap the momentum of the Syrian protests and assuage international opinion. As soon as America discovers that a particular tactic no longer works to her advantage, she introduces another tactic to consume domestic and international efforts to resolve the Syrian crisis.

America's support for the recent UNSC calling for the removal of Assad was another tactic and was based on the fact that she was dead certain that Russia and China would oppose the resolution, and in this way Washington could deflect the anger of the international opinion towards Russian and Chinese obstruction of the UNSC resolution. America may use other tactics such as the creation of a humanitarian zone inside Syria to diffuse international pressure.

---

[75] "GCC Pulls out of Syrian mission", Arab News, (January 25, 2012).
[76] Alex Spillius, "How do we help get rid of Bashar al Assad?", The Telegraph, (February 2, 2012).

Hence it is important to be aware of the devious styles employed by major powers that appear to oppose their interests, while in reality such tactics merely safeguard their interests.

As for Assad, he is a loyal servant of America, and it is his master that allowed him to build commercial and military ties with other powers such as Russia, China and Europe. This did not strengthen the influence of any of these powers in Syria. On the contrary, America adroitly used such ties to support and strengthen Syria and its reach in the region.

February 8, 2012

## 39

# Who Will Rescue the Syrian People from Assad's Bloody Regime?

*"You can't make war in the Middle East without Egypt and you can't make peace without Syria."*

*--Henry Kissinger*

After spending months observing the callous slaughter and atrocious carnage of innocent Syrians at the hands of Assad's brutal regime, the Western powers finally decided to call for Assad's departure. In August 2011, US President Obama said, "The future of Syria must be determined by its people, but President Bashar al-Assad is standing in their way. His calls for dialogue and reform have rung hollow while he is imprisoning, torturing and slaughtering his own people.

We have consistently said that President Assad must lead a democratic transition or get out of the way. He has not led. For the sake of the Syrian people, the time has come for President Assad to step aside."[77] Cameron issued a similar joint statement with Sarkozy and Merkel that read: "Our three countries believe that President Assad, who is resorting to brutal military force against his own people and who is responsible for the situation, has lost all legitimacy and can no longer claim to lead the country.

We call on him to face the reality of the complete rejection of his regime by the Syrian people and to step aside in the best interests of Syria and the

---

[77] "Syria unrest: World leaders call for Assad to step down", The BBC News, (August 18, 2012).

unity of it."[78] The EU foreign policy chief, Lady Ashton, said there had been a "complete loss of Bashar Assad's legitimacy in the eyes of the Syrian people"[79].

It was no coincidence that West's call for Assad's departure came after the failed efforts of some Gulf Arab countries and Turkey. The rulers of Saudi Arabia, Bahrain and Kuwait somehow mustered enough strength to lift themselves from paralysis and did the ignoble deed of recalling their ambassadors from Damascus. Even in their terse statements, one finds little solace for the Syrian people. "The Kingdom of Saudi Arabia stands before its historic responsibility toward her brothers, demanding the stoppage of the killing machine and bloodshed, and the use of reason before it is too late,"[80] Abdullah said in a statement that was read on Saudi state television. The pitiful remark that took months to transpire is by all accounts another bloody stain on the three monarchs that not only share much of the same features as Assad's oppressive regime, but are exemplary masters in their own right at crushing domestic opposition. Hence, the muzzled criticisms and restrained gestures dressed in velvet gloves are hardly going to halt Assad's rivers of blood. The same can be said for the West's condemnation of Assad's regime and pseudo smart sanctions that will invariably preserve the longevity of the regime a little longer, while a suitable alternative is groomed or found.

Then there is Turkey, which has been so boisterous in its chastisement of Assad that many poor souls in Syria have been longing for Erdogan to intervene and rescue them from the barbarism of Assad's Alawite clan. Some members of the clan are responsible for spearheading Assad's war machine and are notorious for their hatred towards Sunni Muslims. They

---

[78] "UK, Germany and France call for President Assad to stand down", The UK Foreign and Commonwealth Office, (August 18, 2012).
[79] "Syria: Assad must resign, says Obama", The Guardian, (August 18, 2012).
[80] N. Bakri, "3 Arab Countries Recall Ambassadors to Syria", The New York Times, (August 18, 2012).

routinely torture and taunt their victims about their devotion and adherence to their *Deen* prior to executing them in cold blood.

On August 9th, 2011, the Turkish foreign minister Mr. Davutoglu visited Assad to supposedly deliver a stern message from Erdogan to stop the horrific bloodshed. He was bluntly told by Assad that Damascus "will not relent in pursuing the terrorist groups in order to protect the stability of the country and the security of the citizens."[81] In other words, leave us alone to kill whomsoever we like.

Out of all the regional countries and Western powers that have hitherto expressed their displeasure towards Assad's regime, Turkey is best place to put an instant stop to the carnage. This is because Erdogan domestically is stronger than ever before, and has achieved the near impossible feat of not only marginalizing the army's role in political life, but has replaced the army's leadership with handpicked generals. This means that under Erdogan's stewardship the executive, the judiciary, the army and much of the civic institutions can be galvanized to support an immediate intervention in Syria and put an end to the targeted massacre of Syrians. Recent history also bears testimony on Erdogan's side. In 1998, Turkey amassed 10,000 troops at the Syrian border and threatened to invade, unless Damascus surrendered the then PKK leader Abdullah Ocalan. Damascus quickly capitulated and asked Ocalan to leave, who was eventually apprehended in Kenya. If the military threat is not enough, then Erdogan could borrow a page from the so-called doctrine of humanitarian intervention invoked by Britain and France as a pretext to invade Libya. He is sure to find little international opposition should he opt for this route. Erdogan can easily divert Turkey's armed forces currently being used to disable PKK positions to immobilize Assad's security forces and slow

---

[81] N. Bakri, "Turkish Minister and Other Envoys Press Syrian Leader", The New York Times, (August 9, 2012).

down their advance. If Erdogan were only to take a small step in this direction, he would enjoy the more support from the *Ummah*.

With all of the odds stacked in his favour, Erdogan continues to drag his heels, as if the spilling of Muslim blood at the hands of Assad is a novel spectator sport. This is very reminiscent of the Jewish state's slaughter of its Palestinians in 2009, followed by Erdogan's fiery rhetoric against Shimon Perez, which in the end was capped by inaction.

In this respect, Erdogan is no different to other rulers of the Arab and Muslim world who are often found floundering at the time of the *Ummah*'s need, despite the capability of their armed forces and the political reality of the situation being in their favour. This is because Erdogan and other Arab rulers do not serve the *Ummah* of the Messenger of Allah (SAW). Rather, they are servants of foreign powers and are the leading custodians of their master's interests in the region. They are merely puppets who speak and act when they are told and not before. For instance, Erdogan's timely expulsion of Israel's ambassador to Turkey, and the suspension of military agreements with the Jewish state were designed to increase pressure on Israel to resume peace talks with the Palestinians, at a time when the Jewish state is extremely anxious about its border with Egypt and Syria. In this way, the US is using Erdogan, Egypt's military junta and the precarious situation in Syria to pressurise Netanyahu to restart peace talks.

As for Syria, both Erdogan and Khamenei, acting under US patronage, are covertly aiding and abetting Assad's regime and giving it enough time to put down the uprising. The toothless sanctions announced by the US underscores just how keen the Obama administration is for the current regime to stymie the domestic revolt. In the meantime, the US continues to explore alternative political solutions to Assad's regime - again with Turkey and Iran's full cooperation. This is the ugly reality of the situation that faces the innocent people of Syria. Erdogan's immediate remit as stipulated to him by his American masters is twofold. First, to gather the Syrian opposition in Turkey and develop a political alternative to Assad. The Syrian opposition has held several meetings since May 2011 under the auspices of the Turkish government, and at the last meeting in Istanbul, the Syrian opposition managed to reach broad agreement on the 120 nominees for the transitional council. Second, is to enable NATO to arm Syrian militants and to use a similar approach to that which resulted in the ouster of Gaddafi from Tripoli. "Turkey's military will protect the arms caches on their passage to Syrian rebels. Syrian protest leaders and army deserters have been training in the use of the new weapons with Turkish military officers at makeshift installations in Turkish bases near the Syrian border" as reported recently by Press TV, citing the Israeli intelligence front, Debka.

The only salvation for the people of Syria, and for that matter the entire Arab and Muslim world, is to cease in the engagement of useless pursuits such as the reliance on Western powers to rescue them from tyrant rulers who were handpicked and planted by the West in the first place.

Afghanistan, Iraq and now Libya are clear examples, where the West used humanitarian excuses to intervene and engineered nation building solutions that cemented Western hegemony through subtly changing the face of the ruling regime. Neither the peoples nor the countries have benefited to date. Instead of relying upon Western solutions, the people of the Arab world must work to find salvation in the restoration of the Khilafah. For only the Khilafah on the way of the Prophethood can give them protection, dignity and justice as history has taught us. The Messenger of Allah (SAW) said,

"The imam is a shield behind whom the people are protected and fight."
[Sahih Muslim].

August 18, 2011

# 40

# UN's 'Bloody' Ceasefire Helps Sustain Assad's Killing Machine

*"The US was instrumental in setting up the UN in the 1940s after the World War II. And of course we have a Security Council with a veto. America can veto all the other countries of the world combined...And as long as you have a UN run like that, the UN is literally a tool of US policy."*

*--Stephen Lendman*

The long awaited UN sponsored ceasefire, accompanied by a few monitors, does very little to prevent the brutality of Assad's regime against the Syrian people. Nor does it put a stop to the numerous killing fields that have become drenched in the blood of innocent civilians and stained with the pure blood of martyrs. The ceasefire is part of an international effort to implement Annan's six point plan.[82]

Excerpts from Annan's one sided plan expose its ineffectiveness in halting the savagery of Assad's henchmen and their insatiable desire to spill the pure blood of the people of *Sham*.

For instance: "As these actions are being taken on the ground, the Syrian government should work with the envoy to bring about a sustained cessation of armed violence in all its forms by all parties with an effective United Nations supervision mechanism...Similar commitments would be sought by the envoy from the opposition and all relevant elements to stop the fighting and work with him to bring about a sustained cessation of armed violence in all its forms by all parties with an effective United Nations supervision mechanism."[83]

---

[82] "Kofi Annan peace plan for Syria", Wikipedia, (2012).
[83] *Ibid.*

How can the UN equate the violence perpetrated by Assad's tyrannical regime and that of those defending their lives and properties from Assad's thugs in equal terms? Who is the one that is relentlessly pursuing men, women, children and babies, and taking all measures to exterminate them? Even the blind, the deaf and the one with below average intelligence can perceive the heinous crimes of Assad's regime, smell the stench of its evil, and comprehend the wickedness of its leader. Then again, what more should we expect from the UN, which is a tool of the colonial powers and has a long history steeped in spearheading the West's campaigns to suppress Islam and Muslims.

The real criminals behind the bloody proposal of Assad and Kofi Annan are Russia, China, US, and Europe. These are the very same countries that pretend to be the friends of Syria, but in reality are the friends of Assad. Each power has its own interest in ensuring that Assad's bloody rule continues along with the oppression of the Syria people. For Russia and China, Assad's regime is a bulwark against political Islam, and is the only outlet for the Russians to project their naval power. On the other hand, European countries under the leadership of Britain view Assad's despotic regime as a last line of defence against the destabilization of the monarchies of the Gulf. Britain fears that Assad's instant fall could trigger a wave of popular unrest in the Gulf that could threaten its influence in the region. As for America, the longevity of Assad's rule is essential for her plans to control the Levant and spread the tentacles of Iran. America is the real reason that Assad is still in power. Washington has manipulated the UN to give Assad ample breathing space to carry on with his killing spree.

Thus, the foreign powers overlook the monstrous atrocities committed by Assad against our brothers and sisters in Syria, hoping to secure their interests and prevent the immediate collapse of Assad's regime until a time when a suitable alternative is found. Meanwhile, their collective aim is to gradually manage the collapse of Assad's oppressive rule, through ineffective peace proposals, and other initiatives that are intended to mollify the wide spread angry sentiments in the Muslim world. What we are witnessing in Syria today is almost a rerun of the slaughter of the Muslims in Bosnia.

The only salvation for the Muslims of Sham is to band together and to reject every proposal advocated by the foreign powers through their agents in the UN and in the neighbouring countries. Know that only through the re- establishment of the Khilafah Rashida will they be able to vanquish the foreign powers, most notably America and Europe from the pure land of Sham.

Recall, how the first Khilafah Rashida forced Rome to flee Syria during the reign of Umar ibn al-Khattab. It is reported that the defeated Heraclius bid a long farewell to Syria knowing that he would never return. He said, "Farewell, a long farewell to Syria, my fair province. Thou art an infidel's (enemy's) now. Peace be with you, O' Syria – what a beautiful land you will be for the enemy hands."[84]

Oh Muslims of Sham! The time has come for you to repeat the feat of your forefathers, by joining forces with your brothers in the armed forces and send a befitting reply to the New Roman Empire (the West) –the main enemy of Muslims –and to vanquish her from this region once and for all.

April 27, 2012

---

[84] "Abu Ubaidah ibn al Jarrah", Wikipedia.

## 41

## Syrian Crisis Halts Persia's Influence

*"Bashar Assad, Iran's red line."*

*--Ali Akbar Velayati*

Lately, Iran has made headline news in a variety of ways. The Jewish entity regards Iran as an existential threat, the West continues to fret over Iran's nuclear programme, the Gulf Corporation Council (GCC) bitterly complains about Tehran's interference in Bahrain and Yemen, and Syrians blame Iranian forces for the slaughter of civilians. Yet there is one piece of news that has only attracted a cursory mention and that is Iran's influence in the region is waning.

The Levant and Iraq is where Iran's influence is diminishing at a spectacular speed and eroding Iran's ability to influence regional politics. The pivot for this transition is Syria. At the beginning of the revolution Iran staunchly stood by its ally Assad. Tehran bolstered Syria's economy with enormous amounts of aid and strengthened Assad's forces with the elite Iranian commandoes to brutally suppress the uprising. On October 1st 2012, The "Times" newspaper reported that Tehran had given $10 billion to prop up Assad and his floundering regime. The revelation clearly demonstrates the value Tehran places on supporting Assad despite the huge economic toll of international sanctions against the Iranian people. In the summer of 2012, Tehran struggled to keep a lid on its clandestine military activities in Syria, and eventually the activities of the Quds Force became so pronounced and widespread that Tehran finally acknowledged its military operations in the country. In September 2012, Guards commander Brigadier General Mohammad Ali Jafari said, "A number of Quds Force members are present in Syria and Lebanon... we provide (these countries) with counsel and advice, and transfer experience to them."[85]

As the Syrian jihadists draw near towards surrounding Damascus, Iran's billions of dollars and military assistance in propping up Assad appears insignificant-a wasted effort. Amongst Sunni jihadist Iran has negligible influence and this is worrying the Iranian leadership as it struggles to grapple with the situation. It is faced with a strategic choice whether to continue to embrace the Alawite faction and their militia the Shabiha after falling from power or to embrace the Sunni Jihadists who deeply despise the Iranian regime. An article entitled "Syria's Fate Hinges on Whom It Hates Most, US or Iran?" in Bloomberg on February 6th 2013, aptly summed up the strategic dilemma for Tehran as: "Thereafter Iran will face a strategic decision: whether to continue supporting a predominantly Alawite militia that represents only a small fraction of Syrian society, or to engage the Sunni Islamists who are poised to wield power in Damascus once Assad falls. Iran's leaders will try to embrace the Sunni radicals, and if that fails they will work with the Shabiha to prevent the formation of a stable, anti-Iranian order in Syria".

Equally troublesome for Iran is the spill over of Syria's instability into Lebanon and Hezbollah's precarious position. At the outset of the Arab revolution, Iran's proxy Hezbollah and its surrogate leader NasrAllah (swt) publicly cheered the fall of autocratic rulers in Tunisia, Egypt and Libya, but openly supported Assad and sent armed men to suppress the Syrian people. The hypocritical stance of Hezbollah jeopardized its ability to garner support amongst the Lebanese populace, especially amongst the Sunnis. Furthermore, the movement was despised by Syrians as aiding and abetting Assad against them, and this prompted the jihadists in Syria to openly warn Nasrallah of dire consequences should he continue to support Assad. Subsequently, Hezbollah's power has weakened both at home and

---

[85] "Iranian elite units rumoured to be in Syria to advise Assad", Russia Today, (September 17, 2013).

across the Arab world. A weaker Hezbollah also implies the weakening of Iranian influence in Lebanese politics.

The weakening of Hezbollah-Assad-Iranian axis has been dealt a further blow by the rising wave of protests in Iraq. Sunni dominated areas in Iraq are witnessing a late Arab spring that is threatening Al-Malki's grip on Iraqi politics. Al-Malki who has close relations with Tehran is struggling to contain the Sunni hinterland after Iraqi soldiers opened fire on unarmed civilians.

Between 2004 to 2008 Iranian influence and power in Iraq was at its apex. It evoked King Abdullah to comment on the reach and magnitude of Iranian power by using the term *Shi'a* Crescent, which described Iranian influence stretching from Damascus to Tehran passing through Baghdad. The other side of the crescent passes through Bahrain, Eastern Saudi Arabia and Yemen. Today, the long reach of Iran is facing an existential threat in Syria, which surely spells the end of the Iranian efforts to create the *Shi'a* crescent and ends her ambitions to dominate the Middle East and its supplies of hydrocarbons.

Nonetheless, Iran is not the only loser in the political reconfiguration that will ensue in aftermath of Assad's demise. The real loser is America. For the past four decades, America has secretly collaborated with Iran in a desperate bid to create a *Shi'a* Crescent that would eventually place oil away from the hands of Sunni despots into the hands of the *Shi'a* autocrats and mullahs who in turn would be more loyal subjects to America than Sunnis. This also explains why America has been so reluctant to punish Iran over its interference in Lebanon, Iraq and Syria, even though Washington has had ample opportunity to chastise Tehran. Similarly, America has gone out of it way to assuage Israeli concerns over Iran's nuclear programme. America knows full well that if Iran is subject to any sort of military attack, Iran's influence that stretches from Yemen to Lebanon will fade. By doing so, America's capacity to fashion political solutions and maintain her hegemony in the region would be severely impaired. Brzezinski has warned about such consequences for America should it choose punish Iran. He said, "A war in the Middle East, in the present context, may last for years. High inflation, instability, insecurity...probably significant isolation for the United States in the world scene. In effect, the American taxpayer should be ready to pay $5 to $10 a gallon for the pleasure of having a war in the Strait of Hormuz."[86]

Hence, America has little choice but to use Iran to prop up Assad and hope that its long-term plan of using Iran to control the hydrocarbons of the Middle East via the *Shi'a* crescent remains intact.

March 18, 2013

---

[86] T. Beamon and K. Walter, "Brzezinski to Newsmax: War With Iran Could Last Years, Devastate Global Economy", Newsmax, (July 18, 2012).

## 42

## Palestine Question: America is Deceiving Both Palestinians and the Jews

*"There are people who control spacious territories teeming with manifest and hidden resources. They dominate the intersections of world routes. Their lands were the cradles of human civilizations and religions. These people have one faith, one language, one history and the same aspirations. No natural barriers can isolate these people from one another ... if, per chance, this nation were to be unified into one state; it would then take the fate of the world into its hands and would separate Europe from the rest of the world. Taking these considerations seriously, a foreign body should be planted in the heart of this nation to prevent the convergence of its wings in such a way that it could exhaust its powers in never-ending wars. It could also serve as a springboard for the West to gain its coveted objects."*

*--Sir Campbell Bannerman, Prime Minister of Britain [1905-08]*

On October 6th 2011, the Executive Council of the United Nations Education, Science and Culture Organization (UNESCO) approved Palestine's entry into this UN agency as member. The resolution was approved by 40 votes in favour and 4 against (the United States, Germany, Latvia and Romania), while 14 other countries abstained. UNESCO's move to admit Palestine was vehemently criticized by America. Speaking to reporters US Secretary of State, Hilary Clinton said," I think that this is a very odd procedure indeed and would urge the governing body of UNESCO to think again before proceeding with that vote."[87] Just three days earlier, the US Congress 'punished' the Palestinian people by withholding $200 million dollars of aid. The two events clearly demonstrate that the international mood to support Palestinian statehood is divided. America's opposition intensified last month, when President Mahmoud Abbas again reaffirmed his commitment to seek UN approval for official recognition of the Palestinian state. On September 17 2011, Abbas said, "We are going to the security council. The world is sympathizing with the aspirations of the Palestinian people."[88] This unilateral move is detested by the Zionist state and is also opposed by America. In August 2011, Wendy Sherman, Under Secretary of State for policy, and ranked third at the US State Department categorically stated: "If any such resolution were put in front of the Security Council, then we would veto it."[89] On September 21st US President Obama publicly confirmed at the UN that the US would veto any attempts by the Palestinians for statehood. Nonetheless, despite the frantic effort of the Obama administration to undermine Palestinian struggle for statehood, the actions of America's surrogates in the region tells an entirely different story.

But first it is important to understand why Obama cannot make good on his desire to see a two state solution, which he defiantly defended at the UN last year. It is well known that President Obama is running for re-election in 2012 and is constrained by the amount of pressure his administration can apply on Netanyahu to commence negotiations with the Palestinians. The Jewish votes during US general elections are priceless for both democratic and republican contenders. Both sets of politicians vie with each other to demonstrate their loyalty to the Israeli cause in return for Jewish votes. The Republican Party is exploiting Obama's weakness to

---

[87] J. Rogin, "Palestinian membership in UNESCO is just the tip of the iceberg", Foreign Policy, (October 7, 2011).

[88] C. McGreal, "Palestinian leader ignores US warnings on UN statehood bid", The Guardian, (September 16, 2011).

[89] "It's Official: US Will Veto PA's UN Statehood Bid", IsraelNationalNews, (August 9, 2011).

unequivocally support the Jewish state on this matter, and has started to make inroads amongst the Jewish voters, who traditionally are staunch democrats. The Jewish electorate makes up only 3% of American voter, but is pivotal in the swing states of Florida and Ohio. More importantly, the Jewish community is a very important constituency for fund raising, and the Palestinian statehood issues have become a significant source of concern for them. "Mr. Obama does not want to get into an unproductive fight with Israel," said Aaron David Miller, a long time State Department expert on the Middle East, who is now at the Woodrow Wilson Centre. Hence, the Obama administration cannot take a public stance that supports the Palestinians but ignores the demands of the Jewish state. However, America's allies in the region have no such qualms, and are doing their utmost, to make the Jewish state vulnerable and to urge Netanyahu to negotiate and finalize a two state solution with the Palestinians.

For example, the military junta of Egypt has used the ouster of Mubarak to give a clear indication that the thirty odd years of invincible peace the Jewish state enjoyed is now precariously poised. The attacks by militants in Sinai, the frequent disruption of gas supplies, and the recent ransacking of the Israeli embassy in Cairo that forced the ambassador and his staff to flee have clearly reminded the Jews how vulnerable their border with their Egypt neighbours has become. This was made worse by the killing of Egyptian border soldiers and the subsequent pseudo apology released by Netanyahu's government. His government is also anxious from the rising tide of Islamic opposition to the Jewish state — a development that does not bode well for their future survival.

Additionally, Turkey's deteriorating relations with Israel have also accentuated the weakness of the Jewish state. The expulsion of the Israeli ambassador, cessation of military ties, threat of legal action over the Marvi Marmara incident and Erdogan's vocal opposition to Jewish state's treatment of Palestinians has begun to erode Israel's confidence and increased its isolation. Erdogan's recent statements have made Turkey extremely popular in the Arab world, which is spearheading American efforts to isolate the Jewish state. For instance, on his visit to Cairo he said, "Israel is the West's spoiled child.[90] To this day it has never executed a decision by the international community. It (Israel) acts irresponsibly and without hesitation in smashing human dignity and international law by carrying [out] assaults on international convoys, which carry nothing but food and toys for children..."

Compounded with the problematic relations with Turkey and Egypt is the growing unrest in Syria, which earlier spilled over into the Golan Heights and drove home the message to a distraught Jewish populace that its border with Syria is no longer impregnable. Thus in a space of a few weeks, the Jewish state finds its three pillars of territorial stability, shaken to the core, and now many Israelis are uncertain about the future.

Complicating matters further, Netanyahu now faces the actions of pro-British contingent of countries. The 'harsh' remarks by King Abdullah of Jordan, and the pledge of the Saudi's to provide $200 million aid to the Palestinian authority to enable it to function is a resounding warning that the Jewish state is fast losing old friends amongst British and American surrogates. It is against this backdrop that Abbas has intensified his efforts for pronouncing statehood. His tongue could not have moved, unless he was given explicit permission by America to do so.

America's intention behind all of these manoeuvres is to forcibly goad Netanyahu's government to accept the fact that the Jewish state's security is not sustainable with its neighbours, unless it commits to peace and presses ahead with the two-state solution. In a visit to the Jewish state last week, US Defence Secretary Leon Panetta warned that Israel was at risk of becoming isolated and more vulnerable if it did not take steps to repair ties with neighbouring countries and restart negotiations with the Palestinians.

---

[90] D. KirkPatrick, "Premier of Turkey Takes Role in Region", The New York Times, (September 12, 2011).

He said, "The question you have to ask is: 'Is it enough to maintain a military edge if you are isolating yourself in the diplomatic arena? Real security can only be achieved by a strong diplomatic efforts as well as a strong effort to protect your military strength.'"[91] This is especially true now, as the Arab uprising has brought to the fore a new set of public expectations that cannot be simply swept under the carpet as before. This was also echoed by Panetta. He said," It is pretty clear at this dramatic time in the Middle East when there have been so many changes that it is not a good situation for Israel to become increasingly isolated. And that is what has happened."[92]

Thus at home the Obama administration stands shoulder to shoulder with the Jews fully expecting their votes, but in the Middle East she uses her loyal allies and agents in the region to compel the Jews to pursue peace with the Palestinians and her neighbours.

The Palestinian people must be careful not to be smitten by the actions of their neighbouring countries—particularly Turkey— all of whom are working tirelessly to implement the colonialist agenda and prevent their true liberation from tyranny. How can any person call for a Palestinian state that for all intents and purposes is a prison state entirely dependent on Israel for its existence? Whether it's the single state solutions as advocated by Britain in the past or the two-state solution promoted by the US; the people of Palestine and the Jews will never find peace under such colonialist projects. Jews, Christians and Muslims of Palestine would do well to look and learn from the Islamic alternative that guaranteed peace for hundreds of years under the auspices of the Khilafah state.

October 13, 2011

---

[91] "Turkey & Iran war", Global Post, (October 2, 2011).
[92] *Ibid.46*

## 43

# Are the GCC States Planning Closer Ties?

*"Nothing but Failure? The Arab League and the Gulf Cooperation Council as mediators in Middle Eastern conflicts."*

*--Marco Pinfari*

Over the years much has been said about the merits of closer unity between the countries of the Gulf Corporation Council (GCC)- Bahrain, Kuwait, Qatar, Oman, Saudi Arabia and the UAE that was formed in 1981. However, in recent months the urgency amongst some member states to forge ahead with stronger political and fiscal ties has grown tremendously. In December 2012, Saudi Arabia's King Abdullah Bin Abdul Aziz Al-Saud at the GCC summit, called upon the member states to move from the phase of cooperation to the phase of 'union' within a single entity. Saudi Arabia and Bahrain have already taken steps to build strong military and economic relations between them.

Yet despite such developments, smaller member states like Oman and the UAE feel overtly threatened by Saudi Arabia and fear relinquishing certain aspects of their sovereignty to Riyadh. Earlier this month, Oman went as far as rubbishing the whole idea of the union. Yousuf Bin Alawi Bin Abdullah, the Minister Responsible for Foreign Affairs said, "There is no Gulf Union."[93]

No matter how hard some member states try to resist closer unity, there are many factors that practically compel the GCC states to press ahead with unity and these include:

1. Intellectual revival in the Muslim world

---

[93] "Oman's foreign minister says there is no Gulf union", Gulf news, (June 6, 2012).

To the Arab masses-long before the present uprisings-the notion of nation statehood was in decline. More and more Arabs felt that their identity had less to do with the artificial states that were crafted as a consequence of the Sykes-Picot agreement in 1916, and more to do with the state of the *Ummah*. This notion of the *Ummah* draws its strength from Islamic legislative sources and the history of the region. For all intents and purposes it undermines the nation state model. Furthermore, it acts like a unifying force amongst Muslims of various backgrounds, and its political expressions are centred on the Khilafah with its foreign policy being jihad. The Arabs of the GCC are no different and also feel more affinity towards the *Ummah* than their respective countries. For instance, last week, Sheikh Ali al-Hikmi from the Saudi Council of Senior Scholars, issued a fatwa forbidding jihad for Syria. He said, "The Syrian people are facing injustice, persecution and the force of an arrogant and haughty regime, and needs our prayers and help in every possible way. The support for the Syrian people should be in harmony with the country's policy. Everything is linked to a system and to the country's policies and no person should be allowed to disobey the guardian [Saudi Government] and call for jihad."[94] Coinciding with the Saudi fatwa was another fatwa issued in Moscow that banned the term jihad and Khilafah to be used for political goals. The meeting attracted theologians from Gulf countries: Saudi Arabia, Kuwait and Qatar. Islamic experts from Morocco, Jordan, Tunisia, Bahrain, Iraq, Egypt, Lebanon, Mauritania, Sudan, Afghanistan, and Turkey also attended the meeting.[95] It is not then surprising to find the GCC countries participating in endeavours that prohibit the use of such terms, as these terms strengthen the narrative of the *Ummah* within their people and poses a direct and serious threat to their existence.

2. New political challenges

---

[94] "Saudi religious authority forbids 'jihad' in Syria", Muslim News, (June 8, 2012).
[95] "Islamic theologians ban to use terms jihad and khalifate in political goals", Interfax, (May 29, 2012).

The wind of political change is the second driving factor that is shaping the behaviour of GCC countries. The wellspring of revolutionary movements across the Arab world has unleashed a new set of demands for political reform. These reforms are diametrically opposed to the ruling elites that preside as archaic dictatorships and fiefdoms which dominate the Arab world. The revolt in Tunisia and the departure of the tyrants such Ben Ali, Mubarak and, Gaddafi has sent shivers down the spines of the remaining rulers. The gulf Arabs are not immune to such political upheavals experienced by their fellow brethren in the greater Arab world. Uprisings in Bahrain and Oman and skirmishes in Eastern Saudi Arabia are a portent reminder of how quick events can unfold and change the political landscape. To counter the revolutionary movement and to maintain the status quo, GCC member states have held several meetings and have even contemplated extending membership to Morocco and Jordan.

## 3. Regional security concerns

Lastly, the perceived threat of Iran, or more accurately put - the rise of the 's*hi'a* crescent' adds a strong military dimension to the unification efforts. The GCC states are extremely anxious about the demise of Sunni power in the region—especially in Iraq and Lebanon. They are also petrified by the prospects of their own *Shi'a* populations revolting. The revolt of *Shi'a*'s in Bahrain against King Hammad was a wakeup call for the gulf countries and in particular, their focus has been on the role of Iran in agitating *Shi'a* opposition. Hence, in their efforts to curb Iranian influence, the collective military expenditure of the GCC has risen sharply in the past few years. Market intelligence firm Forecast International predicts: "a 14 per cent rise in spending over the next five years. At the national level, defence investment generally represents 10-20 per cent of total state expenditure annually. For 2010, Forecast estimates total GCC defence/security investment at $68.3 billion, expecting the total to increase to $73.4 billion in 2011 and continue growing to $82.5 billion by 2015."[96]

It is the combination of the aforementioned factors that provides much of the impetus behind the latest unification drive and not ideological considerations. Additionally, given the political differences between states such as Saudi Arabia and Qatar, it is difficult to see how such a union will function without a singular political leadership. A quick glance at the EU's failure to address the Euro crisis, or speak with a single voice on foreign affairs, exposes the fallacy of proceeding with unification without political unity.

The only tried and tested model, which for many centuries provided sound unitary political leadership, security and prosperity to Muslims (irrespective of them being Arab or non-Arab) was the Khilafah. The Khilafah is not a union of countries or a federal state; rather it is a unique political system where the people elect a ruler to rule over them through the implementation of *Shar'iah* rules. It is only a matter of time before the despotic regimes of the Gulf will give way to the return of the Khilafah.

June 13, 2012

---

[96] David Hedengren, "Middle East defence spending will continue to rise", Your Middle East, (October 18, 2011).

44

# Implications of an American Strike on Syria

*"I have decided that the United States should take military action against Syrian regime targets. This would not be an open-ended intervention. We would not put boots on the ground. Instead, our action would be designed to be limited in duration and scope."*

*--US President Barrack Obama*

So once again, Americans find their government on the brink of attacking another Muslim country after having already waged war against Afghanistan, Iraq, Pakistan, Somalia, Yemen and Libya in the past decade or so. However, this is not the first time the US has intervened in Syria. In October 2008, American Special Forces conducted a raid into Syria killing 8 civilians. This time, the US intervention will be more prolonged and the resulting civilian deaths will be much higher.

Many facets of America's second impending strike on Syria can be scrutinized and debated, however, there is only issue that really stands out, and that is the impact of American hegemony and unilateralism on both the region as well as on the prevalent international system.

Even before the Arab spring revolution, anti-Americanism was rife not only in the Arab countries but also in the wider Muslim world. Since then anti-Americanism has reached an all-time high and there is no evidence to suggest that it will subside anytime soon. On the contrary, American military intervention in Syria will only exacerbate such sentiments. This is dangerous not only for America but also for West's relationship with the Islamic world. These negative sentiments form the basis for intellectual and political awakening in the Muslim world. It forces Muslims to explore ways on how to become intellectually and politically independent of American hegemony and perpetual Western interference.

Another factor closely related to negative American sentiments is America's duplicity over the application of its ideology in the Islamic world. For instance, why does America ignore the 100,000 or so civilians killed at the hands of the Butcher Assad by conventional means but raises a huge hue and cry when the same butcher kills 1429 Syrians but this time through chemical weapons. Likewise why does America choose to stand by General Sisi and allow him to use American weapons to kill over a thousand Egyptians and not intervene—Sisi is only gently reprimanded. Additionally there is no mention of American intervention in Palestine and Burma where nothing short of genocide is being perpetrated against Muslims. These are just some of the inconsistencies related to the value of human life placed by America. What about the contradictions regarding the implementation of democracy and freedom in the Islamic countries. The coup in Egypt against the democratically elected leader Morsi and the grotesque episode of Abu Ghraib in Iraq have laid bare American hypocrisy over her two ideological idols: Democracy and Freedom.

The combination of anti-American sentiments and America's ideological duplicity has invigorated Muslim minds to view political Islam rather than liberal democracy as a panacea to their problems. The confidence amongst Muslims in liberal democracy and Western solutions has been further diminished by the sustained economic crisis in the West and the revolt against capitalist policies stretching from Europe to Brazil. Neither have the false Islamic pretenders such as Ennahda, Muslim brotherhood and others have helped the West in their crusade to promote their civilization in Muslim countries. These groups are despised by the masses and are viewed as endorsing capitalism and American hegemony disguised in Islamic garb. Hence, throughout the Arab and Muslim world, more and more Muslims are embracing political Islam as the only exit solution to their colonization by America and the West.

Therefore it is no longer surprising to find Muslim societies across the Islamic world deeply polarized between secular autocrats struggling to maintain the existing order for America and their colonial masters, and the Muslim masses wanting to liberate themselves through political Islam. The polarization has contributed to increasing instability and chaos, and is responsible for much of the political vacuum that pervades the Muslim world. Subsequently, America's primacy has weakened significantly and this means that America has to resort to greater force to maintain some semblance of control in order to protect her vital interests.

The lack of confidence in Western concepts and solutions has made both the implementation and the longevity of political solutions in Muslim countries difficult for Washington. This is despite the fact that America has considerable military might in the region, compliant military generals, and subservient politicians at her disposal. As soon as America takes a political decision it is not long before it unravels and America compelled to rethink. For instance in Syria the US started by supporting Arab monitors initially, which quickly gave way to Annan's Six Point Plan and this was followed by the Lakhdar Brahimi plan, then the Geneva peace plan was born. Now after military strikes it is anticipated that Geneva peace plan 2 will be mooted. America's failure to fashion successful political solution for countries like Egypt, Iraq, Yemen, Libya, Somalia, Afghanistan and Pakistan tells a similar story. In 2006 Pat Buchanan had this to say about America's political failures in the Muslim world. He said, "If Islamic rule is an idea taking hold among the Islamic masses, how does even the best army on earth stop it? Do we not need a new policy?[97]" Several policies later and America is still struggling for a new policy to contain Islam.

On the international front, America's repeated threats to go it alone in Syria have grossly undermined the confidence in the international system. In truth American intransigence to unilaterally invade Iraq in 2003 was the beginning of the end of the international system and a death blow to the UN. As the world increasingly moves towards pre-1920 international

---

[97] P. Buchanan, "An Idea Whose Time Has Come?", Antiwar.com, (June 23, 2006).

framework for dealing with each other—when great powers ruled and international law was just a notion— international law and the UN will no longer be relevant to settle dispute between nations.

Finally, America and its allies in the West have worked tirelessly to craft an international system that for the past 60 odd years has prevented the Muslims masses from establishing their state—the Caliphate. And now by America's own handiwork the Muslim masses are being repeatedly attacked and this has bludgeoned to death any inclining Muslims masses had towards liberal democracy, and ignited their passion for the re-establishment of Caliphate.

The precedence of "humanitarian" intervention established by America, and the subsequent decline in the nation state model together with the fragmentation of the international law all provide a fertile foundation for the Caliphate to not only swiftly unify fifty-five Muslim countries under a single political authority, but also to intervene around the global to protect Muslim populations and spread Islam.

The Caliphate will also reform international relations and dispel the current drivers behind the upkeep of today's international system such as one rule for the West and another rule for the rest, where might is right and fabricated evidences are norm to wage preventative wars. Regarding the latter, the belligerence of America and other European states towards the world will be immediately dealt with by the Caliphate. In such cases no evidence will be required as their crimes against humanity are well documented and recorded. In sum, America through its blind arrogance is paving the way for the 21st century to belong to the Caliphate.

September 9, 2013

**45**

# Syria: Obama's Embrace of Assad is Sign of America's Weakness

*"Now, at the end of 2013, Syria stands as a tale of mismatched commitments, and an example of America's inability to steer events from a distance."*

*--The Wall Street Journal*

What started out as mass protests against Assad's brutal autocratic rule quickly transformed into a bloody conflict— pitting Assad and his international backers against the Syrian people. Since then tough questions have been repeatedly asked as to why America has not intervened in the bloody conflict. The Obama administration even set irrevocable red lines to assuage international criticism regarding US inaction in Syria. And when the rubicon was crossed, Assad escaped punishment for using chemical weapons against his own people. Yet despite Assad's horrific war crimes record, America remains unashamedly supportive of him.

In the past, America attacked countries like Somalia, Sudan, Iraq, Libya, Yemen and others based on the flimsiest of arguments such as humanitarian intervention and weapons of mass destruction. Even today, Washington is employing the pretext of humanitarian intervention in South Sudan to deploy its troops to ensure the free flow of oil. But in Syria, neither the logic of humanitarian intervention applies, nor is the use of chemical weapons an invitation for US military action.

So why is America reluctant to intervene? According to America's former ambassador to Syria, Ryan Cocker, Syria is different. He said, "I think we made a mistake right at the beginning in somehow thinking that

Syria was like Egypt, like Tunisia, like Libya.[98]" This narrative that Syria is somehow different is ridiculously stupid. The numerous air attacks conducted by the Jewish state in Syria, undermines the central pillar of this narrative.

The reason Assad is still in power is that the alternative is not acceptable to the West. Cocker explained: "And do we really want the alternative—a major country at the heart of the Arab world in the hands of Al Qaeda? So we need to come to terms with a future that includes Assad." Russia like America is also petrified at the prospect of the Caliphate's return. Speaking on Russia Today, Russia's Foreign Minister Lavrov said, "... the threat of jihadists coming to power, the threat of creating a caliphate with extremist rules... understanding that changing the regime is not the way to solve this problem." The threat of the Caliphate is what binds America and Russia together in their support for Assad.

America is now openly embracing Assad and is looking towards Geneva 2 to forge a political solution that retains Assad in power, and isolates the jihadists from rest of the opposition. Oddly enough, General Idris of the Free Syrian Army (FSA) has dropped his demand of Assad stepping down from power. A signal that Idris may be contemplating aligning the American backed FSA with the axis of evil - Assad, Iran and Hizb-e-Iran.

Whether, the Caliphate returns to Syria or not, one thing is certain, America's influence is diminished, as it has to increasingly rely on its erstwhile opponent Russia and regional outcast Iran to stabilize America's precarious control in Syria and the Levant.

January 10, 2014

---

[98] "Syria can only be contained, not extinguished, top former U.S. diplomat Ryan Crocker tells CNN's Amanpour", CNN Amanpour Blog, (September 11, 2013).

46

# Chaos in South Sudan is America's Failing

*"Apparently, those in favor of South Sudan have now been silenced in the harshest manner possible. The country is marching towards failure, and there seems to be no cure...At this junction, one is forced to question: was breaking up Sudan really a wise thing to do? As far as I get it, an undivided Sudan would have been better off."*

--Foreign Policy In Focus

S outh Sudan, a new nation born out of American endeavours to control the country's vast oil supply and provide 'Israel' with access to the African continent to meet its oil and security needs is quickly descending into the abyss of chaos. Washington is struggling to prevent a full-scale civil war. The usual culprits are two Western agents - President Salva Kiir and his former vice-president Riek Machar - at loggerheads with each other. Both are using inflammatory tribal politics to stake their claim to rule the fledgling African nation of 10 million people.

In July 2013, the first signs of a political power struggle surfaced within the Sudan People's Liberation Movement (SPLM), the ruling party when President Kiir sacked his entire government in an attempt to curb the ambitions of his powerful vice president. Tensions within the ranks of SPLM soon engulfed not only the Sudan People's Liberation Army (SPLA) but also South Sudan's two largest communities: Mr Kiir's Dinka, the largest of South Sudan's tribes, versus Mr Machar's Nuer tribe. However, major violence first erupted between two communities on December 15th 2013, when Dinkas in the presidential guard in the capital Juba sought to disarm their Nuer colleagues. The situation worsened when President Kiir publicly accused Machar of plotting a coup against him.

The hastily arranged talks in Ethiopia at the behest of America, threats to rein in Machar by President of Uganda, Yoweri Museveni—America's strong man in the region—the mobilisation of 7500 UN peace keepers and other measures have hitherto failed to halt the violence. What was once touted as President Obama's major foreign policy triumph is now more looking like a major disaster.

In 2005, as part of the Comprehensive Peace Agreement (CPA)[99] signed between SPLM and the Khartoum, Sudanese living in southern Sudan had a right vote to for independence in a referendum. In July 2011, South Sudanese voted overwhelming under US auspices to cede from Sudan. The new country was essentially curved out of Sudan by America to exert greater control over the oil resources in the South, and to limit China's growing influence. Nonetheless, the country was prone to extreme bouts of civil strife, which prompted the CIA in 2010 to issue a warning: 'over the next five years...a new mass killing or genocide is most likely to occur in southern Sudan'.

The marriage of convenience between Kirr and Machar to unite against a common enemy the Sudanese government in Khartoum was bound to fall apart. As soon as the South Sudan became independent and Washington became pre-occupied with other matters, relations between Kirr and Machar nose-dived, eventually culminating into the killing spree witnessed today.

Regardless of America's military superiority and her capacity to generate billions of dollars in aid, America has a terrible record when it comes to nation building. American ventures into Somalia, Afghanistan, Iraq, Libya and other countries have only left behind a trail of destruction and

---

[99] "Comprehensive Peace Agreement (CPA), Sudan", Council of Foreign Relations, January 09, 2005).

disillusionment with freedom and democracy. South Sudan is just another one of America's failed states.

This is ample evidence that America cannot nation build or stabilise countries it invades through diplomacy or political work. The longer this carries on, the more futile becomes America's military superiority in turning battlefield gains into political bargaining chips, which can be exploited by American politicians to implement political solutions that have a more durable shelf-life. But perhaps, more damaging than America's failure to nation build is the perception that America cannot get the job done i.e. America is good at toppling regimes but nothing else.

January 15, 2014

# 47

# America Supports the Continuation of Tyranny in Egypt via Sisi, but Will the People Take Heed

*"Given that Egypt's military sees itself in an existential struggle, the United States cannot stop the slide toward authoritarianism. Yet it is not suitable for Washington to maintain the same kind of assistance package to Egypt that it had in the past. The US government will recognize the new president and work with Cairo on its legitimate security needs."*

*--Michele Dunne*

President Sisi, Egypt's latest but most brutal tyrant to date is on a crusade to rid Egypt of any dissent that is not officially sanctioned by his government. Unrepentant about his anti-democratic credentials, Sisi justifies both the coup against Mursi and his draconian policies aimed at cleansing Egypt of Islamists, as essential measures to bring "democracy" back to Egypt.

Sisi is not alone on Egypt's path to the restoration of tyranny. US Secretary of State, John Kerry on a recent visit to Cairo offered renewed support for the measures initiated by Sisi. Kerry said, *"The road map is being carried out to the best of our perception. I think it's important for all of us, until proven otherwise, to accept that this is the track Egypt is on and to work to help it to be able to achieve that.[100]"* Kerry also bolstered Egypt's capacity to commit terror by saying that US had recently released $575 million in assistance for Egypt's military and that he was confident 10 Apache helicopters would be delivered to Egypt soon. With Sisi rapidly patching up relations with neighbouring countries, one can only assume that the new military

---

[100] "Egyptians Following Right Path, Kerry Says" , The New York Time, (November 03, 2013).

hardware will be used to shore up the border with the Jewish State and commit acts violence on the domestic front.

Yet it was only three years ago that America supported the efforts of the Egyptian people to oust Mubarak from power. Speaking in February 2011, President Obama told the Egyptian people: *"The Egyptian people have made it clear that there is no going back to the way things were: Egypt has changed, and its future is in the hands of the people … They have made it clear that Egypt must reflect their hopes, fulfil their highest aspirations, and tap their boundless potential.[101] "*

America's abrupt U-turn against the desire of Egyptians to free themselves from the rule of tyranny and her penchant for embracing dictators is not surprising. America is more interested in safeguarding first and foremost her national interest. If this means that America has to re-embrace dictatorship at the expense of democracy then so be it. Summing up the Obama administration's attitude towards the Arab revolutions, Kiron Skinner, director of Carnegie Mellon University's Centre for International Relations and Politics said, *"We have seen dictators fall and seen new forms of authoritarian rule. The whole arc of the Middle East is not becoming the democratic experiment the Obama administration had been trying to foster during the Arab Spring."*

There are three valuable lessons to learn from this whole episode:

1. The mere desire to emancipate Egypt from tyranny and establish Islam is not enough for the revolution to succeed. This was wickedly exposed in the early days of the revolution, as Nasserites— the custodians of the regime— stepped in to remove Mubarak by making sure the regime remained intact. It was only later, during the ominous rule of the Supreme Council of Armed Forces (SCAF) that some Egyptians realised the full extent of the

---

[101] "President Obama Issues Stern Statement on Egypt", ABC News, (February 10, 2011).

control exerted by the Nasserites, but most Egyptians remained oblivious to this or chose to ignore it.

What Egyptians require is a clear understanding about what they want their revolution to deliver i.e. to rule by Islam under the shade of the Caliphate state or to live in a pseudo democratic state where a small courtier of people close to the West make laws for the rest to live by. The companions of the Messenger of Allah (SAW) in Mecca had a crystal clear understanding that they wanted to live by Islam. This not only became the sole purpose of their existence, but was the main driving force by which they were able to liberate the whole of Arabia from the rule of tyranny and *jahiliyah*.

2.  Egyptians during their revolution relied on leaders that were part and parcel of the current political landscape. They were bereft of a clear vision, unable to articulate coherent policies and most of all their thinking was imprisoned by the status quo. This included both secularist and Islamists. Hence, it did not come as a surprise to see Mursi fumble and the people live in misery. The same fate awaits Sisi, his government and Egyptians living under his rule. This is because both Mursi and Sisi chose to rule by other than Islam.

    What Egyptians require is a leadership that understands Islam deeply, can clearly articulate the end goal i.e. the re-establishment of Caliphate and has carefully thought about how to rule and what to implement when taking power.

3.  It also became abundantly clear that Islam cannot be delivered via the ballot box. The only practical way to bring about comprehensive change in Egypt where Islamic *Shar'iah* is supreme is to have the army support the transformation of the Egyptian

society. Today, the army stands against the people of Egypt opposing their every move to implement Islam.

For Islam to be implemented the material power i.e. the army must be in the hands of the Muslims not the West. Before the Messenger of Allah (SAW) established the first Islamic state in Madina he sought material support from Al Aws and Al Khazraj, and once he (SAW) had received and secured the authority only then did he (SAW) implement Islam.

It is hoped that Egyptians will deeply ponder on these points, so that they become accustomed to what Islam demands in both of a vision for the Islamic Caliphate and its method of implementation. Allah (swt) says in the Qur'ān:

*"Oh you who have Iman! Answer (the call of) Allah (swt) and His Messenger when he calls you to that which gives you life; and know that Allah (swt) intervenes between man and his heart, and that to Him you shall be gathered."*

[ TMQ Al anfal:24]

June 29, 2014

## 48

# America's Humanitarian Intervention in Iraq, But Not in Gaza, Syria, Burma or Congo

*"When nations send their military forces into other nations' territory, it is rarely (if ever) for "humanitarian" purposes. They are typically pursuing their narrow national interest - grabbing territory, gaining geo-strategic advantage, or seizing control of precious natural resources. Leaders hope to win public support by describing such actions in terms of high moral purposes - bringing peace, justice, democracy and civilization to the affected area."*

*--Global Policy Forum*

On August 7th, 2014 the US President Barack Obama authorized military strikes in Iraq. He said, "When we face a situation like we do on that mountain, with innocent people facing the prospect of violence on a horrific scale and we have a mandate to help - in this case a request from the Iraqi government - and when we have unique capabilities to act to avoid a massacre, I believe the United States cannot turn a blind eye.[102]"He added: "Earlier this week, one Iraqi said no-one is coming to help. Well, today America is coming to help.[103]"

Once again America is eager to intervene in the Muslim world to carry out military operations. This time it is Iraq and the justification is again humanitarian assistance. The delivery of humanitarian relief, in the form of air drops by US jets represents the first aerial mission over Iraq since 2011. This marks the start of the deepest American engagement in Iraq since US troops withdrew in late 2011 after nearly a decade of war.

---

[102] "Obama authorizes air strikes in Iraq", Reuters, (August 07, 2014).
[103] *Ibid*

However, what is interesting to note is that there is no coherent strategy or moral compass guiding American foreign policy interventions where domestic population are being pulverized to smithereens and gross human rights violations occur on a daily basis. The actions of the Jewish State in Gaza clearly constitutes genocide, but there is no American intervention. Likewise, the barbaric acts of Assad against his people does not justify American intervention. In both cases, war crimes are being perpetrated by the likes of Netanyahu and Assad, yet America chooses to turn a blind eye. Beyond the Middle East, Muslim minorities are being merciless wiped out in Burma and the Democratic Republic of Congo (DRC), but there is no talk of humanitarian intervention. The persecution of Muslim minorities in the latter two countries far exceeds both in scale and magnitude to what is happening to minorities in Iraq, but America chooses to intervene in Iraq and ignore the plight of Muslims elsewhere—so where is the moral equivalence?

Over the past twenty years or so, America and her Western allies have slowly eroded the concept of the nation state as enshrined by the Westphalia Treaty. The treaty explicitly forbids the interference in the internal affairs of nations by other nations. But through the pretext of humanitarian intervention, the West has grossly undermined the nation state concept. Moreover, the selective application of humanitarian intervention has further eroded the credibility of the nation state model, and weakened the West's claim of any moral superiority in their foreign interventions.

This is not limited to the Muslim world, and can easily applied to the suppression of minorities in Russia and China. However, America and the West choose not to intervene here, as they do not have the stomach for an all-out war with countries that have the ability to significantly damage Western interests.

What may look like a bleak period in the history of the Muslim world—demonstrated through repeated Western interventions and wars—should not be interpreted as American or Western superiority. Yes, America and the West are militarily superior, but this has not helped them shape political outcomes as demonstrated by both the wars in Iraq and Afghanistan.

In fact, it can be argued, the biggest weapon against America and the West are their ideological inconsistencies in foreign policy matters. The damage wrought by such glaring contradictions far overshadow what any adversary of the West could hope to achieve.

In this lies the silver lining for the Muslim world. For when the real Caliphate returns, it would be relatively easily for the Caliphate in the current international climate to not only unify the Muslims world, but also to expand its frontiers to other continents based upon humanitarian intervention fused with its invitation to Islam. The persecution of Muslim minorities in Europe, and the oppression of the Muslim population together with the suppression of Latinos and Black populations in America would be more than enough reason for the Caliphate to intervene to liberate such people from the tyranny of the West to the justice of Islam. Allah (swt) says:

*"And they planned, and Allah (swt) also planned; and Allah (swt) is the Best of planners."*

[TMQ Al-Imran:55]

August 8, 2014

**49**

## Overblown Security Assessment Suggests Another Western Invasion of a Muslim Country is Likely

*"But terrorists rarely change the world map. Major rogue states can destabilize the world order and everything we cherish. The spies knew that but could do nothing about it because they were told to take their eye off the rogue state threats and instead chase the bearded crazies."*

*--Matthew Dunn*

Earlier in the week, the British Prime Minister David Cameron issued a grave warning and stated that Britain faced its greatest threat. He said, "What we are facing in Iraq now with ISIS (Islamic State) is a greater threat to our security than we have seen before.[104]" He added, "If we do not act to stem the onslaught of this exceptionally dangerous terrorist movement, it will only grow stronger until it can target us on the streets of Britain." The grim warning coincided with the UK's threat level raised to substantial from severe--meaning that a terrorist attack was very likely.

Cameron also went further with his assessment of the threat emerging from ISIS and warned European leaders. He said, "With designs on expanding to Jordan, Lebanon, right up to the Turkish border, we could be facing a terrorist state on the shores of the Med and bordering a Nato member." So the question arises is this just scaremongering or is there a hidden motive behind Cameron's remarks.

Cameron is not alone in his assessment of the ISIS's threat. In America, some government officials as well as a growing proportion of the public

---

[104] "ISIS pose 'greater threat to Britain than we've known before' and are MORE dangerous than Al-Qaida", Daily Mirror, (August 29, 2014).

perceive ISIS to be a real threat. "This is a group of people who are extraordinarily dangerous,[105]" said Senator Dianne Feinstein, the California Democrat. Mike Rogers, leader of the House Intelligence Committee warned: "Isis would like to have a Western-style attack to continue this notion that they are the leading jihadist group in the world."

According to a Pew Research Center report issued recently about the American public's perception of ISIS, Americans feel threatened by the obscure jihadi group. The report states : "Following the beheading of American journalist James Foley, two-thirds of the public (67 percent) cite ISIS as a major threat to the United States. The report said that 91 percent of Tea Party Republicans described ISIS as a "major threat" as opposed to 65 percent of Democrats and 63 percent of independents. The report also said: "Half of the sample was asked about ISIS and the other half was asked about the broader threat of 'Islamic extremist groups like Al Qaeda,' which registered similar concern (71 percent major threat, 19 percent minor threat, 6 percent not a threat).

However, there are number of intelligence analysts that question the severity of the threat posed by ISIS. Matthew G. Olsen, the director of the National Counterterrorism Center at the Brookings Institution said, "As formidable as ISIS is as group, it is not invincible," Mr. Olsen added. "ISIS is not Al Qaeda pre-9/11" with cells operating in Europe, Southeast Asia and the United States. Mr. Olsen's sobering but measured assessment of the organization stood in contrast to more pointed descriptions by other American officials. Olsen's assessment chimes extremely well with Obama's view in June 2014. Back then he conceded that the group had become more powerful in "some places," but downplayed the idea that ISIS's gains in Iraq meant the US was in greater danger. "We've also got a lot better at protecting ourselves," he said.

---

[105] "Feinstein: Obama 'too cautious' on Islamic State militants", The New York Post, (August 31, 2014).

What makes a mockery of American and British assertion about the imminent danger posed by ISIS's is a resurgent Russian state that is well equipped with nuclear weapons, and is more determined then ever to make a stand against West's continued interference in Ukraine. Russia possesses both the motive and the means to really hurt the West, whereas ISIS only has aspirations. Last week, Vladimir Putin pointed to Russia's nuclear arsenal and warned the West: 'It's best not to mess with us' on Ukraine.

The only other occasion such bellicose language was used by Britain and America was when they wanted to invade Afghanistan and Iraq. The same rhetoric is being employed today to justify another American led invasion of another Muslim country, and this time the target increasingly appears to be Syria and parts of Iraq.

As usual the West is aided in her invasion of the Muslim world by corrupt agent rulers, who spare no effort in providing America and Britain the necessary encouragement and pretexts to intervene. King Abdullah of Saudi Arabia said, "If neglected, I am certain that after a month they will reach Europe and, after another month, America. Terror knows no borders and its danger could affect several countries outside the Middle East."

If it was not for the agent rulers providing their airspace, waterways, air bases, intelligence and money, the West would not be able to invade Muslim countries. And even when they did invade--aided and abetted by agent rulers--the West struggled to defeat the brave sons and daughters of the *Ummah* in Iraq and Afghanistan.

What the Muslim world requires is permanent immunization against the virus of Western interventions in the Muslim lands, and this can only be achieved by the re-establishment of the rightly guided Caliphate. The Caliphate will use political guile and intrigue to make the kafir colonialist powers fight each other thereby making them weak before the *Ummah*.

September 4, 2014

# 50

# Is the Breakup of Iraq Part of America's Wider Plan to Reshape the Middle East

*"We view the current period as a turning point, just like 1918 and 1945."*

--*Atlantic Council President Frederick Kempe*

With Iraq's rapid descent into chaos and Maliki's inability to retake territory lost to both ISIS and Kurdish Peshmerga fighters, there is growing posturing amongst Kurdish leaders and their supporters to declare independence.

During an interview with CNN's Christine Amanpour, the president of the northern Iraqi Kurdish Administrated Region, Massoud Barzani made several references to an independent Kurdish state. When asked: "Can Iraq hold together as a nation?" A smiling Barzani replied: "I don't think so." He then went on to say: "We are now living in a new era that is completely different from that Iraq that we always knew, the Iraq that we lived in one or two weeks ago." When asked: "Is this is the time for Kurdistan to seek the fulfilment of its long-time ambitions about self-determination, even independence?" Barzani replied. "During the last ten years we did everything in our power to build a new democratic Iraq but unfortunately the experience has not been successful." Barzani's emboldened remarks come on the heels of Peshmerga fighters securing Kirkuk. The city has reportedly 10 billion barrels of proven oil reserves and is currently part of Kirkuk-Ceyhan pipeline, which runs north to the Turkish port.

Oddly enough, the Jewish Prime Minister Netanyahu welcomed the prospects of an independent Kurdistan. He said, "We should ... support the Kurdish aspiration for independence." And he also described the Kurds "a nation of fighters [who] have proved political commitment and are worthy of independence". The candid support for a separate homeland for the Kurds fails to mask Netanyahu's real delight at finally resurrecting the old British built Kirkuk-to-Haifa pipeline that use to supply oil to the Jewish state.

The events in Iraq coupled with overt support for an independent Kurdish state have rekindled memories of American efforts to redraw the map of the Middle East. Over the years, this process has been given different names by American politicians and think tanks. Zbigniew Brzezinski, former US National Security Advisor used the term "Arc of Crisis" and the Rand Corporation employed the term the "Greater Middle East". In 2006, the US Secretary of State Condoleezza Rice used the words "New Middle East". Speaking at a  press conference organised by the US State department, Rice said: "[w]hat we're seeing here [in regards to the destruction of Lebanon and the Israeli attacks on Lebanon], in a sense, is the growing—the 'birth pangs'—of a 'New Middle East' and whatever we do we [meaning the United States] have to be certain that we're pushing forward to the New Middle East [and] not going back to the old one." Others like Lieutenant-Colonel Ralph Peters have even published a map of the New Middle East. However, there is one common denominator in all of these themes—divide and conquer— that is to exploit sectarian, ethnic and religious differences to curve out new states. Iraq after the dismemberment of Sudan appears to be America's latest target.

America successfully laid the seeds for Iraq's partition during the first Gulf War. The aim was to isolate Baghdad from the Kurdish areas to the North of Iraq and Shiite dominated areas to the South of Iraq. America accomplished this through the implementation of the infamous Operation Northern Watch to enforce the no-fly zone north of the 36th parallel in Iraq, and monitor Iraqi compliance via UN Security Council resolutions 678, 687, and 688. Later, Operation Southern Watch was enforced to protect the no-fly zone south of the 33rd parallel in Iraq and monitor compliance with United Nations Security Council Resolutions 687, 688, and 949.

After the fall of Saddam in April 2003, America deliberately fostered an environment that encouraged sectarian violence especially amongst Iraq's Sunnis and Shias. America accomplished this feat through military operations that disproportionally targeted Sunnis and a biased political process that favoured the Shias. For instance, in October 2006, the Iraqi parliament passed a resolution after a controversial vote, agreeing to revisit how to create a federalist state in 18 months. Sunni parliamentarians boycotted the vote, saying it would divide the country, and the measure passed 140-to-0 by the largely Shiite and Kurdish members. Shortly after the parliament vote, Abdul Aziz al-Hakim the leader of the Supreme Council for Islamic Revolution said,"… the Iraq problem can only be solved with regions."

The subsequent appointment of Maliki as Iraq's Prime Minister was clearly intended to accentuate divisions amongst Sunnis, Shias and the Kurds, and also to create circumstances conducive for America to intervene at any time and partition Iraq if she so desired.

The events in Iraq are indeed a turning point and represent a struggle for two competing narratives for the Middle East as a whole. The first narrative espoused by old Europe is to maintain the status quo i.e. to preserve the current map of the Middle East firmly rooted in the Sykes-Picot agreement of 1916. The second narrative adopted by American policy makers is to redraw the borders of the Middle East. This is what Frederick Kempe envisages i.e. a birth of a "New Middle East", where old European agents and states, are replaced by American surrogates and new countries forever indebted to Pax Americana. However, both narratives are in danger of being trumped by the peoples' narrative for the region. This is the powerful desire to see a borderless Middle East firmly united under the Caliphate.

July 7, 2014

**51**

# American and Iranian Collaboration is Spurring Sectarianism Across the Middle East

Are we witnessing the emergence of a *Shi'a* crescent?

> *"If anybody a year ago had said the United States and Iran might today be cooperating in dealing with a major international crisis, they would have been regarded as deranged."*
>
> --*The Guardian Editorial*

O ver the years, the official narrative advocated by both Washington and Tehran is that America and Iran are adversaries competing with one another for influence in the Middle East. But the civil war in Syria and more recently Iraq's sectarian infighting challenges this assertion on multiple fronts. There is growing body of evidence that points to collusion instead of rivalry as the main factor in shaping relations between the two countries.

Just take a look at some of the recent news headlines. "ISIS is the best thing to happen to Iran-US relations in years", blurts out the Washington Post. "Strange bedfellows: US-Iran cooperate on crisis in Iraq", says The Daily Star. According to CNN: "US and Iran: From sworn enemies to partners on Iraq?" While the Jewish newspaper Haaretz complains: "The US shouldn't beg Iran to act on Iraq and Syria". On economic matters, Russia Today reports: "US company signs billion-dollar energy deal with Iran".

Ever since, US President Obama announced a nuclear deal with Iran back in January 2014, cooperation between the two countries has become more transparent. This apparent openness has forced many to review

America's political actions in Syria and Iraq— where Tehran is actively involved in providing unstinting support to both Assad and Al Maliki.

Take Syria for example—America has patiently watched Iran bolster Assad's floundering regime through billions of dollars in aid, weapons, and Iranian special forces collaborating with Hezbollah fighters and Assad's henchmen. Despite Assad crossing Obama's red lines on several occasions, America has refused punish Assad or its backer Tehran.

Similarly, Iran for several years has provided money, arms and men to help Maliki subdue the Sunni resistance in Iraq. Even today, as Sunni militants advance towards Baghdad, Iran is providing drone surveillance; military advisors and other methods of support to help the Shias in Baghdad and South of the country shore up their defences. Again, despite America's bellowing rhetoric against Iranian interference, the Obama administration has been reaching out to Tehran to explore ways on how best to stop the advance of Sunni fighters. One measure that has been welcomed in Washington is the joint strikes carried out by Syrian and Iraqi jet fighters against Sunni targets.

The picture that emerges from both Iraq and Syria is one in which Alawaite and Shia governments are waging a brutal war against their respective Sunni populations under the patronage of Iran. By America publicly refusing to get involved in both conflicts and simultaneously preferring to solicit Iranian support conveys the impression that America is intentionally backing the current status quo. Hence, one is forced to conclude that perhaps America would like to see the creation of a Shia crescent that stretches all the way from Lebanon to Yemen. Conveniently, such a collection of states aided and abetted by Iran would place the oil of the Middle East into the hands of the Shia, who in turn would be indebted to America's benevolence. In January 2010, King Abdullah of Jordon in an interview with Farid Zakaria at Davos Switzerland warned about Iran's efforts to fuel sectarian hatred and the rise of the Shia crescent. He said,

*"Certain members – of the Iranian government using an agenda to create the perception of a Shia crescent... I saw a political strategy that would as an endgame have the Sunnis and Shias at each other's throats ... the fault line between Shias and Sunnis goes from Beirut all the way to Bombay and it's a catastrophic subject to play with."*

To ensure that Iranian expansionism does not get too big for American policy makers to handle, America in cohorts with Saudi Arabia and the Gulf countries is arming and funding several Sunni jihadi groups. The ensuing result is sectarian strife on a massive scale, where Sunnis and Shias are fighting each other to curve out their zones of influence. Some of these could turn out to be mini states, for instance ISIL's recent declaration is one such attempt. The other is the push by the Kurds for independence. Across the border in Syria there is talk of dividing Syria into several parts. There is little doubt that America has deliberately instigated this, and on the face of it Iran not Saudi Arabia appears to be principal regional benefactor.

Once again it is the people of the region that are suffering, as America works to put its own version of Sykes-Picot agreement in place through sell out rulers. America does not care how many Muslims are killed in the process, so long as she is able secure her vital interests, even if this means new countries are created out of old ones.

The only salvation for the Muslims of the region is to put their differences aside. The first step in this process is to unite on the basis of Islam. Allah (swt) says:

*"And hold firmly to the rope of Allah (swt) all together and do not become divided. And remember the favour of Allah (swt) upon you - when you were enemies and He brought your hearts together and you became, by His favour, brothers. And you were on the edge of a pit of the Fire, and He saved you from it. Thus does Allah (swt) make clear to you His verses that you may be guided."*

[TMQ Al-Imran:103]

The second step is to give the unity a political authority that is independent of America and Western inspired agents. This can only be achieved through the re-establishment of the rightly guided Caliphate by Muslims giving *Bay'ah* to a Caliph who will rule according to the Qur'ān and Sunnah of the Messenger of Allah (SAW). The Messenger of Allah (SAW) said,

"Whoever dies and did not make an oath of allegiance (to a Muslim leader) has died a death of *jahiliyah* (ignorance)."

[ Sahih Muslim, Kitab-ul-Immarah]

The third step is to oppose internationally Western plans and plots that are focussed on dividing and exploiting Muslim lands and making Muslims engaged in cheap struggles. The Caliphate should use all of its might and power to cut the hand of any foreign power that dares divide the Muslim *Ummah*. Only then will Muslims be able to live in peace and security. Allah (swt) says:

*"And in that day believers will rejoice. In Allah (swt)'s help to victory. He helpeth to victory whom He will. He is the Mighty, the Merciful."*

[TMQ Ar-Rum:4-5]

July 9, 2014

52

# The Pakistanization of Turkey

*"The Balkanization of Iraq has become more evident than ever with the recent sectarian violence…Iraq is moving closer to a civil war and almost unavoidable disintegration, prompting serious but less-mentioned worries in Turkey."*

--*Ayhan Simsek*

On October 2nd 2014, the Turkish parliament authorized the government to carry out cross-border military operations in Iraq and Syria to fight the Islamic State of Iraq and the Levant (ISIL) and other armed groups. The motion, put forward by the ruling Justice and Development (AK) Party, passed with 298 votes in favors and 98 against. The vote also allows foreign soldiers to be stationed in Turkey and to use its military bases for the same purposes with no limit on the troop numbers. Speaking before the parliament, Ismet Yilmaz, Turkish defence minister said, "The rising influence of radical groups in Syria threatens Turkey's national security. … The aim of this mandate is to minimise as much as possible the impact of the clashes on our borders." He added, "The only target of this text is a terrorist organisation that wants to disturb the peace of Iraq and Syria."

The vote was immediately welcomed by America. "We have been closely engaged with Turkey. We welcome the Turkish parliament's vote to authorize Turkish military action," Jen Psaki, the State Department spokeswoman, said.

The vote passed by the Turkish parliament raises several interesting questions. Will Turkey permit America to use Incirlik air base and allow American troops to be stationed on its soil? Will Turkey's fear of Kurdish self-determination hamper its fight against ISIL? Will Turkey now close its borders to jihadis wanting to cross over to Iraq? Will Turkey target other Islamic groups in Syria in addition to ISIL, thereby strengthening Assad's grip on power? Will Turkey strike Kurdish militants groups operating in Iraq and Syria under the pretext of fighting terrorism? These are just some of the questions being asked of Turkey.

However, the most dangerous dimension to Turkey's parliamentary approval, is that it precariously brings Turkey close to fighting those Islamic elements in Iraq and Syria that Ankara helped to create. In many ways, Turkey is now mirroring what happened to Pakistan some decades ago[106].

In the eighties, Pakistan in collaboration with the US and Saudi Arabia radicalized the Pakistani population during the Soviet invasion of Afghanistan, and later recruited Afghans from more than three million Afghan refugees residing in Pakistan. These Afghans were given religious schooling in madrassas backed by Saudis as well as military training by ISI. Thus the Taliban movement was born, and with ISI guidance Taliban were able to conquer large parts of Afghanistan. Later the movement turned on Pakistan under the banner of Tehrik Taliban Pakistan.

Today Turkey's current situation resembles the early years of Pakistan's sponsorship of the Taliban. ISIL and other groups are recruiting militants in Turkey, as well as from Syrian refugee camps. By starting a fight against ISIL and other Islamic groups in Syria, there is real danger that Ankara will quickly become embroiled in a protracted guerilla war confined within Turkish borders.

Such a situation does not benefit Turkey or the Muslims of Iraq and Syria. The only beneficiary is America, which has unashamedly embarked upon an elaborate plan to change the map of the Middle East—after

---

[106] M. Tanchum, H. Karaveli, "Pakistan's Lessons for Turkey", The New York Post, (October 5, 2014).

dismemberment of Iraq and the partitioning of Syria, Turkey will become America's next victim.

The Pakistanization of Turkey is intended to weaken Turkey both economically and militarily before the next phase of balkanization can begin. In Pakistan's case, America has wasted little opportunity in talking about the balkanization of Pakistan by hosting independence movements such as Balochistan nationalists. How long before Turkey ends up where Pakistan is today.

Indeed the real lesson to learn from Pakistan's folly is that America along with other Western powers can never be trusted. And in this context, the Turkish government should have taken the following steps:

1. To announce the closure of all Western embassies and the immediate expulsion of their diplomats. It is well known that Western embassies are the cauldron of conspiracies and intelligence operations directed against the Turkish state.

2. To sever all military ties with Western powers which also includes NATO. To seize all military equipment that belongs to their armed forces and to expel or imprison their personnel, especially American armed forces and NATO personnel, who are actively at war with the Muslim world.

3. To immediately address the grievances of the Kurdish population and sign an agreement with the warring Kurdish militants to lay down their arms and join the ranks of the Turkish army.

4. To mobilize all Islamic militants opposed to Assad to join the ranks of the Turkish army and then to march to Damascus to remove Assad and his henchmen from power. Those groups that  that refuse to join should be isolated and dealt a fatal blow. This includes ISIL.

5. To persuade other Muslim countries allying with America to sever ties with her and join Turkey in liberating Syria and returning refugees safely home to both Syria and Iraq.

6. To send a stern message to Iran that if it fails to withdraw its support to Assad, Abadi and Hezbollah then Tehran will pay a heavy price.

These are just some of the actions that are well within the grasp of Turkey's leadership and if performed sincerely and correctly, can prevent America and her allies from executing their evil plans against the Turkish state and the wider Muslim *Ummah*.

But for Turkey to be taken seriously by the Muslim *Ummah*, Turkey must abandon her secularism, whole-heartedly embrace Islam and re-establish the rightly guided Caliphate. Under the Ottoman Caliphate the Muslim world was protected from the nefarious designs of the European crusaders for many centuries and at its peak i.e. during the rule of Suliman Qanooni Muslims from Africa, Middle East, India and the Far East enjoyed unrivaled peace, prosperity, and security which was the envy of the West. So think what will happen today, if Turkey decides to resurrect the days of the Caliphate, not the days of the Ottoman, Abbasid or Ummayad Caliphate, but the days of the Caliphate on the way of the prophethood?

*"Oh you who have Iman, respond to Allah (swt) and to the Messenger when he calls you to that which gives you life. And know that Allah (swt) intervenes between a man and his heart and that to Him you will be gathered."*

[TMQ Al-Anfal:24]

October 7, 2014

53

# Egypt and GCC Spearhead Plans to Create a Regional Intervention Force to Serve the West

*"And cooperate in righteousness and piety,but do not cooperate in sin and agression..."*

*--[TMQ Al-Maida:2]*

This week it was revealed that Egypt, Saudi Arabia, the United Arab Emirates and Kuwait are discussing the creation of a military pact to take on Islamic militants, with the possibility of a joint force to intervene around the Middle East. The discussions reflect a new assertiveness among the Middle East's Sunni powerhouses, whose governments — after three years of post-Arab spring turmoil in the region — have increasingly come to see Sunni Islamic militants and Islamist political movements as a threat.

This is not the first time that Egypt, Saudi Arabia, the United Arab Emirates are coming together to forge an alliance to intervene in other Arab countries. Egypt and the UAE cooperated in carrying out airstrikes against Islamic militants in Libya during the summer, according to US officials, and last month Egypt carried out strikes of its own. Separately, Saudi and UAE fighter planes have already carried out attacks against militants in Iraq. However, what is noteworthy about the recent announcement is that there are now plans to create a permanent Arab military intervention force to fight Islam. The military dimension of the partnership between these countries is to supplement the ideological fight against political Islam. This fight will be waged on two fronts: ideological and military.

On the ideological front, Saudi Arabia is eager to fight political Islam worldwide and has donated $100 million for the United Nations Counter-Terrorism Centre (UNCTC) in August 2014[107]. "The goal is to help provide the tools, technologies and methods to confront and eliminate the threat of terrorism," Adel al-Jubeir, the Saudi ambassador to the United States, said in presenting a cheque to UN Secretary General Ban Ki-Moon. In October 2014, the UAE Emirates Policy Centre (EPC) organized a two day conference to discuss measures to fight Islam under the guise of terrorism. Dr Anwar Gargash, UAE Minister of State for Foreign Affairs, told the conference: "The UAE has repeatedly warned about the growing threat that extremist actors and ideologies pose to our region. We need to acknowledge that these actors and their radical ideologies by their nature cannot be moderated, manipulated, or contained. They are fundamentally opposed to the tolerant values and moderate agenda that unite us in the UAE with many of our international partners." He said that combating extremism requires a broad range of tools and a sustained effort by the international community.

The alliance comes at a time, when Western powers most notably America and Britain are suffering from military defeat from wars in Iraq and Afghanistan, and popular dissent at home means that further interventions are problematic. Subsequently, it is not surprising to find Arab countries stepping up efforts to do the West's dirty work to fight political Islam. Additionally, several other observations can be made about these developments:

1. Egypt and the GCC have been at odds with each other for several decades, however the rise of political Islam has galvanized their patrons America and Britain to press Egypt and the GCC countries to actively fight political Islam. Political Islam is now viewed as an existential threat by both the Arab regimes as well as

---

[107] "Saudis Give $100 Million to UN Fight on Terrorism", New York Times, (August 13, 2014).

their colonial masters—America and Britain.

2. The West will no longer oppose the political system of secular autocracies such the military dictatorship in Egypt or the monarchies of the Gulf countries. On the contrary, the West will buttress these political systems to become a bulwark against the of the Caliphate.

3. The military alliance between these countries is only directed at thwarting the rise of political Islam, and there is no mention of removing Assad from power. America is seeking to keep Assad's regime intact, even though it has repeatedly violated the red lines set by Obama.

4. The alliance is intended to check the rise of Iran's influence, which extends from Yemen to Lebanon and is increasingly taking on a strong military shape. In this way, the West is preparing the grounds for perpetual war to produce a new map of the Middle East.

Thus it is imperative for the Muslim *Ummah* to seriously think about changing their situation from being slaves of the West under the present colonial systems guarded by watchmen loyal to their colonial masters to becoming full slaves of Allah (swt) through the re-establishment of the rightly guided Caliphate state. Allah (swt) says in the Qur'ān:

*"Indeed, Allah (swt) will not change the condition of a people until they change what is in themselves. And when Allah (swt) intends for a people ill, there is no repelling it. And there is not for them besides Him any patron."*

[TMQ Al-Raad:11]

November 7, 2014

## 54

## Overblown Security Assessment Suggests Another Western Invasion of a Muslim Country is Likely

*"But terrorists rarely change the world map. Major rogue states can destabilize the world order and everything we cherish. The spies knew that but could do nothing about it because they were told to take their eye off the rogue state threats and instead chase the bearded crazies."*

*--Matthew Dunn*

E arlier in the week, the British Prime Minister David Cameron issued a grave warning and stated that Britain faced its greatest threat. He said, "What we are facing in Iraq now with ISIS (Islamic State) is a greater threat to our security than we have seen before.[108]" He added, "If we do not act to stem the onslaught of this exceptionally dangerous terrorist movement, it will only grow stronger until it can target us on the streets of Britain." The grim warning coincided with the UK's threat level raised to substantial from severe--meaning that a terrorist attack was very likely.

Cameron also went further with his assessment of the threat emerging from ISIS and warned European leaders. He said, "With designs on expanding to Jordan, Lebanon, right up to the Turkish border, we could be facing a terrorist state on the shores of the Med and bordering a Nato member." So the question arises is this just scaremongering or is there a hidden motive behind Cameron's remarks.

Cameron is not alone in his assessment of the ISIS's threat. In America, some government officials as well as a growing proportion of the public

---

[108] "ISIS pose 'greater threat to Britain than we've known before' and are MORE dangerous than Al-Qaida", Daily Mirror, (August 29, 2014).

perceive ISIS to be a real threat. "This is a group of people who are extraordinarily dangerous,[109]" said Senator Dianne Feinstein, the California Democrat. Mike Rogers, leader of the House Intelligence Committee warned: "Isis would like to have a Western-style attack to continue this notion that they are the leading jihadist group in the world."

According to a Pew Research Center report issued recently about the American public's perception of ISIS, Americans feel threatened by the obscure jihadi group. The report states : "Following the beheading of American journalist James Foley, two-thirds of the public (67 percent) cite ISIS as a major threat to the United States. The report said that 91 percent of Tea Party Republicans described ISIS as a "major threat" as opposed to 65 percent of Democrats and 63 percent of independents. The report also said: "Half of the sample was asked about ISIS and the other half was asked about the broader threat of 'Islamic extremist groups like Al Qaeda,' which registered similar concern (71 percent major threat, 19 percent minor threat, 6 percent not a threat).

However, there are number of intelligence analysts that question the severity of the threat posed by ISIS. Matthew G. Olsen, the director of the National Counterterrorism Center at the Brookings Institution said, "As formidable as ISIS is as group, it is not invincible," Mr. Olsen added. "ISIS is not Al Qaeda pre-9/11" with cells operating in Europe, Southeast Asia and the United States. Mr. Olsen's sobering but measured assessment of the organization stood in contrast to more pointed descriptions by other American officials. Olsen's assessment chimes extremely well with Obama's view in June 2014. Back then he conceded that the group had become more powerful in "some places," but downplayed the idea that ISIS's gains in Iraq meant the US was in greater danger. "We've also got a lot better at protecting ourselves," he said.

---

[109] "Feinstein: Obama 'too cautious' on Islamic State militants", The New York Post, (August 31, 2014).

What makes a mockery of American and British assertion about the imminent danger posed by ISIS's is a resurgent Russian state that is well equipped with nuclear weapons, and is more determined then ever to make a stand against West's continued interference in Ukraine. Russia possesses both the motive and the means to really hurt the West, whereas ISIS only has aspirations. Last week, Vladimir Putin pointed to Russia's nuclear arsenal and warned the West: 'It's best not to mess with us' on Ukraine.

The only other occasion such bellicose language was used by Britain and America was when they wanted to invade Afghanistan and Iraq. The same rhetoric is being employed today to justify another American led invasion of another Muslim country, and this time the target increasingly appears to be Syria and parts of Iraq.

As usual the West is aided in her invasion of the Muslim world by corrupt agent rulers, who spare no effort in providing America and Britain the necessary encouragement and pretexts to intervene. King Abdullah of Saudi Arabia said, "If neglected, I am certain that after a month they will reach Europe and, after another month, America. Terror knows no borders and its danger could affect several countries outside the Middle East."

If it was not for the agent rulers providing their airspace, waterways, air bases, intelligence and money, the West would not be able to invade Muslim countries. And even when they did invade--aided and abetted by agent rulers--the West struggled to defeat the brave sons and daughters of the *Ummah* in Iraq and Afghanistan.

What the Muslim world requires is permanent immunization against the virus of Western interventions in the Muslim lands, and this can only be achieved by the re-establishment of the rightly guided Caliphate. The Caliphate will use political guile and intrigue to make the kafir colonialist powers ineffective against the ascendency of the Islamic state.

September 4, 2014

# Part 6
# AfPak and the West's war against Islam

55

# Pakistan's Army Chief Betrays Pakistan for America

*"Kayani is a moderate, pro-American infantry commander who is widely seen as commanding respect within the army and within Western circles."*

*--Global Security*

Battered and bruised Pakistan's Chief of Army Staff General Ashfaq Parvez Kayani, struggled to gain the confidence of the nation in the aftermath of America's raid on Abbottabad. Even the loyal army officers and the dependable cadres, once the spine of Kayani's support base, openly challenged his version of events. In particular, many officers were not only perplexed, but less than convinced by the inability of the armed forces to detect and respond to the penetration of Pakistani airspace by hostile enemy helicopters.

The episode also emboldened Pakistan's arch enemy and rival India, to the extent that her military chiefs publicly boasted about India's capacity to conduct a similar operation: Army Chief Gen VK Singh said, "I would like to say only this that if such a chance comes, then all the three arms (of the military) are competent to do this..."[110] and India's Air Chief Marshal P V Naik blurted, "India can do it."[111] This deep-seated enmity towards Pakistan expressed by Singh and Naik, is not limited to the Indian armed forces. Rather, the hostility is rampant amongst Indian politicians, intellectuals, columnists etc. Yet, despite this wellspring of animosity, Kayani and his blundering puppet government continue to extend olive branches of peace to New Delhi.

---

[110] "India capable of taking out targets in Pakistan", Dawn News, (May 5, 2011).
[111] Air Cdre Khalid Iqbal, "Without Osama", Pakistan Observer, (2011).

Nevertheless, the disgraced Kayani and his entourage of misfits that includes the liberal elite, the paid media pundits and the nationalistic officers, chose to overlook Indian animosity and American antagonism towards Pakistan and instead decided to join forces to construct a patriotic narrative to compensate for Kayani's monumental failures. The deceptive narrative advocated by the media mercenaries, the pseudo intelligentsia and the cranky nationalists does not focus on declaring India and America the enemy of Pakistan but instead purports that the army is the only institution that can prevent Pakistan's collapse.

Upon a cursory examination of the rationale that underpins this narrative—even by an ordinary person with a modicum of common sense— demonstrates that it is a preposterous claim, peppered with inconsistencies and contradictions. For starters, how can Kayani defend Pakistan's lopsided relationship with America? America is an avowed enemy of Pakistan, in both word and deed, and continues to openly destabilize Pakistan in the tribal areas, whilst simultaneously strengthening its bilateral relations with India through nuclear deals and high-tech military contracts. How can Kayani defend the vicious, indiscriminate drone strikes that have killed and maimed thousands of innocent Pakistani civilians? Perhaps the answer lies in Kayani's appetite for spilling further Muslim blood by demanding that the number and intensity of the drone strikes should increase, as disclosed recently by Wikileaks. Indeed, a long list of Kayani's crimes against Pakistan can be compiled, which would be enough to hang him for treason in any court of law, except Pakistan.

What about Kayani's predecessors? Field Marshall Ayub Khan presided over the humiliating Indus Treaty, which surrendered control of Pakistan's waterways and rivers to India. General Yahya Khan lost East Pakistan (now Bangladesh), only for India to consolidate her grip over the Muslims of Bangladesh. General Zia ul Haq lost Sachin to India. General Pervez Musharraf ceded Kargil to aid Vajpayee's election victory, lost Afghanistan, abandoned the Kashmiri people, compromised Pakistan's nuclear assets and laid the foundations for unprecedented American hostility and hegemony in the region. Furthermore, the appalling state of Pakistan's political landscape over the past five decades is a direct result of the collective efforts of its military leadership. Under its auspices, politicians are bought and sold - most of them are jesters and puppets of the army; elections are routinely rigged courtesy of the ISI and the majority of political decisions usually bear the hallmarks of the military high command. Is there any aspect of political life that the military does not influence or control? The same can be said about the economy. Apart from the vast business interests that have mushroomed under successive military chiefs, the military continues to consume a significant share of the fiscal budget year on year, as opposed to other institutions.

In return for allowing complete domination of Pakistan's politics and economy, has the military leadership successfully defended Pakistan's national interests? The answer is simply No! The facts listed above speak for themselves. So the deceitful mantra of 'Pakistani army is a saviour of Pakistan' is a barefaced lie. Those who spearhead such a campaign are either smitten by their Western master's empty promises or are misguided transgressors, intellectually bankrupt and unable to think for themselves.

This is the true nature of the military leadership of Pakistan. A leadership that for decades felt no shame and expressed no remorse for squandering the resources of the Pakistani nation in the pursuit of serving and protecting the interests of its foreign colonialist masters. Kayani's treachery, however, has even put his predecessors' accomplishments to shame. Kayani has actively placed the authority of the armed forces in the hands of his American masters. They decide where and when the Pakistani army should be deployed, and whom they should fight. The brutal slaughter of civilians in Swat and the tribal areas, and the subsequent displacement of millions of Pakistanis is ample proof of Kayani's surrender of authority to his American masters. Kayani has clearly transgressed the limits prescribed by

Allah (swt) in granting the authority of the armed forces to the disbelieving colonialists.

Muslims of Pakistan must oppose at every juncture the evil alliance between Pakistan and America that Musharraf brokered in 2001 to fight Islam, but Kayani nurtured it, brought it to extraordinary levels of American subjugation that saw the release of the killer Raymond Davis, whilst the innocent Aafia Sidiqqui languished in prison. Even after the humiliation of the Abbotabad raid, the disgraceful Kayani continues to protect this evil alliance and claims that Pakistan's strategic assets are safe. His obedience to his American masters and his loyalty to the evil alliance is so firm that the cut in US aid to Pakistan has not diminished his zeal or enthusiasm. Allah (swt) forbids Muslims from entering, supporting and remaining quite about alliances with disbelieving colonialist powers that seek to destroy Islam and Muslims:

*"O you who have Iman! Take not the Jews and Christians as Awliyaa (friends, allies) they are Awliyaa (friends, allies) only to each other. And he among you that turns to them is of them…"*

[TMQ Al-Maidah:51]

and

*"Give to the hypocrites the news that for them there is a painful torment. Those who take disbelievers for Awliyaa (friends)' instead of believers, do they seek I'zzah (honour, power) with them? Then verily, all the I'zzah belongs to Allah (swt)."*

[TMQ An-Nisa:139]

and

*"Oh you who have Iman Take not for Awliyaa (friends, allies)' disbelievers instead of believers. Do you wish to offer Allah (swt) a manifest proof against yourselves?"*

[TMQ An-Nisa:144]

The Muslims of Pakistan can take some immediate steps to pressurise the military leadership to cut its alliance with America.

1. Do not extend any forms of cooperation to the leadership of the armed forces in its sin of supporting America's war against Pakistan. Halt all supplies and logistics, until the army leadership relents and severs its ties with America.

2. Send messages of defiance to all the local Corp commanders that this evil alliance with America will not be tolerated. Furthermore, engage in all forms of non-violent civil disobedience at all the army headquarters in the four provinces demanding an end to Pakistan's relationship with America.

3. Actively convince your sons and daughters who work for the armed forces not to participate in any activity that supports America's hegemony over Pakistan.

As for the officers of the Pakistani army, they are not like Kayani and his small courtier of mischief advisors. They are sincere to Islam and yearn to defend Pakistan from the enmity of America and India. However, it is not enough for them to be angry in silence and while continuing to serve Kayani in obedience. There is no obedience to the one who seeks to plunder and destroy Pakistan, and sacrifices its brave soldiers for the interests of foreign powers. Nawaas bin Sama'aan reported that the Messenger of Allah (SAW)) said , "There is no obedience to the creation in disobedience to the Creator."[112] 'Ali reported that Messenger of Allah (SAW) said, "...There is no obedience in disobedience to Allah (swt). Obedience is in Ma'roof."[113] Below are a couple of actions you can immediately take to show their obedience to Allah (swt) and their disobedience to Kayani.

---

[112] Baghawi in 'sharhus Sunnah' [10/44] Ahmad, Al Haakim.
[113] Muslim  kitaabul Imaarah [no.4536], Bukhari [Eng vers. Vol. 9 no.259].

1.  You most actively oppose your superior officers who support Kayani and are committed to America's subjugation of Pakistan.

2.  You must work tirelessly, to stop Kayani from using the Pakistani armed forces to execute America's crusade in Afghanistan and Pakistan. This means you must refuse to execute orders, operate military equipment, fly planes etc. that involve the killing of Muslims or aiding American forces to gain domination over Pakistan.

In the long-term, there is only one solution to the domination of America over your affairs and the control of your armed forces. You must join hands with your brothers in the army to re-establish the Khilafah which will bring an end to the American hegemony, and return dignity to the people of Pakistan.

August 21, 2011

**56**

## Pakistan's Policy of High Interest Rates, Devaluation and the Dollar Peg is a Recipe for Disaster

*"Pakistan's economy seems to be experiencing a near-death experience."*

--*The News International*

As the world debates what to do about the financial crises plaguing both America and Europe, very little debate is taking place inside Pakistan about its ailing economy. The policy prescription implemented by the present government, which consists of a combination of interest rate hikes and devaluation, has failed to stimulate growth. On the contrary, this 'quick fix' has so far resulted in inflation, mass unemployment and economic stagnation. Economists and politicians equally seem at loss, on what do next. Some profess that the only solution is more of the same economic medicine prescribed by the West, plus some additional assistance in the form of foreign loans, while others are simply clueless. So what can be done, and how can Pakistan's economy become self-sufficient.

The most powerful tool the Pakistani government believes it has to curb inflation (or for that matter the contraction and expansion of the country's money supply) is through interest rate adjustments. Pakistan's current interest rate stands at 13.5% - one of the highest in the world. A high interest rate is not conducive for economic growth and has a number of implications for the economy. First, businessmen, entrepreneurs and wealthy people are encouraged to either take their money out of investments, or to not invest at all; instead they deposit their money with banks to earn interest. Given Pakistan's precarious security situation and energy crisis, depositing money is seen as an extremely attractive option. In this way, money is taken out of circulation from the real economy and is no longer used in new or existing ventures. Subsequently, no new jobs are created to absorb the millions of new job seekers in the domestic market, and unemployment increases.

Secondly, the banks (on their part) use depositors' money and deposit it with Pakistan's state bank in special accounts to earn 13.5% in interest. As the state bank does not have surplus money to pay interest; it is forced to 'create money' in order to pay interest to the depositing banks. The banks then receive money in the form of interest and use it to pay their depositors at a slightly lower rate of interest, say, 12%. The banks pocket the difference doing absolutely nothing. The depositors either reinvest the interest in the form of additional deposits, or use it to buy goods and services, thereby increasing the inflation rate of certain items, especially luxurious goods.

Thirdly, high interest rates make it extremely difficult for corporations and small businesses to pay off their loans or borrow money. Typically, bank loan charges are at an exorbitant rate of interest e.g. it is typical for borrowers to pay an additional 5% to 8% above the state bank's discount rate of 13.5%. This means that some commercial borrowers (companies and SMEs alike) seek to restructure their debt, which entails paying more over a longer period of time. Others are simply forced to cut their costs, which translates into laying off workers, reducing existing product lines and operating on 'shoestring' budgets. However, some corporations and businesses are not so fortunate and declare themselves bankrupt, or are forced to close for business. Likewise, households are also forced to curb their spending, as some attempt to refinance their debt, while others simply default on their home or car loans, because the bread winner in the family unexpectedly becomes unemployed.

Subsequently, those businesses that survived the initial culling continue to operate in tough economic conditions where demand for their goods and services is substantially reduced, as people have less money to spend.

The drop in domestic consumption over a sustained period will inevitably cause many companies and businesses to go bust (or into receivership). Although high interest rates are aimed at reducing inflation, the real cost for Pakistan is high unemployment, destruction of businesses, stifled innovation and a dramatic decline in economic growth. One of the few organisations that recently posted profits included private commercial banks as they were able to profit from both the depositor and the borrower.

Interest rates aside, Pakistan has also had a bitter experience historically with devaluation. Being a net importer country with a weak manufacturing base, its government recently collaborated with the state bank over devaluing the Rupee. This was primarily done to address Pakistan's balance of trade. This is where the state actively discourages the import of goods and encourages the export of domestic goods. By devaluing the Rupee, the Pakistani government increased the costs of manufacturing inputs, which caused havoc in the agricultural, textile and other sectors that were already reeling from the policy of high interest rates. Hence, the high cost of borrowing together with the increase in manufacturing costs rendered many industries and companies unable to compete internationally. Unable to find buyers for their expensive products, key exports declined and Pakistan's balance of payments deteriorated. This was further compounded by the continued import of basic food stuffs. Despite being the fourth largest agricultural economy in the world, Pakistan is a net importer of foodstuffs. This means it requires Pakistan to pay more for its food imports (after devaluation) thus causing domestic food inflation to greatly rise. In recent years, food inflation has been made worse by the declining value of the Dollar and the Pakistani Rupee's peg to the dollar. To conceal the failure of its devaluation policies, the Pakistani government has relied more and more on expatriate remittance and the export of domestic staple foods to boost Pakistan's balance of payments. The latter is particularly cruel for the Pakistani population, as in a desperate bid to earn foreign exchange and improve the balance of payments, the Pakistani government exports much needed staple foods such as rice and wheat, which leads to shortages at home. The hard earned foreign exchange is not re-invested back into the domestic economy, but is repatriated in the form of debt service payments to strengthen foreign economies. Thus, the Pakistani government is forced to borrow from international institutions to redress a shortfall in its balance of payments. Therefore Pakistan's pursuance of high interest rates and devaluation has failed to curb inflation and stimulate growth.

Strangely enough the economic measures implemented by the present government are at odds with the practitioners of capitalism in the West. In the West, very low interest rates are deemed mandatory to stimulate economic growth in the current financial climate. But in Pakistan, the opposite is considered necessary. The discrepancy is not due to Pakistan's own economic considerations, but is due to the government's continued subservience to international lenders, especially to the IMF and other such like institutions.

The economic policies followed by Pakistan, the West and the world in general, are based on free market principles, which were first advocated by Adam Smith in his famous book 'The Wealth of Nations' published in 1776. Today, economists called neo-liberals such as the late Milton Friedman and his colleagues at the University of Chicago elaborated on Smith's work and the works of other neo-classical economists such as Menger, Jevons and Warlas to develop an aggressive understanding of how the free market should function today. In their view, the most efficient way to run markets is to transfer control of public property to individuals, with the role of the government limited to providing a stable free-market only. Governments should not regulate markets and state intervention in the market is abhorred. This became the corner stone of modern day economic thinking and was the force behind 'Thatcherism' in the UK and 'Reaganomics' in the US. Later, it was used as an economic policy prescription for third world countries and was made part of the Washington Consensus in 1989 by the economist John Williamson. Hence, deregulation of markets, privatization of public and state utilities, trade liberalisation, monetary control via interest rates, floating exchanges etc. became synonymous with the concept of free markets.

The free market idea is conceptually flawed. This is because wealth is never equally possessed by people and this impacts their ability to purchase goods and services from the market place to satisfy their needs. In practice, those who have huge amounts of wealth enjoy permanent access to the market and are able to purchase any type of property (basic as well as luxurious). On the opposite end of the spectrum, many people do not have the means to purchase a loaf of bread to eat, or a piece of cloth to hide their nakedness. Hence, governments around the world are forced to intervene and provide assistance to such people. Moreover, in the aftermath of global economic crisis in 2008, governments ignored free market principles and interfered to nationalise banks and corporations. Thus, Western governments became owners of private properties— a clear contravention of free market principles! Hence the concept of a truly free market is unworkable in practice and as for the idea: "The idea that markets are always right was a mad idea,"[114] declared the French President, Nicolas Sarkozy in 2008.

Solutions to Pakistan's economic problems lie in Islam. Some of these practical solutions are as follows:-

1. The money supply should be based on a bimetallic standard such as gold and silver. This will reduce the volatility in the prices of goods and services and give Pakistan's economy much needed stability.

2. The Rupee, once buttressed by gold and silver, should be de-pegged from the dollar. This will prevent the debasement of the Rupee and increase its purchasing power. In other words, Pakistan should be

---

[114] "Nicolas Sarkozy calls for overhaul of capitalism", The Telegraph, (September 26, 2008).

able to buy more for less, thereby reducing pressure on the balance of payments.

3.  Pakistan must unilaterally end all forms of usury payments to the IMF, WB and other programmes concocted by the colonialists to destroy the country's economic sovereignty. Additionally, Pakistan should categorically refuse to meet any of its $58.34 billion external debt.[115] This will enable Pakistan to divert circa $11[116] billion earmarked for debt servicing to address the need of Pakistan's poor.

4.  All IMF structural conditions imposed on Pakistan, should be reversed, especially those related to the privatisation of Pakistan's public utilities such as electricity, gas, and banks.

5.  The super-rich in Pakistan should be taxed under emergency tax laws as mandated by Islam. Pakistan's top 30 richest people are worth circa $15 billion and these are only reported figures. A 30% tax will net $5 billion.[117] Thus the money raised through the levy of emergency tax on the wealthy can be used to stimulate Pakistan's ailing industries.

6.  Some of the proceeds collected should be used to boost Pakistan's agricultural output, so that its people can be fed. Any surplus food can be exported or exchanged with other valuable goods. This will also enable Pakistan to circumvent international restrictions.

---

[115] E. Zadi, "Pak external debt mounts to $58.39b", The Telegraph, (February 18, 2011).
[116] This is an estimated figure based on 35% of Pakistan's federal budget of $30 billion for 2011. Another way of looking at Pakistan's debt, are the total debt liabilities (public and foreign) which is 55% of Pakistan's GDP $230 billion. This amounts to $126 billion.
[117] This figure is derived by totalling the net worth of Pakistan's top 30 richest people and levying a 30% tax. I believe the figure to be very conservative as the rich have a habit of concealing their true net worth.

These are just some of the Islamic measures that can be applied to turn the Pakistani economy around. However, these measures are likely to be vehemently opposed by the existing political class who are subservient to the interests of the colonial powers and are captivated by their failed free market economic principles.

A new political system is therefore required to implement these solutions. This system is based on Islam and must be able to implement these solutions. This political system is known as the Khilafah and Muslims must work to re-establish it. Only the Khilafah can guarantee economic self-sufficiency and prosperity.

October 11, 2011

57

# Pakistan's Greatest Crisis is the Country's Incompetent Leadership

> *"How tragic is it that in fifty years, the Pakistani nation could not produce a single leader of political ingenuity and moral and intellectual credibility. What would history say that only wicked people, most corrupt and egomaniac and indicted criminals became its leaders – an insult to the idea of Islamic Pakistan, if you can think rationally."*
>
> *--Dr Mahboob Khawaja*

Today the people of Pakistan face a myriad of challenges that threaten the country's very existence. This includes: American threats of unilateral action beyond the tribal area and its efforts to seize the country's prized nuclear assets, the Indian backed insurrection in Balochistan, a dramatic increase in suicide bombs, and the economy in tatters. But perhaps, the most significant issue that has blighted the nation is the leadership vacuum that pervades all segments of society.

A manifestation of this horrible void is the all too familiar troika tussle between the Pakistani army under the ignoble leadership of Kayani, Zardari's reprehensible government, and the pseudo independent judiciary headed by Chaudhary. Those that cling to the vain hope that Pakistan's Tehrike Insaaf (PTI) is no panacea to leadership crisis have numerous reasons to be disappointed in the current antics of the PTI. Consider the most obvious—PTI's recruitment policy of flooding its ranks with ex-Musharraf cronies, and other sleazy politicians (footstools of America) to supersede sincere PTI workers in a desperate bid to win the upcoming general election. If Imran Khan could so easily forgo the party's ideal of meritocracy in favour of nepotism, and treat his own workers unfairly then one can only imagine what Imran Khan's 'corruption free' Pakistan would look like.

Politicians are not the only culprits. Military top brass, bureaucratic big-wigs, industrialists and civic leaders are just as guilty of putting themselves ahead of Pakistanis. Put it another way, all have either abdicated responsibility or simply buried their heads in the sand. The only thing common amongst the nation's leaders is the beseechment of foreign powers. Politicians, unashamed of courting American and British officials, frequently plan and execute trips to Dubai, London and Washington for even the smallest of issues.

A large proportion of them, openly desire servitude to Western powers and shamelessly promote their interests. Then there are the pseudo-Islamist politicians, whose contributions to date include none other than adding corruption to the political landscape, legitimizing the abhorrent actions of the rulers and destroying the confidence of the public in political Islam. The behaviour of the military top brass is equally callous. Kayani, like his fraudulent predecessors, has moved heaven and earth to secure American interests in Pakistan. The indiscriminate slaughter of Pakistanis at the robotic hands of blood-thirsty American drones taking off from Pakistani airbases; the farcical response of the Pakistani army to the Abbotabad attack are some of his noteworthy accomplishments.

The business community and industrialists are not exempt from this critique. History bears testimony that they are content to be bedfellows with any government—civilian or military—as long as the tax bill is kept to a minimum and they are granted immunity from loan defaults. When the achievements of the business community is measured in terms of transfer of technology and contribution to the nation's self-sufficiency they score naught. In sum – Pakistan's leadership since its inception in 1947 has repeatedly failed to emancipate Pakistan from the intellectual, political and economic subjugation of colonialist powers.

The root cause of Pakistan's leadership predicament can be attributed to a single factor – namely the continuation of the economic and political system left behind by the British – later amended by the US. This system has meticulously cultivated a plethora of civilian and military leaders who were defeated, corrupt and infatuated with the West. In their eagerness to serve Western powers—Western solutions were relentlessly borrowed and applied to all walks of Pakistani life. The cut and paste mentality was bound to fail, as the adopted solutions were disconnected from the problems of Pakistan and opposed to the beliefs and cultural values coveted by the people. Consequently, Pakistan witnessed years of turmoil and polarization which has reached a tumultuous climax today.

The only salvation for Pakistan is for a new dynamic Islamic leadership to take the reins of power and reverse Pakistan's decline. This leadership must be radically different from the past and cannot be an existing player in the nation's corrupt systems and institutions. It must possess an acute sensation of the problems of Pakistan and an ideological vision that reflects the beliefs and values of the people. It must eschew violence, but be bold enough to lead the masses to a comprehensive revolt against the present secular order and raze all vestiges of Western domination. The West has already described this political trend as the movement to re-establish the Khilafah.

February 3, 2012

58

# The Balkanization of Pakistan: Is Balochistan the Next to Cede?

*"In particular, there is a general acknowledgement that Pakistan will very likely continue to be destabilized and ultimately collapse. What is not mentioned in these assessments, however, is the role of the military and intelligence communities in making this a reality; a veritable self-fulfilling prophecy."*

*--Andrew Gavin Marshall*

Recently, some senior American politicians have initiated efforts to support the separation of Balochistan from Pakistan. Californian Republican, Dana Rohrabacher is leading the campaign for Pakistan's dismemberment, and he has been joined in this crusade by fellow Republican Congressmen Louie Gohmert and Steve King. On February 18, 2012, the three Republican politicians tabled a bill before congress that stated that Balochistan is currently divided between Pakistan, Iran, and Afghanistan with no sovereign rights of its own, the resolution explained that "in Pakistan especially, the Balochi people are subjected to violence and extrajudicial killing," and therefore, the Balochi people "have the right to self-determination and to their own sovereign country; and they should be afforded the opportunity to choose their own status."

The three politicians are not alone in fomenting a new assault on Pakistan's territorial sovereignty. Earlier, on February 8, 2012, the US subcommittee on 'Oversight and Investigations of the House Committee on Foreign Affairs' convened a hearing on the extrajudicial killings and human rights situation in Balochistan. Rohrabacher who chaired the meeting invited retired Lieutenant-Colonel Ralph Peters, to testify. Lt. Col. Peters was the architect of the infamous 2006 - New Middle East map and is a passionate advocate for the disintegration of the Muslim world along sectarian and religious fault lines. His map shows the truncation of a number of Muslim countries (including Pakistan) truncated. Speaking before the committee Peters said, "We need to ask honestly why Balochis are not entitled to a Free Balochistan, why the Pashtuns—despite their abhorrent customs—are not entitled to a Pakhtunkhwa for all Pashtuns, why forty-million Kurds aren't entitled to a Free Kurdistan..."

The US government on the other hand was very quick to distance itself from the Congressional hearing conducted by Rohrabacher and from Peters' testimony. The spokesperson for the US State Department Victoria Nuland said, "Our view on Balochistan has not changed. We are aware of this hearing. As you know, Congress holds hearings on many foreign affairs topics. These hearings don't necessarily imply that the US government endorses one view or another view. I'd underscore that the State Department is not participating or involved in this hearing."[118] However, denials from the US government do not square well with overwhelming evidence that the US through its think tanks, non-governmental organizations, US sponsored websites and dubious Balochi movements are instigating a domestic uprising in the Balochistan province.

Way back in 2006, the eminent US think tank Carnegie Endowment for International Peace published a report titled, "Pakistan: The Resurgence of Baloch Nationalism". The report highlights the rich natural resources of Balochistan and then makes the case to use Balochi rebels against Islamabad and Tehran. Furthermore, the US State Department-funded National Endowment for Democracy (NED) and the Voice of Balochistan (VOB) have been instrumental in fomenting dissension and nationalistic feelings. NED has been funding the Balochistan Institute for Development (BIFD) which claims to be the leading resource on democracy, development and human rights in Balochistan, whereas the VOB on the

---

[118] "US govt distances itself from Balochistan hearing", Dawn News, (February 10, 2012).

other hand, has been active in carrying propaganda messages on behalf of the American government. Also, there is the Balochi Society of North America, which openly carries messages of support from Rohrabacher. Over the past few years, the US has also been pressing Pakistan to allow it to open a consulate in Quetta, which is the capital of Balochistan. No doubt the consulate is central to US plans to have eyes and ears on the ground to execute its nefarious intentions against Pakistan.

Yet despite all these obvious signs that America has an open hand in orchestrating nationalistic sentiments in Balochistan, the leadership (both civil and military) of the country refuses to accept this narrative and considers America its friend and continues to maintain its unstinting support to Washington.

Have these leaders forgotten that this is the same America that abandoned Pakistan during the 1971 war with India, which resulted in Pakistan's dismemberment? And the same was repeated after the withdrawal of the Soviets from Afghanistan, which resulted in millions of displaced Afghans seeking refuge in Pakistan. This is the same America that has repeatedly invaded Pakistani sovereignty since September 2001. Not forgetting the slaughter of thousands of innocent Pakistani citizens through drone strikes, the humiliation of the army during the US Abbotabad operation, the release of Raymond Davis, and the innumerable losses in economic activity and international trade that are some of the ridiculous features of this lopsided relationship.

America's relationship with Pakistan has not only weakened the country, but has strengthened its arch rival India. The plight of the Kashmiri people has all but been forgotten and Pakistani leaders are eager to strike a deal that retains India's domination of Kashmir. Thanks to America, Pakistan now faces a hostile Western border that is dotted with Indian consulates that pose an impending mortal danger to Pakistan. What the Pakistani rulers will not admit to is that they have helped America transform Pakistan into the new Balkans of Asia, and they have known this all along. For instance, former Pakistan High Commissioner to UK, Wajid Shamsul Hasan admitted that Pakistan is slated to become a "failed state" by 2015, "as it would be affected by civil war, complete Talibanisation and struggle for control of its nuclear weapons[119]." Rather than opposing this trend the rulers of Pakistan are complicit with America in Balkanizing the country. Allah (swt) says in the Qur'ān:

*"And never will Allah (swt) grant to the unbelievers a way (to triumph) over the believers."*

[TMQ An-Nisa:141]

They have lost their moral compass, betrayed the Pakistani people and have chosen a path to please America. Surely they lead a life of misery.

*"But whosoever turns away from My Message, verily for him is a very distressful life."*

[TMQ Taha:124]

The only way for the Pakistani people to keep Pakistan's integrity intact and away from the evil intentions of America and other major powers is to forge their unity on the basis of the Qur'ān and Sunnah alone. Allah (swt) says:

*"And hold fast, all of you together, to the rope of Allah (swt), and do not separate."*

[TMQ Al-Imran:103]

The practical way to accomplish political unity is by working for the establishment of the Khilafah Rashida. Only then will the people of Pakistan find unity and peace.

April 20, 2012

---

[119] Quoted by former Pakistan High Commissioner to UK, Wajid Shamsul Hasan, Times of India, (February 13, 2005).

# 59

## Pakistan's Marriage with America is Unsustainable

*"They believe they have been let down by the leadership across the board, that they do not believe that the government is a truly independent government."*

---*Tariq Pirzada*

Recently, two decisions have come to epitomize the corruption and the inaptitude of the Pakistani elite to lead their people away from the precipice of crisis and chaos that has engulfed the country. Both the civil and military leaderships bear equal responsibility for putting the country on the path of self-destruction and ignominy.

Firstly, President Asif Ali Zardari's decision to nominate Raja Pervez Ashraf – popularly known as 'Raja Rental'—as Prime Minister underscores the determination of the civilian leadership to continue with the rampant corruption and incompetence that has become the mainstay of his government. Raja Rental was famously derided by both his peers and the Pakistani public for his miserable record as the Minister of Water and Power. During his tenure Pakistan suffered incessant power shortages and black outs. Rather than reprimanding him and banishing him from the government, Zardari rewarded Raja by officially appointing him as the Minster of Information Technology.

However, allegations of misuse of power and sleaze never left his side, and most probably elevated his importance to Zardari, so much so, that Raja Rental eventually landed the top job and became Prime Minister Gilani's successor. Mr. Gilani you will recall was unceremoniously dismissed by the Supreme Court for refusing to entertain corruption allegations against Zardari.

Thus the never ending saga of rampant corruption was not only set to continue, but was given a huge boost when Raja Rental created the unnecessary position of the Deputy Prime Minister and gave it to Chaudhry Pervaiz Elahi — the grand daddy of political sleaze. The position was created as part of a power sharing deal brokered between Zardari of PPP and the Chaudhry brothers of PML (Q). Chaudhry Pervaiz Elahi was once an arch nemesis of Zardari, but now they are bedfellows in a hideous corruption team that includes 'Mr 10%', Raja Rental and the Chaudhry of sleaze.

Secondly, the Chief of Army Staff (COAS) Kayani, anxious not to be left behind, mounted his own campaign to go down in the history books as Pakistan's most corrupt and subservient general. After putting up with eight months of nominal resistance to American demands to reopen NATO supply lines, the COAS all of a sudden capitulated. In return, Pakistan received an apology from Clinton— which was not meant to be an apology but a mere expression of regret—for killing Pakistani troops and no extra cash for the delivery of supplies to NATO forces as initially demanded. This incident was touted as a diplomatic victory for Pakistan, but people were truly left bewildered by the development and wondered why had Kayani provided the means for NATO to accelerate the sharpening of knives to dismember Pakistan?

As for America, she was quick to shower praise on her stooges and hoped for greater subservience to her interests. On July 1st, 2012, the US Secretary of State Clinton called Prime Minister Raja Rental and said that she hoped US-Pak relations would improve further during his tenure. A week later, Clinton expressed her hope for better relations with the military. She said, "We want to use the positive momentum generated by our recent agreement to take tangible steps on our many shared, core interests."[120] Obviously, this means more drone strikes, greater incursions by US troops

---

[120] "Clinton looks for better US-Pakistani cooperation", Dawn News, (July 8, 2012).

and an escalation of Pakistani military operations against militants opposed to America's occupation of Afghanistan. Many Pakistanis are now wondering how all of this is going to help them.

With America showcasing and supporting Pakistan's corrupt leaders, the Pakistani public is becoming increasingly anti-American. According to a new poll released a few weeks ago by the Pew Research Centre, about 75% of Pakistanis regard the US as an enemy. Three years ago, 64% of Pakistanis surveyed said they viewed America as an enemy. A growing number of Pakistanis also feel that improving relations with Washington isn't a major priority, the poll found. Furthermore, around 40% of Pakistanis surveyed said that they thought that US economic and military assistance actually had a negative effect on their country. Only 12% said they believe that economic assistance from Washington helps solve Pakistan's problems. The same poll found that Muslims in Pakistan wanted a greater role for Islam in political life. Pakistanis turning towards Islam to adopt alternative solutions to the current milieu is an ominous sign for America and Pakistan's leadership.

America on her part is either oblivious to this trend due to her arrogance, or somehow thinks that she can carry on calling the shots despite the apparent wavering of her primacy. There is no doubt that the present model is unsustainable, even if Pakistan did somehow manage to divorce America. It is only a matter of time before the Pakistani people opt for an Islamic state, and America along with her surrogates will be banished from the country.

July 23, 2012

# 60

## America's Failure in Afghanistan Spells the End of the West's Dominance in Eurasia

*"The West has already failed in Afghanistan, just as the Soviets failed in the 1980s and the British way back in the nineteenth century."*

*--John Humphrys*

After having fought for more than a decade in Afghanistan, America has yet to show any considerable gains for its brutal occupation. Nonetheless, there are some diehard American strategists who beg to differ, and argue that America has achieved its primary objective, which was to establish a few military bases in Afghanistan to counter Russia, China and the future Khilafah state for the eventual supremacy over Eurasia. But, even this lofty ideal when measured against the reality on the ground appears too remote to be categorized as a useful accomplishment. On the contrary, the rampant instability in Afghanistan not only puts into jeopardy the viability of such strategic objectives, but more importantly raises questions about how long America can afford to stay stuck in the Afghan quagmire and continue to post failure after failure.

Clues about this very prospect were provided at the NATO summit convened in Chicago back in May 2012. Speaking about America's ubiquitous nemesis the Taleban, Obama candidly admitted that they were a hardened opponent and whatever gains NATO had made could easily be undone. He said, "The Taliban is still a robust enemy, and the gains are still fragile. But think about it. We've been there now 10 years. Ten years in a country that's very different, that's a strain, not only on our folks but also on that country, which at a point is going to be very sensitive about its own sovereignty."[121] Just how much time does the world's lone super power need with all of its sophisticated weaponry to defeat a rag tag army of no more than 25,000 or so? America has assembled under its supervision 400,000 soldiers—not to mentions the tens of thousands of private contractors— on both side of the Afghan-Pakistan border, and after several years of warfare it is still unable to crush them. Outgunned and outmanned the Taliban are definitely proving to be more than a robust enemy.

Equally unfathomable is that it has taken several years for the US to accept the fact that NATO is not only fighting the Taleban but also the Afghan people. The reference to "be very sensitive about its own sovereignty" is an admission by President Obama that NATO faces a popular resistance which cuts right across ethnic fault lines and trumps traditional tribal loyalties.

Another fiasco of America's Afghan war is its exorbitant cost, which has placed a huge toll on the defence budget and this has been further exacerbated by the economic crisis of 2008. America has spent circa $550 billion on the Afghan war since 2001. Other NATO member states like Britain have spent in the region of $20 billion. Yet despite squandering billions of dollars of tax payers' money, NATO has very little to show. Karzai's government is corrupt to the core and hated by ordinary Afghans. Karzai's writ does not extend beyond parts of Kabul, and if it does exist elsewhere, it is totally reliant on foreign forces. According to some estimates Taliban controls around 80% of Afghanistan and this probably explains why it is so difficult for NATO to hold on to territorial gains. All attempts to co-opt the Taliban into a political solution have also failed. The Financial Times summed West's sorry state: "Five years ago the Americans were refusing to speak to the Taliban. Now the Taliban are refusing to speak to the Americans. That is a measure of how the balance of power has shifted in Afghanistan. The Western intervention there has failed." Added to this

---

[121] "President Obama's Press Conference", CNN Transcripts, (May 21, 2012).

is the human toll on NATO forces, which cannot be quantified in monetary terms. So it came as no surprise to find that the joint communiqué issued at the end of the Chicago summit expressed the collective desire of all the NATO countries to draw the curtain on their Afghan misadventure. The statement read: 'After 10 years of war and with the global economy reeling, the nations of the West no longer want to pay, either in treasure or in lives, the costs of their efforts in a place that for centuries has resisted foreign attempts to tame It'[122]. Allah (swt) says:

*"Indeed, those who disbelieve spend their wealth to avert [people] from the way of Allah (swt) . So they will spend it; then it will be for them[source of] regret; then they will be overcome. And those who have disbelieved - unto Hell they will be gathered."*

[TMQ Al-Anfal:36]

Whilst 2014 (a date revised several times) is the final withdrawal date for most NATO countries, America and her junior partner Britain, both steeped in arrogance, have still not learnt their lesson and plan to stay beyond this date. But the writing is on the wall; America and NATO are heading for a catastrophic defeat and no matter how hard they try to dress up their failings their only success will be to unite and embolden Afghans along with their brethren across the border in Pakistan to claim the scalp of Pax-Americana and deal a devastating blow to NATO's first ever mission in Eurasia.

*"On that Day shall the believers rejoice- With the help of Allah (swt), He helps whom He will, and He is Exalted In Might, Most Merciful."*

[TMQ Al-Room:4-5]

July 24, 2012

---

[122] "NATO Agrees on Afghan Security Transition in 2013", New York Times, (May 21, 2012).

**61**

# Karimov Supported by the West and Russia Commits a Heinous Crime

*"Uzbekistan's dictator is another Gaddafi-in-waiting. Realism is one thing, but the United States can't be afraid to call the devil by his name."*

*--Tom Malinowski*

To most people, Islam Karimov—the ruler of Uzbekistan, is viewed as a brutal dictator, responsible for the massacre of thousands of innocent people in Andijan in 2005. Away from the bloody suppression of his people, Karimov and his henchmen are renowned for carrying out inexplicable acts of torture on political prisoners that routinely leave victims dead, or scarred for life. Now another atrocious crime can be added to Karimov's catalogue of evil acts committed against his people.

Recently, the BBC reported that Karimov has been running a secret campaign to sterilize women without their knowledge or consent. Speaking on a condition of anonymity from Tashkent, an Uzbek gynaecologist revealed to the BBC details of the programme. She said, "Every year we are presented with a plan. Every doctor is told how many women we are expected to give contraception to; how many women are to be sterilized. There is a quota. My quota is four women a month."[123] The programme is not confined to the capital and is operational in other parts of the country, most notably in the Ferghana Valley and the Bukhara region—both of which are the hotbed of Islamic revival.

The first case of sterilization was reported in 2005, and in 2007 it was brought to the attention of the UN. Then the United Nations Committee

---

[123] "Uzbekistan's policy of secretly sterilising women", BBC News, (April 12, 2012).

Against Torture (CAT) reported forcible sterilizations and hysterectomies in Uzbekistan, but little notice was taken and the matter was quickly forgotten, until now. Given the regime's fondness for secrecy it is difficult to estimate how many women have been robbed of their God given right to have children, however the numbers probably run into tens of thousands. In 2010 the Expert Working Group (EWG) which consists of independent experts conducted a survey of medical professionals based in Uzbekistan, and collated evidence of some 80,000 sterilizations. The numbers are likely to be much larger as both medical professionals and victims often conceal the facts for fear of reprisal from Karimov's henchmen.

But the real question to ask, is why Karimov has resorted to such a heinous act against defenceless women who pose no obvious threat to his regime or to the longevity of his reign. For those who subscribe to Thomas Robert Malthus's theory about population control, Karimov's actions are easy to explain. In fact, Karimov would find himself in the company of distinguished Western thinkers who ardently support vile means to curb population growth.

There is another sinister motive that lurks deep within Karimov's cursed soul. It causes him much distress and is the foremost of his adversaries. This nemesis is political Islam that not only threatens to extinguish Karimov's rule, but also the combined hegemony of both the West and Russia in the region. Having tried all the means available, Karimov has invoked sterilization of Muslim women as a desperate measure to fight the growth of political Islam that has now enveloped Uzbekistan into a renewed frenzy of Islamic revival, and is slowly but surely edging its way to the establishment of the Islamic State. For this reason alone, both the West and Russia have overlooked Karimov's barbaric acts and in particular, the West has made their coveted standard of human rights inapplicable to the plight of Uzbeks. Furthermore, they have bolstered his regime with money, weapons and experts to discover innovative ways to halt the growing tide of Islamic revival in the country.

Have not Karimov and his masters pondered on the circumstances surrounding the birth of Isa and Musa? Have they not reflected on how the tyrants of that age, King Herod and Pharaoh used all their might and wealth to extinguish the light of Allah (swt) and resorted to the killing of male babies to safeguard their kingdoms? Both of these ancient tyrants concocted sterilization programmes of their own—and in the end, both failed to prevent the message of Allah (swt) from reaching their peoples. Allah (swt) says in the Qur'ān about the disbelieving tyrants:

*"They wish to extinguish the light of Allah (swt) with their mouths, but Allah (swt) will not agree except that He will perfect His light, even though the Unbelievers may detest (it)."*

[TMQ Al-Tawba:32]

Likewise, Karimov and his masters will be unable to prevent the sons and daughters of the Muslims of Uzbekistan from carrying the Islamic dawah to every city, town and village. By Allah (swt)'s permission no corner of Uzbekistan will be left untouched by the Islamic revival and every government official and associate of Karimov will hear the call for restoring the Khilafah and tremble with fear.

*"Allah (swt) is the master of His affair, but most people do not know."*

[TMQ Yusuf:21]

April 20, 2012

# 62

## Americans Pay to Shield the Architects of Torture

*"If you're an American president who wants to promote a pro-torture policy, there are two rules you must follow. First, call it something else. Second, don't leave a mark."*

--*Civil Liberties*

Not too long ago, it was reported that the CIA used $5 million dollars[124] worth of American tax payers money to pay legal fees in order to protect two of its employees accused by the federal government of torturing suspects. Psychologists Jim Mitchell and Bruce Jessen are infamous for having invented the brutal interrogation programme that employed water boarding—a form of drowning, and is classified as torture in America. Additionally, Mitchell and Jessen personally subjected suspects to water boarding inside secret prisons administered by the CIA. It is the first time those who carried out this horrific torturing technique have been publicly identified.

Internationally the US has supported the outlaw of torture and is a signatory to the Convention Against Torture and Other Cruel, Inhuman or Degrading Treatment or Punishment, which was signed by President Ronald Reagan on April 18, 1988 and then later ratified by the Senate on October 27, 1990. The main elements of the definition of torture contained in the convention are:

1. The intentional infliction or threatened infliction of severe physical pain or suffering.

---

[124] "The CIA secretly agreed to pay $5million to shield the architects of its water-boarding programme", Daily Mail, (December 17, 2010).

2.  The administration or application, or threatened administration or application, of mind altering substances or other procedures calculated to disrupt profoundly the senses or the personality.

3.  The threat of imminent death.

4.  The threat that another person will imminently be subjected to death, severe physical pain or suffering, or the administration or application of mind altering substances or other procedures calculated to disrupt profoundly the senses or personality.

Hence, it is quite evident even to a layman, that water boarding constitutes torture. Indeed in 1947, the United States thought the same and prosecuted a Japanese civilian who had served in World War II as an interpreter for the Japanese military and engaged in water torture. Yet despite these public pledges and aversion to water boarding, America saw nothing wrong in using this form of torture against al Qaeda suspects in the aftermath of September 11, 2001. For instance in 2002 Mitchell and Jensen flew to Thailand and water boarded Abu Zubaydah 83 times. Furthermore, the Bush administration upheld the technique as instrumental in thwarting terror attacks despite the illegality of such views. Writing in his memoirs Bush said, "We DID use water boarding... because it saved the lives of many Americans."[125]

Such glaring violations of international law and breach of the American constitution are the norm when it comes to prosecuting America's war against Islam— poorly disguised as a war against terror. Prisoner abuse and the torture of detainees in Abu Ghraib, Bagram and Guantanamo are well documented, as is the extrajudicial torture and killing of unarmed civilians in Iraq and Afghanistan. In fact, so rampant is the torture and abuse of

---

[125] "'We DID use waterboarding... because it saved the lives of many Americans, George Bush defends 'torture' of terror suspects", Daily Mail, (November 9, 2010).

Muslims at the hands of the American crusaders that it belies America's claim to be the bastion of freedom and human rights.

In contrast, Islam stipulates that prisoners of war should be treated kindly. In general, prisoners of war must be treated with compassion, where the aim is to win them over to Islam. In the Qur'ān, Allah (swt) says:

*"And they give food, in spite of their love for it (or for the love of Him), to the Miskeen (the poor), the orphan, and the captive,(Saying): 'We feed you seeking Allah (swt)'s Countenance only. We wish for no reward, nor thanks from you."*

[TMQ Al-Insaan:8-9]

Ibn Katheer said: "Ibn 'Abbaas said: in those days their prisoners were mushrikeen; on the day of Badr the Messenger of Allah (SAW) commanded them to be kind to their prisoners, so they used to put them before themselves when it came to food... Mujaahid said, this refers to the one who is detained, i.e., they would give food to these prisoners even though they themselves desired it and loved it."[126]

In another example, after Al-Kamil defeated the Franks during the Crusades, Oliverus Scholasticus praised the Islamic laws of war, commenting on how Al-Kamil supplied the defeated Frankish army with food[127]. He said, "Who could doubt that such goodness, friendship and charity come from God? Men whose parents, sons and daughters, brothers and sisters, had died in agony at our hands, whose lands we took, whom we drove naked from their homes, revived us with their own food when we

---

[126] Hasan Abi'l-Ghuddah, "Ahkaam al-Sijn wa'l-Sujana' wa Mu'aamalat al-Sujana' fi'l-Islam", p257.
[127] Judge Weeramantry, and Christopher G. Justice without Frontiers. Brill Publishers. pp. 136, (1997).

were dying of hunger and showered us with kindness even when we were in their power."[128]

By Allah (swt)'s leave, when the Khilafah returns it will set a benchmark in how wars are fought and how prisoners of war and non-Muslims in general are treated.

December 21, 2010

---

[128] *Ibid,69 at pp 136-137.*

63

# The Pentagon is a Conveyor Belt for Hatred and Enmity Towards Islam

*"We are not at war with Islam."*

-- *US President Barrack Obama*

It was only last month that Pentagon officials repeatedly implored Pastor Terry Jones not to burn copies of the Qur'ān fearing that Jones's inflammatory action could arouse Muslim sentiments and endanger the lives of US soldiers serving in Afghanistan and elsewhere. Yet, a month later the Pentagon managed to outdo the bigotry of Terry Jones and had been caught red handed for spearheading America's crusade against Islam and seeking its total annihilation. Lt Col Matthew Dooley, who was responsible for conditioning hundreds of US officers with a distorted view of Islam, said in one of his presentations: "We have now come to understand that there is no such thing as moderate Islam...It is therefore time for the United States to make our true intentions clear. This barbaric ideology will no longer be tolerated. Islam must change or we will facilitate its self-destruction."[129]

One does not have to look very far to discover the depth and breadth of the Pentagon's enmity towards Islam. In Afghanistan, the US war machine's vilification of Islam is a routine occurrence. This includes the cowardly act of burning the Holy Qur'ān by bigots within the American military. Elsewhere, US troops playfully urinated on dead Afghans and took great pleasure in mutilating their dead bodies. Not forgetting the horrific

---

[129] R. Devereaux, "Anti-Islam teachings 'widespread' in US law enforcement, campaigners warn", The Guardian, (May 11, 2012).

abuse of prisoners in Bagram, the rape of young girls and mindless civilian massacres have become the hallmark of America's malicious crusade in Afghanistan. No matter how hard the US tries to downplay its efforts to indoctrinate its soldiers to hate Islam, these vitriolic incidents, the latest episode is a vivid reminder to the rest of the world that barbarism and not emancipation from tyranny is the hallmark of America's policy in the Muslim world.

It is a well-known fact that wherever in the Muslim world America's military intervenes it leaves behind a trail of death and destruction—a reputation unworthy of a leading nation that also prides itself on tolerance. Look, for instance, at the indiscriminate killings of unarmed civilians by the US drones and Special Forces in Pakistan, or the immunity granted to Raymond Davis for his cold blooded murder of Pakistanis in broad daylight. This clearly undermines America's penchant for promoting human rights it so evangelically preaches to the rest of the world. Take America's war in Iraq: The cruel humiliation of Iraqi prisoners at Abu Ghraib and the senseless killing of unarmed civilians in Haditha are portent reminders about the fruits of America's Iraqi occupation. Yet, despite such barbaric acts perpetrated by USA's military, its soldiers are lavished with praise and their crimes against humanity are overlooked. At the end of last year, President Obama told the troops coming home from Iraq: "As your Commander-in-Chief, and on behalf of a grateful nation, I am proud to finally say these two words—welcome home."[130]

Worse still, there are no serious efforts by America's political establishment or senior officers to change the uncivilised conduct of US troops. Wherever they are stationed, the Pentagon immediately seeks immunity from prosecution as a mandatory condition in exchange for

---

[130] H. Cooper, "Obama praises troops as he ends the war he opposed", New York Times, (December 14, 211).

security pacts or military aid. In other words, there are no repercussions for the evil acts committed by US soldiers against indigenous populations.

If by chance a US soldier is found guilty, sham trials are convened by the US military (the conclusion of Haditha massacre trial early this year) to ensure that punishment does not fit the crime. The US military goes to great lengths to instil savagery within its ranks by making certain that this kind of behaviour is institutionalised. The recent National Defence Authorisation Act passed by the US Senate epitomises such measures, which legalises sex with animals and permits sodomy.

As the US military is committed to preserving its barbarian code and despicable values, one can only imagine what type of training the US military imparts to nations around the globe. So, what is the root cause behind such reckless behaviour that defies human logic? The explanation that "a few rotten apples" are to blame is no longer plausible and does not merit a discussion. Nor can America's military culture institutionalised by the Pentagon, be held solely responsible for nurturing a generation of young men and women who show scant respect for foreign cultures and people.

On the contrary, the military culture is based on the very foundations that the rest of American society is built upon. The sole driver for such behaviour is freedom, which is the bedrock of USA's cherished ideals and is responsible for shaping popular culture, corporate culture, social values and ethics. It is on this very basis that the military in Western countries, especially in America, is responsible for moulding the attitudes of its military personnel.

Men and women, fed from a young age on a diet of freedom enlist in the army as defenders of freedom, undergo weapons training and are eventually deployed overseas. Here, they find themselves in a different environment; laws and restrictions of the home country no longer impinge on what one can say and do, and the weapon in their possession makes them feel that they can finally say and do whatever they desire. Naturally, the indigenous populations' beliefs, values, property, life and dignity are quickly trounced upon—all in the name of freedom.

Freedom is a fanciful idea and always leads to disputes and violence. The West claims that individuals are free to do whatever they choose and indoctrinates within its populace the desire to be free. But, in practice, this leads to unending conflicts amongst the people, as the views expressed by a few, or the behaviour exhibited by some, can be interpreted as offensive and insulting to others. Hence, the Western governments are persistently intervening in disputes and resort to severity of the law to protect the freedoms of some people by depriving others of their freedom to express thoughts and behave in a certain way.

Often, the real benefactors of freedom are those individuals or groups whose views or conduct coincides with the interests of the government, or the powerful capitalists who possess the ability to exert influence over the government. So many institutions, including military establishments in the West, are given free rein to attack Islam because their fiery rhetoric and discriminatory policies are in full harmony with the West's unfinished war on Islam. However, if the Western media, or its numerous institutions, were to insult Jews or the Zionist state of Israel, the Western governments would swiftly adopt stern measures to restrict their insults.

Islam does not believe in the whimsical idea of freedom, where a handful of men decide which thoughts and behaviours are legally beyond censure, and which thoughts and practices are subject to criticism and can be tried in a court of law. Islam stipulates that life, honour, blood, property, belief, race and the mind are to be protected by the Islamic State. All the citizens of the Khilafah are guaranteed these rights, irrespective of whether they are Muslim or non-Muslims.

Islam also protects the rights of non-Muslims to worship without any fear of retribution, or vilification of their beliefs. The Messenger of Allah (SAW) said:

"One who hurts a Dhimmi, he hurts me and the one who hurts me, hurts Allah (swt)." Therefore, it is prohibited for a Muslim to insult the beliefs of a non-Muslim, spill their blood, harm their places of worship and desecrate their property.

The Islamic history is unrivalled in its capacity to guarantee the religious rights of non-Muslims under the shade of the Khilafah. At the time of Umar ibn al-Khattab, the Islamic army conquered Syria, but quickly returned the Jizya[131] collected from Homs, a town inhabited by Christians and Jews. The Muslims reasoned with the non-Muslims that they were returning the money as they were unable to protect their life, blood, honour and property from the regrouping Roman Army. So impressed were the non-Muslims that they said: "We like your rule and justice far better than the state of oppression and tyranny in which we were. The army of Heraclius we shall indeed, with your 'amil's' help, repulse from the city." The Jews rose and said: "We swear by the Torah, no Governor of Heraclius shall enter the city of Homs, unless we are first vanquished and exhausted!" Saying this, they closed the gates of the city and guarded them.[132]

If America's military really wants to reach out to the Muslim masses and win their hearts and minds, the very least it can do is to radically alter the indoctrination of its military officers by representing a more balanced view of Islam that is fully inclusive of the Khilafah and Islam's contribution to human civilisation. Perhaps the Pentagon's trainers can draw on the writings of Bernard Shaw who said, "I have always held the religion of Muhammad in high estimation because of its wonderful vitality. It is the only religion which appears to me to possess that assimilating capacity to the changing phase of existence which can make it appeal to every age. I

---

[131] Jizya is a tax applied within the Khilafah on adult non-Muslim males who have the capability to pay.
[132] Al-Baladhuri, "The Battle of the Yarmuk (636) and after",(1972).

have studied him—the wonderful man and in my opinion far from being an anti-Christ, he must be called the Saviour of Humanity."[133]

Or more recently from one of America's leading business personalities, Carly Fiorina who said, "There was once a civilization that was the greatest in the world. It was able to create a continental super-state that stretched from ocean to ocean and from northern climes to tropics and deserts. Within its dominion lived hundreds of millions of people, of different creeds and ethnic origins...its military protection allowed a degree of peace and prosperity that had never been known. The reach of this civilization's commerce extended from Latin America to China, and everywhere in between. ..While modern Western civilization shares many of these traits, the civilization I'm talking about was the Islamic world from the year 800 to 1600, which included the Ottoman Empire and the courts of Baghdad, Damascus and Cairo, and enlightened rulers like Suleiman the Magnificent."[134]

Failing to conduct root and branch revision of the educational curricula for the US military and indeed for many of America's institutions will only reinforce the impression in Muslim minds that America is hell bent on the destruction of Islam. Americans like to use labels such as extremists and moderates to describe the Muslim world, yet they are oblivious to the fact that they are being held hostage by a small group of neo-con extremists, who are unwavering in their determination to terrorise another civilisation in America's name.

May 14, 2012

---

[133] Quote from Sir George Bernard Shaw found in "The Genuine Islam," Vol. 1, No. 8, (1936).
[134] "Technology, business and our way of life: What's next", Hewlett-Packard Company Website, (September 26, 2001).

# 64

# Breivik's Mentality Shaped by the West's Dislike for Islam

*"Breivik an exemplary product of Western decadence."*

*--Richard Millet*

The despicable nature of the attacks in Norway have laid bare Europe's deep seated hatred towards Islam and seriously belittles one of the main tenets of Western values – religious freedom. Breivik's vilification of Islam is not just an isolated event as the Western media would like to portray. On the contrary, Breivik's demagoguery and Islamophobic views are a product of Western civilization that resonates with many in the West. This could be clearly seen in the way the Western media and her 'experts' quickly branded Islam and Muslims for the attack.

Spurred on by this media frenzy against Islam, several Muslims in Norway were physically assaulted. Mehtab Afsar, Secretary General of the Islamic Council of Norway, said, "We heard some Muslims had already been beaten up in Oslo, and women who were scared phoned me asking for help."[135] The attacks against Norwegian Muslims only abated when the true horror of the terror crimes committed by the Christian fundamentalist, Anders Behring Breivik emerged.

Nevertheless, this did not prevent some European politicians from publicly expressing support for Breivik's anti-Muslim views. Jacques Coutela, a member of France's right-wing National Front party wrote: "The reason for the Norway terror attacks: fighting the Muslim invasion, that's what people don't want you to know."[136]

---

[135] "Whose wake-up call is outrageous Oslo massacre?", Today's Zaman, (July 31, 2012).
[136] "Italy MEP backs ideas of Norway killer Breivik", BBC News, (July 27, 2012).

Coutela also called Breivik: "the main defender of the West." In Italy, Francesco Speroni, a leading member of Italy's Northern League and an ally/partner in Berlusconi's conservative coalition, said "Breivik's ideas are in defence of Western civilization". Also, European parliamentarian Mario Borghezio told Il Sole-24 Ore radio station, "Some of the ideas he expressed are good, barring the violence. Some of them are great."[137] This is not the first time Italian politicians have endorsed disparaging remarks directed towards Islam. A few years ago, Italy's Defence Minister, Antonio Martino[138], praised Fallaci, who wrote a book entitled 'Anger and Pride' in which she described Muslims as 'vile creatures who urinate in baptisteries' and 'multiply like rats'.

No doubt such views are a conveyor belt towards radicalization, which eventually leads to the shaping of the Western government's domestic policy against Muslims. The banning of hijab, the restriction on building of mosques, the blatant spying upon Muslim communities and the incarceration of Muslims without trial are just some of the draconian measures taken by Western governments.

The West claims that individuals are free to worship whatever deity they choose. But in practice, this leads to perpetual conflicts amongst people, as religious beliefs and practices professed by some can be interpreted as offensive and insulting to others. Hence, Western governments are constantly intervening in the disputes and resort to legislation to protect the religious rights of some people while at the same time depriving others. Often, the real benefactors of freedom of religion are those individuals, or groups, whose beliefs coincide with the interests of the government, or those who possess the ability to exert influence over the government. That is why so many institutions in the West are allowed to attack Islam: their fiery rhetoric and discriminatory policies are in full harmony with the West's

---

[137] *Ibid.* 77

[138] R. Carroll, "Liberal voice of Italy savages 'Jew-hating' Left", The Guardian, (June 2, 2012).

unfinished war on Islam. However, if the Western media, or its numerous institutions, were to insult Jews or the Zionist state of Israel, Western governments would swiftly adopt stern measures to restrict their insults.

Likewise, Western governments manipulate religious freedom as part of their foreign policy agenda to either pry open societies closed to Western values, or totally ignore religious freedom when it does not concur with their interests. In the case of the Arab uprising and the massacre of Muslims at the bloody hands of Western agents, the West has chosen to water down its response, as the protestors are avid supporters of Islam and not democracy. Such hypocrisy only serves to underscore the perception amongst Muslims that the America and Europe are solely interested in the utter destruction of Islamic values and practices.

Islam on the other hand, does not believe in the fanciful idea of freedom of religion, whereby a handful of men decide which beliefs are legally beyond reproach and which beliefs and practices are subject to unfettered criticism and legislation. Islam stipulates that life, honour, blood, property, belief, race and the mind are to be protected by the Islamic State. All the citizens of the Khilafah are guaranteed these rights, irrespective of whether they are Muslim or non-Muslims. Islam also protects the rights of non-Muslims to worship without any fear of retribution or vilification of their beliefs. The Messenger of Allah (SAW) said: "One who hurts a Dhimmi, he hurts me and the one who hurts me, hurts Allah (swt)". Therefore it is prohibited for any Muslim to insult the beliefs of a non-Muslim, or to damage their places of worship. Islamic history is unrivalled in its ability to guarantee the religious rights of non-Muslims under the shade of the Khilafah. One only has to look at Spain and Palestine, to find that in the past Jews and Christians lived peacefully with Muslims.

As for Muslims living in the West or residing in the Muslim world, they must redouble their efforts to support the re-establishment of the Islamic state. For only the Islamic state is capable of protecting the rights of

Muslims, whether they choose to live within the confines of the state or outside it. Until the very last days of the Khilafah, the rights of the Muslims were protected. During the rule of Sultan Abdul Hamid II, France decided to stage a play, which depicted the life of the Messenger of Allah (SAW) in a derogatory manner.[139] On hearing this Sultan Abdul Hamid II complained to the French government to put an immediate end to the play. The French government defended its decision to hold the play by citing free speech. But when Sultan Abdul Hamid II threatened France only then did she relent.

August 7, 2011

---

[139] C. E. Bosworth, 'A Dramatisation of the Prophet Muhammad's Life: Henri de Bornier's "Mahomet"' , Numen, Vol. 17,p. 116, (Aug., 1970).

## 65

# Norwegian Bombing a Death Blow to European Multiculturalism

*"Multiculturalism is dead."*                                        *--Horst Seehofer*

T
he horrific slaughter of 85 people by the Norwegian Anders Behring Breivik has surely closed the door on Europe's multiculturalism experiment. Media reports indicated that Breivik was opposed to multiculturalism and Islam. However, in the immediate aftermath of killings, it was difficult to distinguish between the Western media's rant against Islam and Muslims and Breivik's abhorrent views. Europe's tirade against multiculturalism and its failure to accommodate Muslims is not new.

Earlier this year, David Cameron launched a devastating tirade against 30 years of multiculturalism in Britain. He warned that multiculturalism was incubating extremist ideology and directly contributing to home-grown Islamic terrorism. He said, "We have failed to provide a vision of society [to young Muslims] to which they feel they want to belong. We have even tolerated segregated communities behaving in ways that run counter to our values. All this leaves some young Muslims feeling rootless. And the search for something to belong to and believe in can lead them to extremist ideology."[140]

Cameron is not the only European leader critical of multiculturalism. In October 2010, Angela Merkel, the German Chancellor, unequivocally declared: "The approach of saying, 'Well, let's just go for a multicultural

---

[140] "Prime Minister David Cameron has delivered a speech setting out his view on radicalisation and Islamic extremism.", The British Prime Minister's Office, (February 5, 2011).

society, let's coexist and enjoy each other,' this very approach has failed, absolutely failed."[141] Merkel's remarks came soon after Thilo Sarrazin's diatribe against multiculturalism.[142] In August 2010, then a board member of Germany's central bank, Thilo condemned multiculturalism and claimed Germany's intelligence was in decline because of Muslim immigrants.[143] Elsewhere in Europe, boisterous voices are reverberating in the corridors of power warning about dangers of multiculturalism. And all too often, Muslim adherences to Islamic values in Western societies are cited as demonstrative examples of the failure of multiculturalism.

The rallying cry against the concept of multicultural societies extends beyond European shores. On September 29th, 2010, Australia's former Prime Minister John Howard said, "This is a time not to apologize for our particular identity but rather to firmly and respectfully and robustly reassert it. I think one of the errors that some sections of the English-speaking world have made in the last few decades has been to confuse multiracialism and multiculturalism."[144] He further added that some sections of society have gone too far in accommodating Muslim minorities.

In America, the daily assault on multiculturalism by conservatives and other right wing politicians is polarizing American communities and is accentuating tensions between Americans and Muslims. The plan to build a mosque close to ground-zero is just the latest manifestation of this struggle. Clearly then, multiculturalism as envisaged by its proponents has failed to deliver what it was supposed to do, i.e., protect groups or communities against intolerance and discrimination perpetrated by society or dominant groups.

---

[141] "Merkel: Multiculturalism has 'failed'", CNN Top blog spot, (November 13, 2010).
[142] "Why Sarrazin's Integration Demagoguery Has Many Followers", Spiegel International, (September 6 2010).
[143] *Ibid. 82*
[144] S. Tandon, "Former Australia Prime Minister John Howard Attacks 'Multiculturalism'", The Jakarta Globe, (September 29, 2010).

Concepts like multiculturalism and diversity signify that in liberal democracies coexistence can be fostered between different groups without the erosion of their respective identities or cultural norms. However, these concepts although widely employed in the lexicon of modern political philosophy are not new. Rather they are derived from one of the main pillars of Western liberal political thought called pluralism. Like other Western concepts, the origin of pluralism is firmly rooted in the birth of secularism. Back then, some philosophers were incensed at the manner by which various Christian denominations were forced to assimilate and conform to the standards and virtues mandated by the papacy.

They endeavoured to safeguard the religious practices of such groups by campaigning for greater tolerance and leniency to be shown to them by the rest of society and other dominant groups. Initially, this meant that such groups were spared physical punishment and financial penalties. However, they were barely tolerated, and were subject to torrents of racial abuse, extreme discrimination, and forced exclusion from different facets of society. For instance, they were denied employment, precluded from educational institutions, suffered from restrictions on travel movements, etc.

But as time passed, other thinkers sought to extend the boundaries of pluralism and pressed for weaker groups to be granted greater opportunities to express their religious and cultural identity in all aspects of societal life, besides the designated areas of worship. In some cases, the thinkers managed to convince the state to extend protection against persecution of a group's cultural identity and race, and remove impediments to employment previously barred. Hence over the centuries, the concept of pluralism underwent progressive elaboration by Western philosophers and thinkers, as well as selective application by Western States. Despite numerous revisions and reviews, divergent views over pluralisms meaning, its applicability and value to society still persist. Some advocate that pluralism should be limited to a mere tolerance of a group's cultural identity and nothing more. Others equate pluralism with the right for diverse groups to freely express and celebrate their cultural identity without fear and restrictions imposed by society or dominant groups.

Towards the middle of the last century, the labour crisis in Europe spurred an influx of immigrants to European shores. Attempts by Europe to absorb people from numerous diverse cultural and ethnic backgrounds posed a number of challenges to the cohesiveness of their respective societies—chief amongst them were housing, marriage, education, health care, welfare benefits and employment. Tensions frequently surfaced between the indigenous populations and the immigrants, as both competed for limited resources. During this period, several thinkers and a handful of politicians criticized the inability of Western governments to assimilate immigrants. They suggested alternative solutions to preserve social cohesion based on pluralism, and advocated cultural diversity under the guise of integration.

In 1966, Roy Jenkins, a British politician, presented a new pluralistic vision for Britain. He said, " I do not think we need in this country a 'melting pot' which will turn everybody out in a common mould, as one of a series of carbon copies of someone's misplaced vision of the stereotyped Englishman… I define integration therefore, not as a flattening process of assimilation but as equal opportunity, coupled with cultural diversity, in an atmosphere of mutual tolerance."[145] This became known as Jenkins formula and was widely employed by policy makers to establish guidelines and laws for multiculturalism.

Over the next 40 years, pluralism or multiculturalism—as it came to be widely known—was introduced in almost every aspect of life; so much so that indigenous populations perceived immigrants and other minority groups to enjoy greater benefits than themselves. Subsequently, relations between the host and immigrant communities rapidly deteriorated, many

---

[145] "Integration and cohesion in Europe: An Overview", Institute for Strategic Dialogue.

questioned the wisdom behind multiculturalism, and some even went as far as calling for its abolition. Therefore, even before the events of September 11, 2001, multiculturalism which was coveted as a panacea for social cohesion was an abject failure.

Multiculturalism or pluralism is a whimsical idea that is conceptually flawed and unworkable in practice. This is because pluralism encourages groups to promote their cultural identity irrespective of their political influence or financial strength. Naturally, the strongest group uses its political prowess and financial muscle to persuade politicians to define legislation, which vigorously defends and endorses their culture and values at the expense of other groups. Additionally, the most powerful group manipulates the media and the educational establishments to actively promote its culture, which leads to widespread acceptance amongst the indigenous population. In this way, the strongest group's culture becomes indistinguishable from the state's culture. Weaker groups find themselves culturally squeezed, discriminated against, and in conflict with the state. Such groups are coerced by both the state and society to dilute their cultural identity to fit in. Those groups that refuse to temper with their cultural identity are ostracized and consigned to live in ghettos. In extreme cases, they are expelled from the host nation, like what happened to the Roma gypsies in France.

What the Norwegian incident illustrates is that the preoccupation of mainstream society to stigmatize Muslims has provided ample opportunity for other marginalized groups to implant their ideas and attract new recruits to their detestable ideologies. One must wonder how many other home grown right-wing extremists lurk in European cities waiting to pounce against their governments and fellow citizens, whilst politicians struggle to replace multiculturalism with other fad ideas like assimilation, and integrations that will no doubt lead to the same result.

July 25, 2011

**66**

# The West, Russia and China are United in their Hostilities Towards Muslims

*"No. The West is really not concerned about the human cost. They want any of the Arab or Muslim states weakened, and if they can be destroyed, and if they can pit the various ethnic and religion communities against each other, they can just sit back and watch as Syria will be destroyed much like the way Iraq was."*

*--Edward Corrigan*

It is absolutely shocking to observe major powers struck by an apparent bout of paralysis in their approach to prevent the massacre of Muslims in Syria and Burma. What makes their stance even more abhorrent is that some of them passionately espouse human rights and have made it the epicentre of their civilization, but have conveniently overlooked such lofty ideals where Muslims are the victims. The outgoing international war envoy Kofi Annan epitomized the collective inaction at the UN when he said, "Syria can still be saved from a worse calamity."[146] Is not the massacre of 20,000 Syrians enough to mobilize the collective global consciousness to prevent the tyrant Bashar Al Assad from mercilessly slaughtering his people on a daily basis?

Equally hard to fathom for any sane person is the indifference displayed by major powers to stop the callous killing and the whole-sale slaughter of Muslims in Burma. This apathy has allowed the so called peaceful Buddhist monks to develop an incredulous appetite for spilling Muslim blood, debasing Muslim women and ostracizing Muslim communities.

---

[146] K. Annan, "My departing advice on how to save Syria", Financial Times, (August 2 2012).

Incidentally, these are the same monks that are held in high esteem in Western capitals because of their recent struggle to bring democracy; however, their ugly crimes perpetrated against Muslims have apparently gone unnoticed.

Yet for several years now, major powers have been fully aware of the persecution of Muslims in both Syria and Burma. The evil nature of Assad's regime and the wickedness of the Burmese military junta are vividly etched in the annals of history. In 1982 the world watched in utter silence as the butcher Hafiz Al-Assad bombed the city of Hama and killed 30,000 people including women and children. Likewise, the world has chosen to muzzle its voice concerning the extermination of Rohingya Muslims in Burma. The very same UN that has meticulously portrayed itself as a bastion of peace and security described the Rohingya Muslims as the most persecuted community in the world, and refers to them as the Palestine of Asia. It is documented that in 1962 the Burmese military junta began its programme of ethnic cleansing, which continues with unabated ferocity today.

Should we as Muslims be surprised by the conduct of major powers and the demeanour of the UN? Take for instance the five permanent members of the United Nations Security Council (UNSC) and their unstinting oppression of Muslims. America's history is steeped in soiling the earth with the blood of innocent Muslims through wars of attrition, coups, sanctions, covert operations and invasions. One only has to look at America's vicious terror campaign against Muslims in Iraq, Somalia, Afghanistan, Pakistan and Yemen to get a sense of her scorn towards Muslims. Whereas the old colonial powers—Britain and France have spilt the largest amount of Muslim blood through the partition of India and the war of independence in Algeria. Both powers still persist in their hostilities against Muslims, and are at the forefront of many campaigns with their crusading partner America.

Russia and China are just as guilty. Russia has tried to conceal the killing fields of Chechnya by giving the region's capital Grozny a makeover. China continues to subjugate Muslims of Xinjiang under horrific conditions and purposefully denies them their basic rights. These crimes against humanity have not diminished in the slightest their thirst for Muslim blood and their desire to see Islam destroyed. Allah (swt) says:

*"Oh you who have Iman! Do not take for intimate friends from among others than your own people. They will not fail to corrupt you. They only desire your ruin: Rank hatred has already appeared from their mouths: What their hearts conceal is far worse. We have made plain to you the Signs, if ye have wisdom."*

[TMQ Al-Imran:118]

Furthermore, such acts have emboldened other countries to commit treacherous acts against their Muslim populations. Israel continues to oppress Palestinians and India—West's newfound darling—has outdone her protagonists by turning Kashmir into the world's largest prison.

Clearly then there is one standard for the Muslim world and another standard for the rest. In short, the major powers have declared an open season on Muslims everywhere and are avid enemies of Islam. Allah (swt) says:

*"Verily, Satan is an enemy to you: so treat him as an enemy. He only invites his adherents that they may become Companions of the Blazing Fire."*

[TMQ Fatir:6]

Oh Muslims! After all of this it is not befitting for you to seek the help of the major powers or beseech their politicians to lift the aggression against fellow Muslims knowing full well how their governments use international law and the UN to craft solutions that are intended to divide and weaken you. Allah (swt) says:

*"Oh you who have Iman! Choose not My enemy and your enemy for friends. Do ye give them friendship when they disbelieve in that truth which hath come unto you, driving out the messenger and you because ye believe in Allah (swt), your Lord? If ye have come forth to strive in My way and seeking My good pleasure, (show them not friendship)."*

[TMQ Al-Mumtahina:1]

The major powers are not alone in their sheer hatred towards Muslims. They are joined in their crusade to suppress the Muslim masses through their agents in the Muslim world. The enmity of the agent rulers is far worse and deeper in magnitude than compared to their masters. The aim of such rulers is to stand firm together against the Muslim *Ummah* and help their foreign masters protect their interest. Look how they fall over each other to protect the strategic and commercial interests of the foreign powers in Syria and Burma. Their half-hearted condemnations of Bashar and the military junta in Burma do not go beyond finger pointing, empty promises and cheap slogans. They openly forbid the good and encourage the evil. Their hypocrisy towards Muslims knows no bounds. And Allah (swt) says about them:

*"The Hypocrites, men and women, (have an understanding) with each other: they enjoin evil, and forbid what is just, and are close with their hands. They have forgotten Allah (swt); so He hath forgotten them. Verily the Hypocrites are rebellious and perverse."*

[TMQ Al-Tawba:67]

Later this Ramadan you will see them gather in Mecca at the behest of King Abdullah the Custodian of the West's interests in the region. They will feast on lavish banquets, whilst the *Ummah* suffers from oppression and bloodshed. They will deliberate the plight of Muslims in Syria and Burma, but nothing will come of the meeting, unless the major powers decide otherwise. Their real aim is to protect their thrones from the revolution and safeguard the interest of their foreign masters. So do not be dazzled or moved by their speeches. Allah (swt) warns:

*"There is the type of man whose speech about this world's life May dazzle you and he calls Allah (swt) to witness about what is in his heart; yet is he the most contentious of enemies."*

[TMQ Al-Baqara:204]

Oh Muslims! You have already had a major hand in exposing the heinous crimes of Ben Ali, Mubarak, Gaddafi, Saleh and Assad before the world, and now during the nights of Laylal Tul Qadr the time has come to multiply your efforts and work hard for the complete elimination of the non-Islamic systems that shackle you and the agent rulers that eagerly allow the foreign powers to subjugate and abuse you and your Islam. This can only be achieved by working with members of the armed forces to re-establish the Khilafah State and only then will persecution and humiliation in places like Syria and Burma be permanently removed.

The Messenger of Allah (SAW) said, "The Imam is a shield behind which the people fight and are protected." [Sahih Muslim]

And remember the words of your lord as you seek the night of power!

*"If Allah (swt) helps you, there is none to overcome you. And if He abandons you, then, who is there to help you after that? In Allah (swt) the believers should place their trust."*

[Al-Imran: 160]

August 12, 2012

67

# The Capitalist Elite Caused the Global Debt Crisis

*"The world with its billions does not have too many people, but it does have too many in their thousands who think that they are worth a million others."*

*--Daniel Dorling*

The tumultuous performance of the financial markets over the past month has again precipitated fears that the global economy is on the precipice of another disaster. The latest apprehensions stem from Europe's inability to meet its debt obligations and the downgrade of America's debt by Standard and Poors.

Barely a year after European governments and the IMF had lent Greece $156bn[147] to lighten its debt burden, Europe is now embroiled in a new debt crisis. The magnitude of this crisis is such that it threatens to engulf some of Europe's biggest economies such as Spain and Italy. The debt 'contagion' is not limited to Europe alone. Across the Atlantic, America, a country that once boasted a 50 percent share of the world's GDP, controlled 75 percent of the world's gold and once a creditor nation[148], is closer to default after the debt deal agreed by Washington. The convergence of these two debt crises is driving home the point to investors around the world that the longevity of the Anglo-Saxon economic model is nearing its end.

Unsurprisingly, one can witness investors fleeing stock markets and investing in tangible commodities like silver and gold. The latter has already

---

[147] A. Cala, "Portugal could require $107 billion bailout from EU-IMF", The Christian Science Monitor, (March 24, 2011).
[148] "Zionists Pessimistic Impacts on US Economy", Asian Tribune, (August 4, 2011).

surpassed $1900 per ounce, as more and more people realise that fiat money is worthless as central banks around the world continue to debase currencies. There are already indications that the US Federal Reserve may initiate another around of Quantitative Easing – QE 3 to be precise— to stimulate the US economy. This will further debase the value of the dollar, lead to high inflation and contract the US economy. A recipe for economic chaos!

The underlying cause behind the current economic crisis—is yet again— the stubbornness of the super-rich who are unwilling to share their wealth. In the aftermath of the global financial crisis in 2008, the super-rich were able to manipulate governments to undertake key actions and enact laws that legalized the daylight robbery of ordinary citizens. This included:

1. Western governments were quick to bail out debt laden banks, with billions of dollars of tax payers' money. Without any consideration for the laymen, governments adeptly converted the private debt incurred by the super-rich into public debt by moving it off the balance sheet of troubled banks and onto the balance sheet of governments. Hence, government debt increased substantially. For instance, UK debt as a percentage of GDP has gone up from 38% of GDP in 2008 to 89% of GDP in 2011.[149]

2. Western governments also reduced interest rates to historic lows— almost to zero in some countries. This encouraged the super-rich to withdraw their deposits from banks and invest in the stock market for higher returns. Hence, governments had to intervene to capitalize banks. Moreover, it became easy for the super-rich to borrow more money at very low interest rates and invest in the stock market. Naturally, the economy began to stagnate and

---

[149] There are a number of web sites that go into a lot of detail on how UK debt is calculated as a percentage of GDP.

contract, as very little was ploughed back into the domestic economy.

3.  In a further bid to protect the material interests of the super-rich, governments engaged in the printing of money. The money was used to buy government bonds (treasury bills) and corporate stock. Subsequently, stock markets around the world posted huge gains, which gave the public the illusion that an economic recovery was on its way. For instance, the Bank of England had purchased around £165 billion of assets by September 2009 and around £175 billion of assets by end of October 2010. In March 2009, the US Federal Reserve announced $1.2 trillion dollars to purchase assets.

4.  This swiftly led to further devaluation of currencies around the world, and heaped misery on the people through the rapid rise in the price of basic commodities and services, which most could ill afford. In 2011, for example, it took $23.26 to buy what $1 bought in 1913.[150] The super-rich, on the other hand, were shielded from the effects of currency debasement, through their immense wealth and their ability to convert cash into tangible goods.

The measures such as intervening in the markets and capitalizing banks (even owning a stake in them) runs counter to free market economics. But this did not deter the super-rich and their paid servants.

Three years on, the super-rich are again manipulating on both sides of the Atlantic: the political class, the media and the financial institutions collude to defend their wealth at the expense of peoples and nations. For instance, at the heart of Europe's economic woes is in the reluctance of the super-rich to write off debt owed to them by countries like Ireland, Greece, Italy, Spain and Portugal. The super-rich would rather see countries

---

[150] "Inflation Calculator", DaveManuel.com

indebted to them, paying exorbitant interest rates and their respective populations stripped off wealth, than the cancellation of debt payments and a reprieve for indebted countries to recover.

Likewise in America, it is the super-rich that are demanding that the American public must pay for their economic mismanagement and excessive lifestyles. Both the Democratic and the Republican parties compete with one other to protect the interests of the super-rich. On July 31st 2011, the debt deal agreed by both parties cuts fiscal spending, but protects the super-rich from tax hikes. There is no doubt that such a deal will safeguard the wealth of the super-rich, and hurt the majority of Americans. Furthermore, the Republican Party, which represents wealthy capitalists, treated the debt deal as a piece of political theatre and was more interested in hurting Obama's chances of re-election in 2012 by insisting on reducing government spending, which will inevitably hurt the Democrat support base, as the government will be creating fewer jobs. On July 17th, the head of the Democratic Governors Association, Governor Martin O'Malley said, "I think that there is an extreme wing within their party [Republican] who have as their primary goal not the jobs recovery, but the defeat of President Obama in 2012."[151]

Since the rest of the world is dependent on the West's demand for goods and services, and Western financial institutions, billions of people will suffer more than the average Westerner, and the super-rich will continue their robbing spree unabated. Nothing epitomizes this better than the saying of the former US Secretary of State John Foster Dulles, who said, "…somehow we find it hard to sell our values, namely that the rich should plunder the poor."[152] The monopoly of the super-rich over the world's

---

[151] "Democratic Governor: GOP Wants to Hurt Economy to Win in 2012", Fox News, (July 17 2011).
[152] "John Foster Dulles Quote", Quotes Liberty Tree.

wealth, treasures and resources exists only because there is no other ideology to challenge their greed and hegemony.

Islam is the only ideology in the world that categorically forbids the super-rich from hoarding their wealth. It is mentioned in the Qur'ān the translated meaning of which is:

*"And what Allah (swt) restored to His Messenger from the people of the towns - it is for Allah (swt) and for the Messenger and for [his] near relatives and orphans and the [stranded] traveller - so that it will not be a perpetual distribution among the rich from among you. And whatever the Messenger has given you take; and what he has forbidden you - refrain from. And fear Allah (swt); indeed, Allah (swt) is severe in penalty."*

[TMQ Al-Hashr:7]

Only in the Khilafah Rashida will you find the super-rich are unable to hoard and are forced to share their wealth with the people through a variety of economic rules based on Islam. In this way, the citizens of the state are not deprived of the basic necessities of life and have an opportunity to live prosperously. Even non-Muslims recognize the Islamic alternative as the best hope for mankind. Former US Attorney General Ramsey Clark said, "Islam is the best chance the poor of the planet have for any hope of decency in their lives. It is the one revolutionary force that cares about humanity."[153]

September 8, 2011

---

[153] E. Saalakhan, "Five Mistakes of US Policymakers in the Muslim World", Washington Report, (March 1999).

# 68

# Demise of Steve Jobs and the Fall of the West

*"As we look at our own civilization, we should steer clear of the assumption that a gentile decline is all we have to worry about. We should be much more worried about collapse, than decline."*

*--Niall Ferguson*

As Steve Jobs personal biography by Walter Isaacson hits bookshops around the world, a fierce debate rages about his rank amongst America's greatest innovators. President Obama fired the opening salvo when learning about Steve Jobs's (Ibn Jandali) demise. He said, "Steve was among the greatest of American innovators—brave enough to think differently, bold enough to believe he could change the world, and talented enough to do it…The world has lost a visionary. And there may be no greater tribute to Steve's success than the fact that much of the world learned of his passing on a device he invented."[154] For some, however, Steve Jobs has earned the right to be included amongst the world's top inventors. David Ruddock writes: "When history remembers Steve Jobs, it will be not as part of Apple, but as one of the world's great minds. We have lost not just one of the icons of the technological world, but one of the greatest contributors to humanity of the last four centuries."[155]

Americans feel proud about his achievements and given America's domination of the Nobel Prize, there is strong belief that America's pre-eminence in science and technology is set to continue. Indeed, some would

---

[154] "President Obama on the Passing of Steve Jobs: "He changed the way each of us sees the world."
", Whitehouse Blog, (October 5, 2011).
[155] David Ruddock, "Steve Jobs, 56, Co-Founder Of Apple Computer, Has Died",
AndriodPolice.com, (October 5, 2011).

argue that under America's stewardship the West will continue to dominate the globe for years to come. Ambrose Evans-Pritchard states: "The American phoenix is slowly rising again. Within five years or so, the US will be well on its way to self-sufficiency in fuel and energy…Assumptions that the Great Republic must inevitably spiral into economic and strategic decline – so like the chatter of the late 1980s, when Japan was in vogue – will seem wildly off the mark by then."[156] Others point to the dominant role of American popular culture and the pre-eminence of American universities in the provision of education as evidence that America leads the world in thoughts and ideas. For instance, on 15th of August 2011, the English newspaper The Times stated: "US universities continue to dominate the upper echelons of world rankings, taking 17 of the top 20 spots in the Shanghai Jiao Tong ranking." But just how true is the assertion that Western thoughts will enjoy unfettered primacy for the foreseeable future.

Let's examine Western advancement in scientific thoughts. By scrutinising the annals of scientific thoughts over the past four centuries it is quite apparent that scientific discoveries or technical innovations fall into two categories: revolutionary and evolutionary discoveries. Revolutionary discoveries are associated with a step change in the scientific thoughts of a designated discipline. In other words, the discovery of the idea radically changes the fundamental precepts of the subject, and propels innovation and discoveries to new heights; existing limitations on thinking is superseded by a new wave of concepts and ideas. Progress in the subject is by leaps and bounds, and benefit to humanity is immense.

On the other hand, evolutionary discoveries are focussed on the progressive elaboration of the fundamental principles and thoughts about a particular subject. The edifice of the subject remains intact, but the application of basic thoughts crosses existing thresholds, and produces a new body of secondary and tertiary concepts that push the boundaries of

---

[156] "World power swings back to America", The Daily Telegraph, (October 23, 2011).

existing research further and gives newfound impetus to explore fresh lines of inquiry. Advancement is small and the benefit to mankind is of diminutive proportions.

So in physics, its evolutionary moments are many, but its revolutionary moments are very few indeed. Newtonian physics dominated the subject for centuries and was eventually turned on its head by Einstein's theory of relativity. Over a hundred years later, there is yet to be a revolutionary moment (although the recent discovery of neutrinos travelling faster than the speed of light might change this). It was Einstein's theory of relativity and its views on the sub-atomic world that paved the way for the discovery of the computer chip and mobile communication technology. Steve Job's did no more than use computer chips, 3G and WIFI technologies to produce the Apple suite of products such as the iMac, iPhone, iPod and the iPad. The same can be said for other scientific disciplines such as biology, chemistry and others. It can be argued that in the past 100 years or so the discoveries in science and technology are not revolutionary at all; they are merely evolutionary a sort of natural progression.

Leaving aside scientific thoughts, the same classification standards can be applied to other disciplines such as philosophy, literature, sociology, politics, economics etc. Of these disciplines, the subjects of paramount importance are politics and economics, as they have the greatest effect on human thinking and progress, and play a pivotal role in the development of science.

A close inspection of Western economic thinking reveals that two men revolutionized economic theory in the West. The first was Adam Smith who is regarded by many as the father of capitalism. The other is Karl Marx who developed Communist economic theory as an alternative to capitalism. The rest of the economists hitherto have either based their economic works on these two schools of economy or they have amalgamated capitalist and communist principles economic ideas to produce a third way. In sum, their collective efforts to date have only produced evolutionary changes.

Furthermore, although the ideas of Smith and Marx are widely studied, it can be safely said that both are discredited. Communism as an economic model is dead and Smith's free market ideas are facing a catastrophic crisis of confidence. The collapse of Lehman Brothers in 2008 ushered in an epoch of enormous economic turmoil across the globe, exposing the erroneous nature of the 'free market' and inspiring millions to protest against these ideas. Even those who are charged with the responsibility of spreading capitalism to the four corners of the globe candidly admit to its failure. "The idea that markets are always right was a mad idea," declared the French President, Nicolas Sarkozy in the autumn of 2008.[157]

Likewise, the advancement of Western political thought is dominated by a handful of thinkers most—if not all—of whom was present in the enlightenment period. In fact, in the past one hundred and thirty years no one has produced any revolutionary changes in Western political thinking. On the contrary it can be argued that Western political thinking has stagnated over the past century and the West lacks solutions to contemporary political problems. The concepts of nation state, freedom, democracy, international law etc., when applied in practice are found to be flawed and unworkable. The current economic crisis in Europe and the colonial wars in the Muslim world have exposed the fallacy of these ideas. It's not surprising then, that some eminent Western politicians understood the limitations long ago and the erroneous nature of such ideas. Churchill famously remarked: "Democracy is the worst form of government, except for all those other forms that have been tried from time to time."[158]

---

[157] "Nicolas Sarkozy calls for overhaul of capitalism", The Telegraph, (September 26, 2008).

[158] Excerpt from House of Commons speech given by Churchill, (November 11, 1947).

Hence, the demise of the West has been long in the making. Its political and economic thoughts are gradually losing credibility amongst the people of the world and dying a slow death. As a countermeasure, the West is left with no other option but to employ force, both at home and abroad, to ensure that the elite who benefit from it retain their hegemony over other people and nations. Once the political and economic thoughts are discredited and abandoned, scientific progress will also come to a halt. The demise of the Soviet Union is an apt example of when people abandon an ideology, scientific advancement comes to a standstill.

So which nation will take the helm of the leading state after America is dislodged from its perch and Europe follows suit? Some advocate China, Brazil and India as the up and coming nations to lead mankind. But this view is short sighted and lacks thorough analysis. The question is not which nation will lead mankind, but which ideology will lead mankind in the 21st century. China, Brazil and India are fast embracing the very same Western thoughts that are discredited and responsible for West's demise. Hence, the problem is one of thoughts and ideology, not people.

Islam is the only true ideology that is capable to lead humanity today. It has a proven track record of leading mankind in all walks life for over a thousand years, and it produced revolutionary thinking for well over five hundred years, as long as the people exercised *Ijtihad*.[159] The Islamic *Ummah* was blessed with an abundance of revolutionary thinkers, a feat unparalleled in the history of civilisations. Much of the inspiration and guidance responsible for the great Islamic thinkers of history was Islam's prophet and messenger, Mohammad . He is considered to be the greatest leader, thinker, strategist and teacher of all time. He left behind the Qur'ān and the Sunnah, so that generation after him would continue and implement the message of Islam. This is what one of the most renowned thinkers of the 20 century had to say about him. "The world much needs a man with

---

[159] *Ijtihad* is a process where a Mujtahid (one qualified to carry out *Ijtihad*) derives a divine rule by extracting it from the divine texts in relation to a problem.

Muhammad's bright thinking. I believe that if a man like Mohammad's calibre were to assume the dictatorship of the modern world he would succeed in solving its problems in a way that would bring it the much needed peace and happiness: I have prophesied about the faith of Muhammad that it would be acceptable to the Europe of tomorrow as it is beginning to be acceptable to the Europe of today." — [George Bernard Shaw].

November 22, 2011

## 69

# The waning of America's Global Domination and the Coming Khilafah

*"The fall of America doesn't have to be a complete collapse — it is, after all, a country that has managed to reinvent itself many times before. But today it's no longer certain — or even likely — that everything will turn out fine in the end."*

*--Der Spiegel*

The world as we know it is embroiled in a protracted political crisis that threatens to reshape the existing political order for decades to come. At stake, is the fate of two political systems that are inextricably linked and are slowly unravelling on opposite sides of the globe.

In the West, the mighty EU, once a bastion of stability and power is teetering on the brink of implosion. The Euro-debt crisis that has engulfed the European continent threatens to unleash dark forces of nationalism that have remained dormant for over six decades.

In the East, the Arab world enslaved by the autocratic regimes implanted by the old European colonialist powers are falling like dominoes and unveiling forces of change that are dynamic and untested.

These events, when seen through the lens of optimism, are interpreted positively by some: Europe will emerge stronger and more united than before and the Arab world will be transformed into an oasis of liberty and democracy. When viewed through the prism of realism, a completely different picture emerges. The post-modern European experiment is fast coming to an end and the Arab world is finally freeing itself from the vicious shackles of colonialism by dislodging pro-Western autocratic regimes. The demise of both political systems is no accident and is tied to America's global decline. In many ways, the political systems of Europe and the Arab world are a product of American hegemony and ingenuity.

The Marshall Plan provided the edifice for America to control Europe's propensity for war and curb her ambitions to seek and maintain colonies abroad. Post World War II, American leaders sought to diminish Europe's domination of the world. As the historian John Lumberton Harper put it; US President Roosevelt wanted "to bring about a radical reduction in the weight of Europe" and thereby make possible "the retirement of Europe from world politics."[160]

Under the shadow of American economic aid and security architecture, Europe, ravaged by war, charted a new route towards postmodernism—a break from the warring nation state which had consumed the continent in the past. Eventually, the EU was born, where nationalism was finally suppressed and national sovereignty gave way to a transnational authority that presided in Brussels. Europeans marvelled at their postmodern creation and touted it as the 'natural evolution from the nation state model'. A foremost proponent of this model, Robert Cooper (an advisor to former Prime Minister Tony Blair), said, "The postmodern system in which we Europeans live does not rely on balance; nor does it emphasise sovereignty or the separation of domestic and foreign affairs. The EU has become a highly developed system for mutual interference in each other's domestic affairs, right down to beer and sausages…It is important to realise what an extraordinary revolution this is."[161] However, the birth of the postmodern state came at a cost. The EU was no position to challenge America's supremacy in the world and lost many of its colonies to the US in the process. America employed several tactics to subdue the EU especially its most powerful member Germany: the enlargement of NATO, the

---

[160] Harper, "American Visions of Europe: Franklin D. Roosevelt, George F. Kennan, and Dean G. Acheson", Cambridge UK, (1996).

[161] "The new liberal imperialism", The Guardian, (April 7, 2002).

expansion of the EU to include new member states and the use of a single currency i.e. the Euro.

Through this approach, America was able to control levers of economic and military power in Europe. This continued until the collapse of Lehman brothers (one of the world largest investment banks), which triggered the onset of the current economic depression. The American financial crisis is the real cause behind Europe's economic and political turmoil. It is precipitating the collapse of the EU, thereby undermining over sixty years of American supremacy over European affairs. Probably, Germany will arise from the EU rubble as a major power, capable of not only thwarting American interests in Europe, but supplanting her as the main provider of peace and security on the continent. The euro-crisis and not Germany's military might, has handed Berlin a carte blanche to cast European politics in its own image.

Another indication is that within the context of European history, the postmodern experience is truly an anomaly. Europe's characteristic disposition is to eschew peace and engage in feudal disputes fuelled by unbridled nationalism and the quest for dominance over other nations.

As for the present day Arab world, it owes much of its political structures and institutions to the old European powers that colonised it. However, after 1945, America emerged as the world's leading state and entered the Arab world with the intention of displacing British and French influence and usurping the abundant oil fields of the Middle East. The US state department described the find as "[the Middle East is] a stupendous source of strategic power, and one of the greatest material prizes in world history."[162]

America had no intention of dismantling the despotic regimes; rather she sought to place her own agents to administer them while making false

---

[162] N. Chomsky, "A Modest Proposal", Znet, (December 3, 2002).

pretences about delivering freedom and democracy around the world. America, armed with the "Truman Doctrine" proceeded to deprive the Arab world freedom from tyranny and the ability to rule for themselves. She covertly buttressed these regimes to keep the Arab population imprisoned and subdued. But in 2011, popular revolts erupted throughout the region that removed a few tyrants and destabilised the political order America had so painstakingly put together over past decades.

Today, the political landscape is no longer dominated by secularists; a new wave of Islamic revival has hastened to fill the void. In Morocco, Tunisia and Egypt, political Islam is on the rise and its dominance permeates the political medium. Most probably Libya and Yemen will follow suit. Nothing epitomises the Islamic trend better than the stir caused by the moderate Tunisian Prime Minister Hammadi Jebali who referred to the present time as "a divine moment in a new state and in hopefully a 6th Caliphate[Khilafah]," and that "the liberation of Tunisia will, God willing, bring about the liberation of Jerusalem."[163] If the moderates possess grandiose designs to resurrect the Khilafah then one can only image what most of the Arab masses yearn for.

The nation state concept is alien to the Arab world and was imported to the region by European powers in the last century. The natural inclination of the Arab masses is to gravitate towards the Khilafah —a political system that kept them united under a single leader for well over a thousand years. And certainly the Arab world is firmly on that trajectory, no matter what the American government contrives to portray.

As America struggles to manage its decline, the fate of two political systems is about to change for good. The world will then return to the pre-1945 model: a multi-polar world, dominated by different centres of

---

[163] S. Ajmi, "Ennahdha Discourse: The Sixth Caliphate or a Misunderstanding?", Tunisialive, (November 16, 2011).

geopolitical influence, with the sleeping giant awakened the Khilafah will be at its helm.

December 08, 2011

# 70

# The Reasons Behind America's Withdrawal from Afghanistan

*"Ironically, I think that many in the Obama administration, many in the Pentagon, some in Congress, as well as in governments allied to the US, have recognized that there's not going to be any military victory in this war."*

*--Phyllis Bennis*

Recently, there has been a lot of coverage about America's planned exit from Afghanistan, which is scheduled to take place at the end of 2014. Hence, it would be good to review whether America has changed its strategic vision for Afghanistan or is the withdrawal purely a tactical move. If it is the latter then what are the factors involved in pushing Washington to leave Afghanistan.

So let's begin by recapping the importance of Afghanistan for America. America's strategic goals behind the invasion of Afghanistan are:

1. Prevent Russian and Chinese domination of Eurasia

2. Prevent the emergence of the Caliphate

3. Control the hydrocarbon resources of the Caspian Sea and the Middle East

4. Control the security and the transit of hydrocarbons from the Caspian Sea and the Middle East

This is based on the following evidences:

"Eurasia is home to most of the world's politically assertive and dynamic states. All the historical pretenders to global power originated in Eurasia.

The world's most populous aspirants to regional hegemony, China and India, are in Eurasia, as are all the potential political or economic challengers to American primacy. After the United States, the next six largest economies and military spenders are there, as are all but one of the world's overt nuclear powers, and all but one of the covert ones. Eurasia accounts for 75 percent of the world's population, 60 percent of its GNP, and 75 percent of its energy resources. Collectively, Eurasia's potential power overshadows even America's. A power that dominated Eurasia would exercise decisive influence over two of the world's three most economically productive regions, Western Europe and East Asia...almost automatically control the Middle East and Africa. What happens with the distribution of power on the Eurasian landmass will be of decisive importance to America's global primacy and historical legacy.[164]"

"The US has had the ultimate aim of preventing the emergence of any major power in Eurasia. The paradox however is as follows—the goals of these interventions was never to achieve something—whatever the political rhetoric might have said, but to prevent something. The United States wanted to prevent stability in areas where another power might emerge. Its goal was not to stabilize but to destabilize, and this explains how the United States responded to the Islamic earthquake. It wanted to prevent a large, powerful Islamic state from emerging. Rhetoric aside the United States has no overriding interest in peace in Eurasia. The United States also has no interest in winning the war outright...the purpose of these conflicts is simply to block a power or destabilize the region, not to impose order.[165]"

There is no dispute between the Republican Party and the Democratic Party over these strategic goals. Consequently, there are no competing visions between Bush and Obama in foreign policy matters over this region of the world.

---

[164] Zbigniew Brzezinski, "A Geostrategy for Eurasia", Foreign Affairs, (October 1997).
[165] G. Friedman, "The next 100 years, a forecast for the 21st Century", (2009).

The difference between the two parties is related to operational strategy i.e. how to legitimise America's occupation of Afghanistan and retain some semblance of stability, so that Washington can pursue the aforementioned strategic goals. The operational strategy has been the constant source of dispute between Bush and Obama governments, as well as between officials within the Obama administration. The operational strategy has changed several times, but despite successive revisions under Obama, the strategy has settled on four key objectives. These are:

1.  Increase the capacity of the Afghan government to establish its writ over the country. This means building the Afghan security forces, police and army, appointing competent and loyal governors and minimizing corruption in the Afghan government.
2.  Destroy al-Qaida and those Jihadis amongst the Pashtuns opposed to US occupation.
3.  Encourage moderate Taliban fighters to defect and join the central government.
4.  Enlist the help of NATO, Pakistan, Iran, India, Russia, China and other states to participate with the US in solving Afghanistan's problem in a regional context— more of a multi-lateral approach to addressing the challenges posed by Afghanistan.

There is no question that America has struggled to achieve the forgoing operational strategic objectives, and therefore under Obama and his allies there is intense realisation that Afghanistan is no longer winnable i.e. it cannot be stabilized as set out by the objectives of the operational strategy. There are several factors that have caused America to reconsider its position in Afghanistan. These are:

**International factors**

1.  In 2008, in the aftermath of the collapse of Lehman Brothers, the global financial system came under extreme pressure and almost collapsed. This had a profound impact on the economies of

America and Europe to finance wars and intervene in countries abroad.

2.  America's wars in Afghanistan and Iraq have exposed the strains in America's military. Simply put. America is facing "military over reach" and cannot maintain its current level of military commitments abroad. Washington is under intense pressure to reduce its military foot print to a manageable level.

3.  Since its intervention in Iraq in 2003, America is no longer the super power it used to be, and is facing increasing pressure from other major powers like Russia, Britain and France in different parts of the world. In the Asian Pacific, America is increasingly worried about the emergence of China, which Washington fears if left unchecked Beijing will challenge its hegemony in the Asian Pacific region. Graham Fuller former vice chairman of the National Intelligence Council in 2006 described the challenge faced by America from its adversaries. He said, "In the last few years, diverse countries have deployed a multiplicity of strategies and tactics designed to weaken, divert, alter, complicate, limit, delay or block the Bush agenda through death by a thousand cuts. That opposition acts out of diverse motives, and sometimes narrowly parochial interests, but its unifying theme usually unspoken is resistance to nearly anything that serves to buttress a unipolar world.[166]"

The combination of international factors has had a profound impact on America foreign policy in two areas over the last year or so:

A. America has spent circa $550 billion on the Afghan war since 2001. Furthermore, successive budgetary cuts in the military have rendered it difficult for America to fight wars on multiple fronts. This has placed a huge toll on the defence budget. In January 2012, The New York Times in

---

[166] "Strategic Fatigue", National Interest, (2006).

an article entitled "Panetta to Offer Strategy for Cutting Military Budget" stated:

"In a shift of doctrine driven by fiscal reality and a deal last summer that kept the United States from defaulting on its debts, Mr. Panetta is expected to outline plans for carefully shrinking the military — and in so doing make it clear that the Pentagon will not maintain the ability to fight two sustained ground wars at once. Instead, he will say that the military will be large enough to fight and win one major conflict, while also being able to "spoil" a second adversary's ambitions in another part of the world while conducting a number of other smaller operations, like providing disaster relief or enforcing a no-flight zone."

So America, which once boasted about its ability to fight two simultaneous wars, finally admitted that it could only fight one.

B.   America is now forced to prioritise on which wars it wants to fight. America is faced with multiple challenges and has to cope with wars in Iraq and Afghanistan, and also prepare for war against China in the Asian Pacific, as well as the Middle East. Nonetheless, it is China's dramatic rise that is worrying American policy makers the most. In March 2012, the Congressional Research Service prepared a report for US Congress entitled "Pivot to the Pacific? The Obama Administration's "Rebalancing" Toward Asia". In the report, it clearly states:

"Underlying the "pivot" is a conviction that the centre of gravity for US foreign policy, national security, and economic interests is being realigned and shifting towards Asia, and that US strategy and priorities need to be adjusted accordingly. For many observers, it is imperative that the United States give more emphasis to the Asia-Pacific. Indeed, for years, many countries in the region have encouraged the United States to step up its activity to provide a balance to China's rising influence."

The reduction of America's military footprint in Afghanistan and Iraq, and the repositioning of its military and naval forces in the Asian Pacific signals that America is treating China with utmost importance, and if the need arises, Washington is prepared for military confrontation. This is known as Obama's Pivot to Asia strategy—re-balancing of US interests from Europe and the Middle East toward East Asia.

## Regional factors

There are three regional factors that have complicated matters for America to forge a durable solution to the stability of Afghanistan.

• NATO led by Europe has resisted numerous American attempts to get more engaged in the occupation of Afghanistan. Ever since the commencement of NATO operations in Afghanistan under the guise of International Security Assistance Force in 2003, certain European countries have been reluctant to put their troops and assets in harms way. Belgium, Italy, France and Germany have all invoked specific caveats that allow them to place their troops in quieter areas of Afghanistan. Subsequently, NATO summits have failed to redress this issue, and America has found it difficult to carry on with the burden of the Afghan war considering its priorities have changed. In 2012 at Chicago, NATO countries finally accepted to draw the curtain on their Afghan misadventure. The statement at the summit read:

"After 10 years of war and with the global economy reeling, the nations of the West no longer want to pay, either in treasure or in lives, the costs of their efforts in a place that for centuries has resisted foreign attempts to tame it.[167]"

• America failed to get Pakistan to mobilise more troops to conduct military operations in the tribal area, especially North Waziristan. This is despite

---

[167] "NATO Agrees on Afghan Security Transition in 2013", New York Times, (May 21, 2012).

that fact that its agents Zardari and Kayani, and those in the political medium worked tirelessly on the behalf of their master to make the case for greater involvement.

• India also made it difficult for America to succeed in Afghanistan. New Delhi did this by refusing numerous American requests to reduce hostilities between the common borders of India and Pakistan. Consequently, Pakistan was unable to redeploy troops to its Afghan border and assist America in its plan to subjugate the resistance.

## Local factors

The open tussle between Obama and the military leadership over US troop numbers and the time required to implement the operational strategy, led to General McCrystal's dismissal and greatly served to undermine the morale of US and NATO troops. Furthermore, this further emboldened the Pushtun resistance. US General James Conway, head of the US Marine Corps questioned the withdrawal date. He said:

"In some ways we think right now it's probably giving our enemy sustenance. We think that he may be saying to himself, in fact we've intercepted communications that say, 'Hey, we only have to hold out for so long,'" ... "I honestly think it will be a few years before conditions on the ground are such that turnover will be possible for us.[168]"

The manner, in which US troops conducted themselves, very quickly not only alienated the US from the Afghan population, but increased the ferocity of the resistance against the occupation. These measures included the desecration of the Qur'ān, urinating on dead majhi*Deen*, indiscriminate killing of women and children, employing Tajiks to carry out raids in Pushtun areas, aiding corrupt officials etc.

---

[168] "US General: Afghan deadline 'giving enemy sustenance'", BBC News, (August 24 2010).

In sum the combination of international, regional and local factors have pushed America to abandon aspects of the operational strategy and move towards holding direct talks with elements of the Taleban to seek an honourable exit. However, this does not mean that America has abandoned its strategic vision for Eurasia—it has merely parked it, and Afghanistan in the future will serve as a launch pad.

September 25, 2013

# 71

# Pakistani State is Complicit in US Drone Attacks

*"Despite repeatedly denouncing the CIA's drone campaign, top officials in Pakistan's government have for years secretly endorsed the program and routinely received classified briefings on strikes and casualty counts..."*

*--The Washington Post*

The assassination of Hakimullah Mehsud and the publication of a Pakistani report[169] claiming that only 3% of drone victims are civilians has brought into sharp focus the legitimacy of the drone attacks and the violation of Pakistan's sovereignty. At the heart of the issue is Pakistan's reluctance to take concrete steps to stop drone attacks. In this context Nawaz's latest trip to Washington and his half-hearted protests against US drone attacks killing unarmed civilians smells of hypocrisy.

Consider Pakistan's UN ambassador's condemnation of US drone strikes, when he declared that it was a gross violation of Pakistan's sovereignty and international law. He said, "Killing unarmed, innocent civilians is a clear breach of international law. We call for the immediate cessation of drone attacks inside the territorial borders of Pakistan." Earlier, Pakistan Prime Minister, Nawaz Sharif pleaded at the White House with US President Barack Obama to end drone strikes. He told reporters at the end of his trip that he 'emphasised the need to end such strikes'.

Since 2004, Pakistan's territory has been violated 365 times by American drones. These robotic fixed wing planes have indiscriminately killed thousands of innocent people. According to the Bureau of Investigative

---

[169] "Pakistan says only 3% of drone strike victims were civilians", Russia Today, (October 31, 2012).

Journalism the number of people killed by American drones is estimated to be between 2525 and 3613, this is considerably higher than what has been admitted by the UN, American and Pakistani officials.

Misreporting death figures is not the only item US and Pakistani officials have been accused of. Both inside Pakistan and abroad there is a deep belief that Pakistan's civil and military leadership is collaborating with America to conduct drone strikes. After all, robotic drones —irrespective of their technological sophistication— still require on the ground real-time intelligence to identify, track and confirm kills. This requires an extraordinary level of support and collaboration from the Pakistani state. In the absence of such collusion, American drones would be flying blind and firing way off the mark.

A day after Sharif implored Obama to end drone strikes, The Washington Post published a damning report, revealing that the Pakistani government has for years secretly endorsed the drone strikes and routinely received classified briefings on strikes and casualty counts. The report is based on top-secret CIA documents and Pakistani diplomatic memos. In one quote the paper states: "The documents detailed at least 65 strikes in Pakistan and were described as 'talking point' for CIA briefings, which occurred with such regularity that they became a matter of diplomatic routine. The documents are marked 'top –secret; but cleared for release to Pakistan.

Even present and former Pakistani officials have admitted that Pakistan and US are working in together to launch drone strikes inside Pakistan. In September 2013, Khurram Dastgir-Khan, a senior member of the current government, admitted to the National Assembly that 'tacit support' for US drone strikes by organs of the Pakistan state might be continuing. During an interview in 2013, Pakistan's former President and Army Chief Pervez Musharraf acknowledged that he had given the USA qualified permission[170]

---

[170] "US drone strikes in Pakistan", Amnesty International, (2013).

to undertake some US drone strikes in the Tribal Areas during his tenure, which ended in August 2008. Wikileaks also published details of Pakistani officials consenting to US drone attacks. In 2008, Pakistani Prime Minister Yousaf Raza Gillani personally consented to American drone strikes in Pakistan's tribal areas along the Afghan border to combat the Taliban.

Whilst Nawaz Sharif still likes to deny his involvement in assisting America's drone programme, the joint statement issued after his visit to the Whitehouse only serves to underscore his culpability. The 2500 word statement makes no mention of halting drone attacks, and only makes a fleeting reference to the topic as to respect 'sovereignty and territorial integrity'. It is as if the whole visit was just intended to raise the issue and nothing more.

So clearly then, Pakistan's civil and military leaders are mired in providing America unstinting support to carry out drone attacks and to assassinate Pakistani citizens. There is no remorse and no recompense for the innocent victims. There is only high treason and a deep sense of betrayal executed on such a grand scale by Pakistani leaders that it belittles any overtures made to Washington to stop the attacks.

If Nawaz or any of his predecessors were sincere in halting the attacks, no begging trips to Washington are required. All they have to do is to withdraw ground support and kick-out American military personnel as well as American contractors who are free to roam the country. This action alone would render the drones ineffective. And if any drones violate Pakistan's airspace they should be blown to smithereens. These two actions are more than sufficient to bring an end to America's robotic birds and give Pakistan some respite from America's global war against Islam.

However, the long-term solution requires the Pakistani people to get rid of such leaders who hold the whole country hostage to America's whim. This can only be accomplished by ridding the current corrupt system and replacing it with the Caliphate. The Caliphate will not only defend

Pakistan's borders but also teach a lesson to foreign powers that make the grave mistake to violate its territory.

November 5, 2013

# 72

# The True Cost of Pakistan's relationship with America

*"During the last 10 years the direct and indirect cost of war on terror incurred by Pakistan amounted to $ 67.93 billion."*

*--Pakistan's Ministry of Finance*

Lately, several notable Pakistani public figures have expressed their increased optimism about the Pakistani economy and its future. On November 10, 2013 Federal Minister for Finance, Muhammad Ishaq Dar expressed his desire to see Pakistan become the 11th biggest economy in the world. According to the World Bank statistics in 2012, Pakistan presently holds 44th position[171] with a GDP of $236 billion, whilst Canada is in the 11th spot[172] with a GDP of $1,8 trillion.

A few days later, Dar's confidence was also echoed by Federal Minister for Planning, Development, and Reform, Ahsan Iqbal. On November 12, 2013 at a lecture at Harvard University, in the US, Iqbal said, "The Pakistan 2025 Programme will transform the country into a strong economy of upper middle income countries in ranking." He added, "... by making Pakistan a hub of regional integration through regional connectivity projects, we can create three billion new markets in Asia comprising of South Asia, China, and Central Asia with great opportunities for global economy." It appears that both Dar and Iqbal are basing their economic predictions on a paper entitled: 'Pakistan in the 21st Century: Vision 2030', which has been prepared by Pakistan's planning commission. The paper summarizes the economic vision as: "Growing economically at a rate of around 7-8 percent per annum, Pakistan expects to join the ranks of middle-income countries, with a GDP of around $4,000 billion by 2030. This high

---

[171] "World Bank Data- GDP Ranking", World Bank, (Coverage 2012).
[172] *Ibid 11*

growth rate would be sustained through developing its human resources, and by developing the necessary physical and technological infrastructure."

In a separate but related development, the Pakistani government inaugurated the meeting of a working group on Integrated Energy for Pakistan Vision 2025. On November 14, 2013 the group met under the chairmanship of the Secretary Planning, Development & Reforms, Hassan Nawaz Tarar and consisted of many leading scholars, experts and scientists. The immediate aim of the working group is to address the crippling energy problems plaguing Pakistan. Farkhand Iqbal, Senior Chief Energy said in his opening remarks that the country has been suffering from serious problems, as our industries are being closed, exports being declined, per capita income decreased. In short, he said that the energy sector of economy is badly suffering due to energy shortages in our country. He also emphasized that the 11th five year plan (2013-18) and vision 2025 would not be a plan like the plans of the past, but they should be a realistic, doable and a must, to achieve the desired growth rate for the next decade and to make Pakistan an industrialized knowledge base economy.

Like with all previous Pakistani governments, the present government is no different in trying to address Pakistan's ailing economy and severe energy shortages. No government has succeeded to date, and there is very little evidence to suggest that the current government of Nawaz Sharif will do any better. Without even scrutinising the contents of the vision, it is evident that there is problem in terms of which vision the government is following i.e. the 2025 vision espoused by Farkhand Iqbal, Dar and Ahsan or the 2030 vision advocated by the planning commission. Now one may give the government the benefit of doubt for getting mixed up, but the lack of alignment between ministries and poor communication by ministers amounts to a poor start considering the gravity of the situation, and does not bode well for the future.

Apart from the vision, the government has also miserably failed to articulate a clear and cogent strategy that will help them deliver the vision for 2030. For instance, what is the government's strategy that helps them achieve the vision statement: 'Pakistan expects to join the ranks of middle-income countries, with a GDP of around $4,000 billion by 2030.' The vision 2030 document distributed by the planning commission and public statements by politicians are not only woefully inadequate and but are quite frankly a regurgitation of the same old wine manufactured by Western economic consultants and institutions like the IMF, and then sold to the Pakistan public. For instance, on October 4, 2013 the Nation newspaper reported that the government has decided to privatise 31 public sector entities (PSEs) during the current financial year 2013-14 and this mainly includes banking, petroleum and energy sector companies. In return, Pakistan received a $6.7 billion loan programme under IMF's extended funds facility (EFF).

The strategy of parting with Pakistan's treasured silverware to boost economic growth is a recipe for economic chaos and enslavement to Western institutions. One only has to look at the privatisation under Musharraf and Zardari to see that the real benefactors are foreigners, who are free to set prices as they will, pay minimal or no tax at all, and repatriate profits to their own countries to strengthen their economies at the expense of Pakistan. This is in addition to the massive corruption that ensues and ensnares Pakistani politicians. Some have estimated 1550 billion Rupees (US$23.84 billion) worth of corruption during the privatisation process under 8 years of Musharraf's rule alone ("Pakistan: $23.8 billion corruption from privatization under Musharraf", Asia Pacific Action Online).

Hence, it appears that the 11th five-year-plan is headed in the same direction as the previous fifty years of strategy planning— degrading Pakistan's economic sovereignty and depriving our children of a bright future. Furthermore, such a strategy will not pay off Pakistan's $58 billion in external debt or grow Pakistan's economy sufficiently by 2030 to meet the needs of some 230-260 million Pakistanis as forecasted by the planning commission.

Best practice dictates that any economic vision espoused for Pakistan and any economic strategy advocated must be cognizant of the root causes behind the current economic malaise affecting the country. Any solution that does not treat the root causes will only treat the symptoms and will never return the country to economic self-sufficiency.

The three principal causes behind Pakistan's economic troubles is America, her colonial institutions like the IMF and WBO, and rampant corruption. Let's examine these one by one.

Ever since, America's active involvement in Eurasia, in particularly during the Soviet invasion of Afghanistan, Pakistan's economy has undergone sustained deterioration. This is a widely acknowledged fact but it does not feature in official proclamations or economic reports, as Pakistan's elite wants to continue with its suicidal policy of working with America. No matter how hard Pakistani officials try to conceal this fact they cannot hide the truth, and occasionally reveal information that is locked in the deepest depth of their hearts. Just recently, Minister for States and Frontier Regions Abdul Qadir Baloch said that over a 30 year period, Pakistan has spent approximately $200 billion in looking after Afghan refugees. The Afghan refugee burden is clearly a result of US policy to exploit Pakistan as the epicentre of America's war against its arch cold war enemy the Soviet Union.

Despite Pakistan's best efforts to care for their Afghan brethren as mandated by Islam, Pakistan has received peanuts from America in assistance over the past three decades. Even the latest drive by the so called international community has yielded miniscule amounts. International donors have pledged $600 million for the Afghan Refugees Affected and Hosting Areas Programme, but only $15 million has been delivered. So once again, Pakistan will continue to shoulder the burden of our Afghan brethren, even though the country does not have enough means to meet the needs of its own citizens.

In the beginning of the 21st century America launched a new war against Islam disguised as the war on terror. The central front of this war was Pakistan and its impact on the country was catastrophic, especially on Pakistan's economy. On October 23, 2013, Geo TV revealed that the war on terror had cost Pakistan a whopping $100 billion. In return, Pakistan received over $25 billion during the period 2002-2012 consisting of $17 billion in military aid and $8 billion in economic assistance. This aid pales into insignificance when measured over a 66 year period. From 1948 to 2012, Pakistan has received a total of $68 billion in aid. Of which, the economic aid is $42 billion and the remainder $26 billion is military assistance. In practice, however, this aid has been hampered by American economic sanction, which were first imposed in 1979. Peterson Institute for International economics calculates that from 1979 to 1998 the impact of the sanctions was equivalent to a $1 billion— a relatively small sum compared to the direct fallout that Pakistan has suffered when its foreign policy is aligned to America's national interests.

The other factor, which has wreaked havoc on Pakistan's economy is the menace of IMF and WB policies implemented under American auspices. The country has borrowed heavily from the IMF for 29 out of the 40 years between 1971 and 2010. Pakistan's external debt is currently thought to be around $58 billion – about 24% of GDP and 200% of exports. The IMF and World Bank argue that debts for low-income countries usually become impossible to repay when they are between 30-50% of GDP or 100–200% of exports. Yet despite this, IMF continues ignore its own warnings and is eager to lend billions of dollars to Pakistan.

In fact the Pakistani population has become accustomed to the unleashing of economic devastation, whenever IMF and WB officials visit Pakistan. The common prescription advocated by the IMF is privatisation, increase in the prices of petrol, electricity and gas, devaluation of the rupee, increase in tax revenues through the imposition of sales tax, reduction in import duties and several other notorious measures that always seem to increase the dependency of Pakistan's economy on foreign creditors and piles up unwarranted debt. Simply put IMF policies have never worked to bridge Pakistan's fiscal gap or address the balance of payments. All IMF policies do is to ensure the country commits to the ever increasing interest burden. Over the last five years, Pakistan's foreign debt payments have averaged $2.3 billion. That's the equivalent of 10% of exports, and 10% of government revenue, and is half the amount spent on health and education combined ("Unlocking the chains of debt A call for debt relief for Pakistan", Islamic Relief and Jubilee Debt Campaign, July 2013).

Lastly, under American patronage corruption has flourished in Pakistan. It does not matter whether the government is civil or military, corruption is rife under governments that are directly supported by America. For instance, according to Transparency International, Pakistan lost an unbelievably high amount, more than Rs8.5 trillion (US $94 billion), in corruption, tax evasion and bad governance during the last four years of Prime Minister Yousuf Raza Gillani's tenure.

In sum, since 1979, Pakistan's unstinting support for America has cost the Pakistani economy circa $410 billion[173]. Even the die heard neo-liberals and secular fundamentalists in Pakistan, will have to concede that America's relationship with Pakistan is the sole reason for the rapid erosion of the country's economic sovereignty.

For Pakistan's economy to have any chance of growth and self-sufficiency, economic policy makers must sever ties with the US, and devise a 2030 vision and associated strategies that does not feature America and

---

[173] This is based on costs to host Afghan refugees ($200b), external debt ($60b), corruption during Musharraf and Gilani's tenure ($120b) and war on terror ($100b) costs minus the aid ($68b) received from America.

the influence of its colonial tools. But this is only the first step, a more permanent solution necessitates the complete removal of democracy or dictatorship that always places man-made laws above the laws of Allah (swt)

Through these form of ruling, America repeatedly passes legislation through her supporters in both the executive and the parliament to enact capitalist solutions that only serve to safeguard her interests. This is the real root cause of the misery suffered by the Pakistani people. It is only through the establishment of the Caliphate that sovereignty will return to Allah (swt), and pro-American capitalist policies will be banished.

December 14, 2013

73

# The Menace of Karachi is Bailed to Terrorise the City

*"If Hussain were a suspected London-based jihadi, many Pakistanis believe,*
*he would have been arrested years ago."*

*--Owen Bennett-Jones*

On June 6th 2014, the exiled leader of Pakistan's Muttahida Qawmi Movement Party, Altaf Hussain, was released on bail by police in London after he was arrested and questioned on suspicion of money laundering. It is not the first time Hussain has been investigated by British authorities. In September 2010, Hussain was questioned after senior MQM leader Imran Farooq was murdered in London—but no one was formally charged. In any event, there were celebrations in parts of Karachi, as Pakistan's largest city struggles to return to some semblance of normalcy.

Leaving aside the money laundering investigation, the British government has repeatedly failed to investigate Altaf for the crime of inciting terror on the streets of Karachi. On numerous occasions, Altaf has delivered fiery sermons from his headquarters in London to incite sectarian tensions in Karachi. He routinely employs inflammatory language against his opponents and threatens them with terror expressions such as 'body bags'. Yet, despite this, the British government has never tried him for the offense of glorifying terrorism or even battered an eye-lid in this regard. In contrast, the British government has tried several people for glorifying terrorism on the flimsiest of evidences.

The tacit support of the British government to Altaf Hussein suggests that the MQM leader is being exploited to fulfil Britain's general policy of destabilising Pakistan. Using the Mohajir card to incite sectarian tensions is just one tool in her bag of destabilization tactics. The others include: providing support to the nationalist elements in Balochistan and assisting some of the Taleban to carry out strikes against Pakistan.

The government of Nawaz Sharif is fully cognizant of Britain's clandestine support to Altaf, but instead of pressing for Altaf's indictment, Sharif is offering Altaf all kinds of legal and moral support. Sharif's stance may appear at odds with popular sentiment in Pakistan, but is not surprising. Altaf has always been an ISI asset. The MQM was created by the Pakistani military to erode the popular base of Pakistan's Peoples Party in Karachi

The magnitude of Altaf's complicity to promote the objectives of both Britain and the Raheel-Nawaz government is widely sensed by the Pakistani public. Yet despite this over whelming ground swell of support to take action against both him and his movement, successive Pakistani governments have balked at the idea, and this has left Karachites to rot in the ensuing terror violence.

Only through Islam can the different warring factions of Karachi and its people unify, and leave in peace and harmony. Allah (swt) says in the Qur'ān:

*"And hold fast, all of you together, to the cable of Allah (swt), and do not separate. And remember Allah (swt)'s favour unto you: how ye were enemies and He made friendship between your hearts so that ye became as brothers by His grace."*

[TMQ Ali Imran:103]

And for those who repeatedly question how reconciliation can be achieved should ponder on the meaning of the following ayah:

*"And joined their hearts. Had you given away all the riches of the earth you could not have joined their hearts, but it is Allah (swt) Who joined their hearts. Indeed He is All-Mighty. All-Wise."*                          [TMQ Al-Anfal:63]

June 6, 2014

74

# Internally Displaced Pakistanis: Another Casualty of Pakistan's Unstinting Support for America's War Against Terror

*"...the crisis in Pakistan is by most metrics the biggest internal displacement in recent history."*

*--Institute for Social Policy and Understanding*

I t has been only 2 weeks since the Pakistani army launched an offensive in North Waziristan, and the nation finds itself on the brink of another refuge crisis. But this time of gigantic proportions. On June 25, 2014, the Pakistani government officially announced that 450,681 internally displaced persons (IDPs) had been registered so far, and that the number could top 600,000 as the military operations continue. Federal Minister for States and Frontier Regions retired Lt Gen Abdul Qadri Baloch claimed that the government was fully prepared to look after IDPs, but later he contradicted himself, when he appealed to the Pakistani public to donate money. He said, "It is the national duty of every Pakistani, particularly people with means to open up their pockets for the brethren in need.[174]"

This is not the first time; Pakistan is faced with a massive refugee crisis of its own making. In August 2009, the army under America's tutelage launched Operation Black Thunderstorm[175] against the Taleban in Khyber Pakhtunkhwa province and this resulted in 1.2 million Pakistani citizens being displaced. Judging by the inept response of both Pakistani government and the military in dealing with IDPs in 2009, it is very unlikely

---

[174] "Number of IDPs may reach 600,000: Baloch", Dawn, (June 25, 2014).
[175] "Military offensive displaces 30,000 in north-west Pakistan", The Telegraph, (April 28, 2009).

that Pakistan's present refugees will find any respite from their man-made ordeal. Back then many generous Pakistani appalled by the sheer incompetence of both their government and army leadership stepped in to look after the IDPs. But the size of the task now is simply overwhelming, and frankly speaking is a by-product of Pakistan's lopsided relations with America.

Ever since, Pakistan sided with America's war against Islam in 2001, internally displaced Pakistanis have become a permanent feature of the Pakistani landscape. What started out as a trickle in 2001 has become a flood in 2014, making Pakistan's one of the largest internally displaced populations in the world. Things are bound to become worse, as the Raheel-Nawaz partnership spares no effort in pleasing America by conducting further operations all over Pakistan to weed out not just militants, but anyone opposed to America's hegemony over Pakistan

Let's not forget that when Pakistan sided with America in 1980s to contain the advance of the Soviet Union, Pakistan ended up with 3 million Afghan refugees who are still holed up in the country and are unable to return. Now Pakistan has to contend with circa 4.5 million refugees as a direct consequence of American instigated operations in Pakistan's tribal belt. Added to this refugee calamity are the hundreds of thousands of internally displaced Pakistanis still reeling from Pakistan's earthquake in 2005 and the country's worst floods in 2010. These people were simply abandoned by both the government and the army, as assets and money were diverted to fight militants at America's behest.

In siding with America, the civil and military leaders over the past decade, have lost Pakistan's strategic depth in Afghanistan, gravely undermined Pakistan's stance on Kashmir, compromised the security of Pakistan's nuclear weapons, plunged the economy of the country into an abyss of debt, strengthened Pakistan's arch enemy India and have displaced millions of Pakistani citizens.

Yet for some strange reason many Pakistanis cling to the vain hope that somehow their civil and military leaders will lead the country out of its present predicament and create a better future for them and their children. And how naive they have become. Allah (swt) says:

*"Surely Allah (swt) does not change the condition of a people until they change their own condition; and when Allah (swt) intends evil to a people, there is no averting it, and besides Him they have no protector."*

[TMQ Al Rad:11]

June 25, 2014

# 75

# Pakistan Again Fails to Address the Root Cause of Terror

*"Because the United States itself has a long record of supporting terrorists and using terrorist tactics, the slogan of today's war on terrorism merely makes the United States look hypocritical to the rest of the world."*

*--Lt. General William Odom*

In the aftermath of the brutal attack on the Public Army School in Peshawar, the government under the supervision of the army announced a national plan of action to fight terrorism. Prime Minister Nawaz Sharif addressed the nation through national TV and warned the terrorists saying "your days are numbered..." He also announced a 20 point plan to combat terrorism, which includes the establishment of a rapid reaction force, special courts run by military officers to try terrorists, and greater regulation of madrassas[176]. However, for the umpteenth time the government failed to acknowledge the root cause of terrorism plaguing Pakistan.

Unless Pakistan boldly addresses the primary cause behind the terror attacks, the situation in the country will deteriorate further. Terror attacks were unheard of until America returned to Afghanistan in October 2001. Since then, Pakistan has been plunged into a cycle of violence perpetrated against civilians on a magnitude and scale not witnessed before.

The obvious cause behind the terror attacks is well known by all parties in Pakistan, but rarely is it singled out, ridiculed and eliminated. America's state terrorism masqueraded within the confines of international law and supported by Pakistan's military brass is the chief cause behind terror that continues to engulf the streets of Pakistan. America's principal terror

---

[176] "Days of terrorists are numbered, says PM", Dawn News, (December 25, 2014).

inflicting tools on the Pakistani population are: robotic death drones that indiscriminately kill civilians, numerous US incursions into Pakistan such as the Abbottabad raid and Raymond Davis like operatives free to roam streets of Pakistan to plan the next terror attack. None of these items appear on Nawaz Sharif's list and yet all of these terror inflicting methods are well known and documented.

The other pillar behind America's state sponsored terrorism against the Pakistani people is the unstinting support provided by Pakistan's military rulers. This includes: sharing intelligence with American army personnel, furnishing air bases for American drones, providing safe houses for American operatives in Pakistani cities, and ensuring that the American hegemony over Pakistan continues. The cooperation that began during the Musharraf era, mushroomed under Kayani and is now spearheaded by General Sharif shows no sign of abating.

It has not escaped attention of the Pakistani public how some of the high profile terror attacks and incursion by US forces have occurred in military areas, which are supposedly well guarded and protected. So if the military cannot protect its own kind, how does one expect the military to protect Pakistan and its people from Pakistan's arch enemies? Furthermore, no senior army officer is held accountable or punished for the lapse of security, which only serves to raise suspicion that the army brass is in cohorts with America.

If the Pakistani civil and military leadership are sincere about stopping the terror attacks then they must resolutely address the primary cause. All that is required is the implementation of the following 2 point plan:

1. Sever all links with America. This includes the closure of the American embassy, cessation of intelligence sharing and the confiscation of all air bases provided to the Americans. This must be accompanied by the expulsion of all American civil and military personnel from the country.

2. The Pakistani military top brass should publicly repent, and renounce its subjugation to America. This act of remorse should be augmented by the cessation of military activities against the tribes living in both sides of the Pakistani border, and opening up the ranks of the Pakistani army to sincere militants who yearn to fight for the honour and dignity of Islam. This new pact should be employed to safeguard Pakistan's frontiers from the armies of crusaders and their allies.

Nevertheless, the forgoing points are only a temporary measure to stop terror attacks. A permanent solution necessitates the establishment of the rightly guarded Caliphate. Only the Caliphate can unite the Pakistani army Afghans, Pakistani militants and the Pakistani public under the banner of Islam. Allah (swt) says:

*"And hold firmly to the rope of Allah (swt) all together and do not become divided. And remember the favor of Allah (swt) upon you - when you were enemies and He brought your hearts together and you became, by His favor, brothers. And you were on the edge of a pit of the Fire, and He saved you from it. Thus does Allah (swt) make clear to you His verses that you may be guided."*

[TMQ Al-Imran:103]

Once united under Khilafah Rashida, the crusaders and the enemies of Islam will think twice before lifting their hands to strike Muslims!

January 6, 2015

The Messenger of Allah (SAW) said, "Only the Imam is a shield, behind whom you fight and you protect yourself with, so if he orders by *Taqwa* and is just then he has reward for that, and if he orders by other than that then it is against himself."                                              (Muslim)

## About the author

Aabid Moustapha is a prolific writer on Muslim affairs and global issues. His articles routinely appear in international newspapers and magazines, as well as various online websites specialising in world affairs. Aabid has also participated in a number of international conferences to highlight the injustices of the Muslim world and to propose the re-establishment of the Khilafah as the only viable solution.

The War of Civilisations has begun: 75 Essays on the West's War against Islam is his third book that explores this theme. It is similar in style to his other books.